PRODUCING PUBLIC TELEVISION,
PRODUCING PUBLIC CULTURE

PRODUCING PUBLIC TELEVISION, PRODUCING PUBLIC CULTURE

Barry Dornfeld

PRINCETON UNIVERSITY PRESS   PRINCETON, NEW JERSEY

Library of Congress Cataloging-in-Publication Data
Dornfeld, Barry, 1958–
Producing public television, producing public culture / Barry Dornfeld.
p.   cm.
Filmography: p.
Includes bibliographical references and index.
ISBN 0-691-04468-6 (cloth : alk. paper). — ISBN 0-691-04467-8
(pbk. : alk. paper)
1. Documentary television programs—Production and
direction.   2. Public television.   I. Title.
PN1992.8.D6D69   1998
791.45'75—dc21   97-39819

This book has been composed in Times Roman
Princeton University Press books are printed on acid-free paper
and meet the guidelines for permanence and durability of the
Committee on Production Guidelines for Book Longevity of the
Council on Library Resources

http://pup.princeton.edu

Printed in the United States of America

P

For my mother, Ina Gene Feidelman,
and in memory of my father,
Lionel Allen Dornfeld

One feels, really, that two great gods, Entertainment and
Education, have risen up, and this in a way is okay, is the way
things are, but they have kept out all the other, lesser gods: the
gods of Wit and Unprofessionalism, the nasty gods, the gods
that get into noisy arguments, the dissenting gods (David
Susskind is not a dissenting god), the gods that say things in bad
taste and recite poems and do things for the hell of it; the gods
that exist in this "larger world" that television is always
claiming to bring us—which still exists in books and magazines
but does not exist in television, because the air is not really
available to everyone, and because it apparently costs so much
to put together the equipment for broadcasting through it that
one requires of those great modern American institutions, a
giant Commercial Network Television Establishment, or a giant
National Educational Television Establishment, but in either case
an establishment, to run the show.
(Michael Arlen, *Living Room War*, 1969:32)

I think there is one huge problem that faces us and is common
to virtually all series. One has to bear in mind the awful fact
that most television is second rate. The examples that we have
on television are visually wallpaper, and usually have very little
to do with the arguments that are advanced. So the arguments
outstrip the ability of television to demonstrate it properly. So
it's easy to think of the right arguments; it's very, very difficult
to visualize it and to express it in such a way that it is truly
illuminating on the screen. And I think the problem is not to
think of the arguments or the causes, but to try and work out
how we can illuminate it or actually get it on to the screen.
That is the large problem. It's hugely difficult and there
is no way around it.
(Peter Montagnon, one of *Childhood*'s two executive producers,
December 12, 1989)

Contents

Acknowledgments   ix

Chapter One
Studying Public Television as American Public Culture   3

Chapter Two
Childhood on the Contested Territory of Public Television in   35
the United States

Chapter Three
Negotiating Documentary Production: Authorship and Imagined   61
Audiences

Chapter Four
Public Television Documentary Poetics   89

Chapter Five
Cutting across Cultures: Public Television Documentary and   140
Representations of Otherness

Chapter Six
Public Television Documentary and the Mediation of   168
American Public Culture

Appendix A
Organizational Chart of the *Childhood* Staff   189

Appendix B
List of Academic Observers and Advisors   191

Appendix C
Synopsis of the *Childhood* Series   193

Notes   197

References   221

Filmography   234

Index   237

Acknowledgments

I OWE a debt of gratitude to a number of people and institutions whose support and assistance made this book possible. The staff of The *Childhood* Project enabled me to conduct this research by their willing participation and kind assistance through the research and writing stages. I am especially indebted to Geoff Haines-Stiles, who welcomed me to *Childhood* as a participant observer, opened up his work to the scrutiny of this research with a degree of candidness few of us would welcome, and was generous to me throughout the project, making my stay "in the field" enriching in ways I had not anticipated. His associates Peter Montagnon, Erna Akuginow, Gene Marner, Pamela Loxton, Rudy Gaskins, Nancy Tong, Richard Chisolm, Anne Troise, Larry Silk, Victor Balaban, and Myra Stetser assisted me throughout the research process, and openly shared their work and views. Leo Eaton, of Maryland Public Television, and Jay Ruby, from Temple University, both directed me to The *Childhood* Project as a potential site for this study, and I am thankful to them for their suggestion. I am also grateful to WNET for agreeing to grant me access to the work of the *Childhood* series. Kate Kunz facilitated my access to WNET's photographic archive covering the series, and she, Rudy Gaskins, Lawrence Ivy, and Nancy Tong deserve thanks for allowing me to use their photographs freely.

This book had its first life as my Ph.D. dissertation at the Annenberg School for Communication, University of Pennsylvania. I am grateful to the school for its support, including the award of a Dissertation Research Fellowship. I would like to thank my dissertation committee, Professors Larry Gross, Paul Messaris, Joseph Turow, and Arjun Appadurai for their guidance in steering this project from proposal to finished work. Larry Gross provided a steady source of astute advice, patient encouragement, and confidence in my work, and guided me over a number of obstacles in getting this study underway and completed. I would also like to thank Steve Feld, whose model of intellectual fortitude and expansive scholarship I aspired to, and whose academic tutelage, friendship, and enduring support I have valued throughout my training and work.

Once a manuscript had evolved, it benefited immeasurably from careful readings and commentary from several colleagues and friends. Steve Feld, Faye Ginsburg, and Geoff Haines-Stiles read through several different versions of it and provided excellent advice and a lot of encouragement throughout. Barbara Abrash, Lisa Henderson, Toby Miller, and Jay Ruby all took time to read the text and provided extremely insightful comments. Lewis Freidland, Debra Spitulnik, and a third anonymous reader reviewed the manuscript for Princeton University Press and furnished incredibly thoughtful and detailed advice that steered this work through its rocky early stages. Fred Myers furnished me with the necessary cognitive clearance to continue writing while working through my first years of teaching. I am also extremely thankful for the support and editorial guidance that Mary Murrell, my editor at Princeton University Press, provided. New York University's Goddard Fellowship in the spring of 1996 afforded valuable time to complete my writing. I also acknowledge the contributions of my colleagues and students in the Anthropology Department and the participants in the Social Space of Media Seminar in 1996–97.

I am grateful and indebted (literally and figuratively) to my mother, Ina Feidelman, and, her husband Arnold, who supported this work in every way they could. I will always be thankful and obliged to my wife, Carole Boughter, for spurring me on throughout this project, and for her tolerance in putting up with its duration and weight. I continually relied on Carole's perceptive intellectual and interpersonal advice, her discerning and meticulous readings, and her patience. Our children, Ted and Maura, contributed to my intellectual development in ways I will always appreciate. When Ted turned to me one day while I was screening a *Childhood* episode yet one more time and earnestly asked, "Dad, when are you going to stop watching *Childhood* and come and play?" I understood something about both the importance of the work I was engaged in and the necessity of keeping it in perspective.

PRODUCING PUBLIC TELEVISION,
PRODUCING PUBLIC CULTURE

CHAPTER ONE

Studying Public Television as
American Public Culture

I CAME UP out of the subway at Columbus Circle in midtown Manhattan, stepping into the buzz and hustle of a morning in New York City. I was en route to begin my first day of fieldwork studying the making of *Childhood*, a multipart documentary series being produced for public television broadcast in the United States, Great Britain, and elsewhere. The *Childhood* Project office's location on the tenth floor of WNET-TV's building, stretching between 58th and 59th Streets, situated this series in a central place in the geography of the media production industry. At the same time, I was returning to my own geographic past, the metropolitan center I had grown up around but had left to pursue my education and begin a career in independent filmmaking. The ironies of returning home were compounded several weeks later. I accompanied two of the series' production staff and three freelance crew members on a shoot, on which we followed an African American family transporting their three children to early morning doctor and dentist appointments, then off to their day care center, traversing the suburban town of White Plains, where I had spent my high school years and where my parents still lived. The day care center in this predominantly black neighborhood had, in my youth, been a recreation center, where I had mostly watched, and on occasion played in, some fairly competitive league basketball games (all, quite literally, over my head). But these ironies are probably not uncommon when doing anthropology at home. Although the *Childhood* series closely followed two families from suburban Westchester County, it was both global in content and topic and local in its texture as a New York City-based television production.

After clearing my name with the guard at the 58th Street entrance, I took an elevator to the tenth floor, which The *Childhood* Project shared with several other WNET public television ventures. The series' own offices were painted off-white, the hallway decorated with brightly colored handprints painted on the walls, a graphic motif that also appeared in the series letterhead, brochures, and the opening and closing credits. Some seven or eight offices opened off this main hallway, which led to a reception area in front of executive producer Geoff Haines-Stiles's office. Aware of my arrival, Geoff called out into the waiting area in a humorously acerbic manner that would continually catch me off guard: "He's early. Tell him to go back to

Philadelphia." After a moment, he beckoned me into his office where we shook hands, then took me off on a quick tour of the office, introducing me to staff members who were available. Aside from one Steenbeck flatbed film editing machine, a few monitor and VCR setups, and stacks of videotapes on various half-filled shelves, there was little evidence in this workspace that these dozen people were engaged in the production of documentary television programs. Some months later, this space would fill up, with the project eventually converting three offices into full-time editing rooms, where the sounds and images of families raising children in Russia, Brazil, Japan, Cameroon, and the United States would play forward and back through many of the day's twenty-four hours. But much of the work through the first few months of production centered on writing and talking—writing proposals for additional funding, research reports, letters to scholars in the field of child development, faxes overseas to potential locations, crew members, and the series' London-based partners, and ultimately television scripts—and talking about all these arrangements and ideas over the phone and face to face, often in group meetings like the script meeting I had come up to observe on this first day of my research.

The rest of the tour took me through nondescript and mostly empty offices, which would later be filled with staff members, Macintosh computers, filing cabinets full of paperwork, books and articles, and shelves of videotapes. An assistant editor who would not remain with the project very long labored trying to synch up footage that had come in from Moscow. She and Geoff spoke about how charmed they were with the sequence of a Russian mother bathing her baby, and about needing to tell the Russian crew to provide better shot identifications. The brief tour over, Geoff deposited me at an empty desk outside series producer Erna Akuginow's office, a space I would claim as a resting place for much of this fieldwork project. While waiting for the meeting (waiting became a familiar activity as well), I leafed through the xeroxes of articles on the desk that were ready to be distributed to project staff, presumably to be read for this week's work. Geoff began the meeting a short time later, assembling the three producer/directors (one of whom would later leave the project), an assistant producer, and myself. After briefly introducing me and providing an update on the families already being filmed in other countries, he moved the discussion to the search for the second American family for the series. They had already selected an African American family, the Gholstons, and were looking for a white family whose children were in elementary school, with enough girls to balance the two older boys in the Gholston family. Family members had to be articulate and representative of some American "mainstream." They discussed ethnicity, social class, and production logistics, then progressed through the early drafts for four of the programs that would constitute the series. Sandwiches were ordered as the meeting went well into the afternoon, and I took notes on the discussion, trying to be as exhaustive as possible without being too obtrusive on my first day. Although clearly this was not an exotic site for conducting ethnographic research, I felt that I had been allowed inside an occupational world and was given an immediate glimpse of how television programs like these were made.

Public television documentaries are a primary means through which many Americans encounter conceptions about their social and biological lives and witness representations of unfamiliar cultures both outside and within their national boundaries. Through a variety of formats and program genres, public television in the United States presents viewers with depictions of and assertions about the daily lives, institutions, cultural values, and histories of people like themselves or others, both nearby and in far-off places. Through these media texts, viewers grapple with and reproduce understandings of cultural identity and cultural difference. Yet there is a conspicuous and persistant lack of scholarly attention to public television documentary, despite its prominence in American public culture. This book seeks to redress this lack. As a case study of the production of the *Childhood* series, this book provides a close and grounded view of the production of these programs, while demonstrating what it means to "do ethnography" in a media production context. In doing so, I look at public television representations as a form of popular anthropology within American public culture, a disciplined kind of "imagining" through which producers and viewers construct understandings of themselves and others. Bill Nichols claims that "images help constitute the ideologies that determine our own subjectivity" and "make incarnate those alternative subjectivities and patterns of social relation that provide our cultural ideals or utopian visions" (Nichols 1991:9–10). If so, then I would argue that the documentary material on public television represents a culturally rich and potent corpus of images that needs to be analyzed to better understand how practices of producing and consuming media forms contribute to the constitution of American public culture. This book is going to explore what kind of "larger world that television is always claiming to bring us," as Michael Arlen put it in the epigraph to this book, and what kind of world it cannot. I will illuminate the institutional and cultural forces that create a situation where television becomes "second rate," in Peter Montagnon's words, and how progressive intellectual media professionals struggle with this disconcerting situation.

Public television in the United States is infused with a kind of authority, legitimacy, and importance not given to other channels and formats of broadcast media in what has been termed, following Habermas (1989) and others (Fraser 1990; Garnham 1993), the public sphere.[1] I believe this holds true despite recent assertions about the system's impending irrelevance (i.e., Lapham 1993), and in light of its slipping hold on audience share and ongoing controversies within and around the institutions that comprise it. Despite the sense of vulnerability surrounding it, the public broadcasting system still represents the only American institution devoted to producing and broadly distributing television and radio programs that receives significant funding from federal and state governments (administered by an amalgamation of public agencies and private institutions). The circulation of its programming extends beyond a prime-time television broadcast audience of about two million viewers, it has become institutionalized in the educational system in this country as providing important material in teaching the humanities and the social and physical sciences. Nonetheless, it is revealing to compare the situation of public television in the United States with government-sponsored broadcasting systems in other countries. Outside the United States, state-owned, controlled, or sponsored channels represent most of the programming choices and hold a major chunk of a nation's viewership, and debates around public service and the role of broadcasting in national politics and culture take on a public urgency unfamiliar in America.[2] Still, in the American context, discussions over the notion of the public interest and the state of the civic culture continue to take public television into account in a central way. Whether the imagined but rapidly approaching future of new technologies, new services, and increasing channels and formats of image-based media forecasts a place of decreasing or increasing importance for institutions of public broadcasting remains to be seen and is already being contested. Many find it difficult to conceive of a televisual future without some form of public broadcasting and refuse to give up hope for the system's potentially progressive contribution to a democratic future.

Yet we are still hindered in these debates due to the dearth of scholarly attention given both to the institutions of public broadcasting and to the media culture involved in the production and reception of the programs they offer. While occasional theoretical and policy-oriented treatises have analyzed the politics, economics, and social organization of public broadcasting (Rowland 1986; Rowland and Tracey 1990; Aufderheide 1991; Hoynes 1994; Lashley 1992), and periodic manifestos have recommended strategic futures for its institutions (Carnegie Commission 1967, 1979; Somerset-Ward 1993), there have been few extended studies of the administrative and production institutions themselves (but see Engelman 1996 and Powell and Friedkin 1983, 1986) and only sporadic writing on the production and reception of specific programs. Whole genres of educational programming have been left out of academic and popular consideration of what the media is and does.[3] When seen in relation to the overabundance of scholarly and popular writing on entertainment television programming in its many forms, this lack of attention to a major source of what Nichols terms "discourses of sobriety"—media texts ostensibly produced to advance an argument or disseminate information and knowledge (Nichols 1991)—becomes most conspicuous.

As both a scholar interested in the place of media forms in contemporary social life and a producer of documentary films geared toward broadcast on public television, I became interested in this lack of scholarly attention to a domain of cultural production that I held in high regard. My academic and professional backgrounds oriented me toward areas where the fields of anthropology and communication intersected with media forms and practices, both in the production of documentaries concerned with representing worlds of culture, loosely grouped under the rubric of ethnographic film, and in the analysis of media as cultural forms, an interest that falls into the emerging field of the ethnography of media. I saw in these disparate endeavors a shared concern with the importance of media representation in the forming of social subjectivities and cultural identities, and brought to them a commitment to analyzing these processes of representation in a self-conscious way. Consequently, I reasoned that an intensive ethnographic study of the interpretive frameworks through which producers work and of the media production practices they employ in creating a documentary for American public television would illuminate how some segments of our society grapple with *imagination* fundamental issues of identity: how they define themselves in relation to the rest of the world, how they represent the kind of society in which they imagine or wish themselves to live, and how these representations become part of public culture.

This book is based on an ethnography of the production unit that created the seven-hour educational series *Childhood*, which aired in the United States on public television in the fall of 1991, in England in 1992, and in several other countries subsequently, and then entered educational distribution in several formats. *Childhood* addressed the experience and knowledge that American and British audiences have (or do not have) about child development, as seen across several cultural settings and from specific disciplinary orientations. Executive producer Geoff Haines-Stiles collaborated with WNET-TV, one of the major producing stations in the PBS system, to coproduce and present the series. They added British funding and partnership, as well as a team of producers, freelance crew members, and notable academic researchers in child development, history, and anthropology—disciplines concerned with the life of children and families. A close look at the production of this series reveals a great deal about certain socially situated understandings of ourselves and others; conceptions of biology, culture, and history; and about ideologies of cultural difference and universality across societies at this particular moment in time. What is equally important is what this analysis reveals about the complexities of encoding these understandings in the form of documentary television.

MEDIA AS FORMS OF CULTURAL PRODUCTION

While my principal focus here is on understanding how a public television documentary is produced, I also argue for the value of conducting ethnographies of media as forms of cultural production, examining the social processes of encoding and decoding meaning in media images. While important precedents exist in both anthropology and media studies for this kind of investigation, the ethnographic study of media as a dimension of culture represents a new agenda within these fields. Anthropology, which had historically ignored the study of contemporary societies and the influence of modernizing technologies and social structures in other parts of the world, recently abandoned its proclivity toward a view of cultural holism and traditionalism and its resistance toward the modern and the popular. This shift was largely the result of forceful critiques and a subsequent rethinking of the objectives and politics of doing anthropology in the postcolonial world. Simultaneously, although the field of communication/media studies has long been concerned with global processes and issues of political economy, it has traditionally focused its analytical gaze within the industrialized countries from which imperialist cultural forces emanate.[4] Some thinkers within media studies are only recently working out an appropriate balance between the global and the local, arguing that the field needs to look into places where the proverbial sitting room (see Morley 1991) might not exist. I make an argument throughout this book in favor of an anthropology of the media, of the convergence of anthropology with the subject matter of media studies, and apply this hybrid perspective to American culture.[5]

We can locate the historical roots of this convergence in the subdisciplines of both visual anthropology and the ethnography of communication, which also comprised my own academic training and led to this study. Writing in 1980, Sol Worth articulated a distinction between "visual anthropology" and the emerging area of the anthropology of visual communication (Worth 1980). He called for a transition from the former, which was mainly concerned with the complexity of representing anthropological ideas in visual and sound images, to the latter, which encompasses a broader agenda for ethnographic research on visual culture. Worth's writings (Worth and Adair 1972; Worth 1981) emphasized the semiotic aspects of film communication and represented a pioneering, although preliminary, program for what some of that research could become. He attempted to develop an anthropological approach for studying the encoding of social meaning in pictures (still and motion) that would transcend the psychological and linguistic bases of visual studies. Drawing on the emerging paradigm of the ethnography of communication, this approach incorporated social and cultural dimensions of visual communication into a model of meaning and interpretation.[6] Worth's objective—"trying to understand . . . how, and why, and in what context, a particular articulator structured his particular statement about the world" (Worth 1981:197)—is an adequate condensation of my own goals in this project.[7]

The reflexive crisis within anthropology in the 1980s also contributed to the anthropology of the media by shifting the field's focus away from traditional ethnographic sites and practices and to the process of representation itself. Writing by Said (1979) and Fabian (1983, 1990) broke theoretical ground by articulating a powerful critique of the scholarly enterprises devoted to representing other cultures. Anthropologists and others precipitated a critical process of looking at their own practices of representation, particularly the writing of ethnographies (Marcus and Cushman 1982; Marcus and Fischer 1986; Clifford and Marcus 1986), but also the presentation of anthropological materials and non-Western artifacts in other, more public forms: museum exhibits, public performances, and in media formats (see, for instance, Karp and Lavine 1991). The result has been some theoretically rich analyses of contemporary cultural forms in a variety of national and regional settings, emerging as the critique of "discourses of the other," the phrase that Naficy and Gabriel (1991) use to categorize a broad range of academic and popular texts probing cultural representation more generally.[8] Pointing to new, productive directions, Appadurai and Breckenridge advocated the study and analysis of "public culture" (1988), the concern with cosmopolitan cultural forms which "raise a larger set of terminological as well as interpretive problems about the way in which public life in the contemporary world is being culturally articulated" (1988:5). Their work draws us to engage with more deliberate, self-conscious, and broadly relevant culture-making and consuming activities than the disciplinary ones surrounding ethnographic writing.

Public television programs about other cultures are a rich area for this sort of investigation and generate analogous questions about the representation of cultural worlds in public form. Ginsburg (1988), in tracing the history of anthropology programs on television over the last twenty years, noted the scarcity of substantive television programs that draw on anthropology and anthropologists. She argued that television does not hesitate to intrude on subject matter about which anthropologists feel proprietary: "Broadcasting— with its demand to fill ever increasing programming slots—has the leading edge in terms of resources and access for representing 'the other' to the West. Like it or not, television producers have the interest, means and mandate to gather images of those who traditionally have been anthropology's subject and present these as they will" (Ginsburg 1988:41).

An abundance of television programs represent non-Western or non-mainstream cultures through forms not normally considered ethnographic, from *National Geographic* specials to travelogues to current affairs documentaries. We could collect this range of works within a loose genre of "popular ethnography," in that they share with ethnography the intention of translating another cultural world. The culturally exotic has been a common and historically continuous subject of documentary and narrative film and, earlier, photography.[9] Naficy and Gabriel attribute this interest to psychological needs: "Consuming the other is a continual process of yearning—for meaning, for those qualities which the dominant order has exiled or lost, and for the certainties that ideologies provide in a world that is increasingly uncertain and unpredictable" (Naficy and Gabriel 1991:iii).

Within this invented genre of "popular ethnography," we can distinguish works that articulate an explicit *comparison* of cultures, where the stress is not only on the representation of some "other" and the recognition of cultural difference, but rather on the representation of difference itself through an explicit juxtaposition of cultures within a text. We can place works such as Margaret Mead's popular writings, Desmond Morris's illustrated texts on comparative body communication, photography exhibits like "The Family of Man," and documentary series for public television such as *Millennium* (Grant, Malone, and Meech 1992), within this category of popular ethnology. These works, in different ways, juxtapose images of multiple cultures in succession to illustrate some theoretical or thematic view, usually with an explicit or implicit comparison between "them" and "us." Nature and wildlife films share this comparative structure, though they cut between species rather than cultures.[10] This cross-cultural comparative trope, borrowed from anthropology and repeated in different forms and genres of public culture, is a powerful structure in American culture for the production of ideas about cultural identity and subjectivity, cultural difference and similarity.

I will return to the idea of comparative articulations and how they are negotiated and encoded into the *Childhood* series. I argue for the value of looking at public television programs as public culture, as discourses trafficked both within and across social and national boundaries, produced and consumed through conventionalized and socially determined practices (media making and media watching), by individuals located in specific, historically situated, but changing social formations. This framework is built on a view of media as a set of cultural forms that is mobile, argumentative, and emergent, and more complex and encompassing than traditional views of culture as articulated in text-based media theories. Placing the material for this study within such an overarching context forces us to confront complex questions about agency and power, interpretation and evaluation, and the negotiations surrounding the encoding and reception of complex, multicultural representations.

ETHNOGRAPHIES OF MEDIA

Looking at media production as public culture entails not only a consideration of the representations produced by media organizations, but more fundamentally the practices of media production that drive the creation of those representations. Ethnographies of media practices present significant challenges for determining the locus of cultural production in contemporary societies, inviting us to rethink the ways in which we situate ethnographic research. Contemporary societies, increasingly mobile and atomistic, dominated by institutions and corporations and having greater temporal pressures on daily life, feature more difficult landscapes for ethnographic research than the characteristic settings that defined traditional anthropological fieldwork. With research on the production of dominant media, the obstacles presented by contemporary society get multiplied by the difficulty of gaining access to powerful corporate or public institutions, and, once gaining access, finding a research role that is both comfortable and productive. Appadurai (1991) notes how this new conceptualization of public culture calls for new ways of thinking about the place and practice of ethnography, and for situating the local occurrence within more global processes. The strategy I employ approaches the production of media forms by integrating the investigation of multiple discourses (oral, written, imagistic) and socially grounded practices (professional, administrative, intellectual), and suggests we refocus on how studies of media have struggled with these issues.

I begin from a position analogous to what Urban and Sherzer term "a discourse-centered approach to language study," which "looks to discourse to understand how culture is carried and replicated" and sees speech behavior "as a sign vehicle operating in specific contexts" (Urban and Sherzer 1988:287). Building on the study of communication in its enacted social context, we can modify this approach to include communicative modalities in addition to language, as argued by those advocating the ethnographic study of media forms (Gross 1974; Worth 1981; Worth and Adair 1972; Spitulnik 1993; Ginsburg 1994). The resulting perspective avoids what I see as interpretive excess in media studies' approach to image-based texts as unanchored "discursive formations" or "semiotic systems." In short, this approach strives to understand media texts in relation to specific agents, practices, and social contexts.

The programs in a PBS documentary series are part of public discourse in this more focused sense. They are designed, adjudicated, legitimated, and received as representations of and contributions to public understanding, essentially a distribution of scholarly and scientific information to broad publics. Institutions engaged in their production and distribution—government agencies, nonprofit public television stations, media production entities, academic institutions, libraries—treat this material with a degree of seriousness akin to that reserved for written scholarly documents yet support their production with an intense investment of capital and labor. In the case of *Childhood*, this discursive form embodies and brings to public debate (Turow 1985) arguments about and understandings of "American culture" and cultural others, the development of life, nature versus nurture, and a popular sense of cultural relativism. Programs like *Childhood* are part of American society's negotiations over what Appadurai calls "a rich, ever-changing store

of possible lives" (Appadurai 1991), engaging issues from the most pragmatic (birthing position, child care, breast feeding) to the most global (the
nature of cultural difference, the impact of human evolution). Public television's venues of circulation insert these works into public discourse with a
legitimacy and seriousness unlike that of other more popular forms of media
culture. The debates around the institutions of public broadcasting reveal a
great deal about the cultural politics surrounding critical issues in American
public culture: the struggles over multiculturalism, the place of television in
education, the nature and role of intellectual life and scientific knowledge in
public culture, and the legitimation of delegates of cultural and political
power.

My analysis of this form of public culture begins with an understanding of
how social agents (producers, viewers) conceive of (interpret, evaluate) these
textual forms and the meanings they encode in and interpret from the texts
they produce and consume. At the same time, I look at the actual processes
of work, leisure, and forms of socialization in which agents engage, and how
practice is shaped by and in turn shapes larger social structures. Bourdieu's
approach to situating cultural production and consumption as practices taking place in specific cultural fields is foundational to this study.[11] I attempt
here the integration, suggested by Marcus and Fischer (1986), between an
anthropology based on an interpretive or symbolic perspective and a practice-oriented approach, to focus on "both form *and* content, on meaning in
action" (Marcus and Fischer 1986:85).[12] Ethnographic models drawn from
the study of performative and representational domains of expressive culture
view culture as produced and consumed by interpreting agents through sym-
bol-based interactions within a social context, and offer both a theoretical
stance and research approach applicable to work on media forms and practices.[13] The study of ethno-aesthetics or ethno-theory, research into native
categories of artistic knowledge and performance, focusing on the observation and elicitation of native terms and conceptualizations of aesthetic value,
have explicated native theoretical systems for encoding meaning in communicative form.[14] The limitations of these approaches have been in their tendency to deemphasize practice (Ortner 1984) and in their failure to illuminate patterns of use and distribution of knowledge (i.e., between performer
and audience).[15]

I apply the model of ethno-theory to open up the theoretical formulations
of documentary producers, not abstracted from, but in relation to production
practice and aesthetic forms. I attempt to move between theory and practice,
to elicit and articulate the scholarly, aesthetic, and cultural frameworks that
motivate the practices of public television documentary while observing
these practices themselves. An ethnographic approach to cultural production
offers the possibility of rethinking and bridging the theoretical dichotomy
between production and consumption, between producers' intentional mean-

ings and audience members' interpreted meanings, and between production studies and reception studies. In doing so, it transcends disabling debates in media studies, moving beyond the binaries of media power versus resistance, ideology versus agency, and production versus reception.

DISCOVERING THE AUDIENCE AND MISPLACING THE PRODUCER

In her book *Desperately Seeking the Audience*, Ien Ang argued that "the television audience is not the innocent reflection of a given reality" (Ang 1991:35) but is rather a "discursive construct" providing specific advantages to the institutions that define it and, as Turton (1992:288) added, depend on it. Ang took as her concern the industrial machineries of broadcast audience research, looking at how large institutions in several national culture industries produce analyses of their viewership to rationalize marketing decisions. This theoretical move converged with the flourishing interest in theorizing and researching processes of consumption, but with a provocative reversal, locating the notion of audience within the production process. That Ang was less concerned with how various actors within institutions involved in the production of media forms conceive of and construct their audience is understandable, given her focus on large-scale organizations within these industries and their relationship to national cultural policy. But it also reflects what I see as a general deficiency in the study of media production. The profitable reorientation toward the study of audiences has left in its wake a shallow pool of research on production processes, and a limiting theorization of producers as the conduits of corporate ideologies. We need to rethink producers as particular types of agents, producing media texts within contexts constrained by both culture, ideology, and economy, but operating within particular social locations and frameworks, not floating above society, as many approaches to the study of media forms seem to imply. This kind of reorientation would allow us to discuss with greater specificity and clarity the relationship between media forms and practices and the larger public spheres they produce and are situated within.

I focus here on this more grounded sense in which producers seek and, in seeking, construct their audiences. I argue that these constructions have a critical relationship to flows of information in which these larger institutions are engaged. Producers' projections about their audiences greatly affect the selection, encoding, and structuring of the media forms these institutions distribute, whether they are mainstream television programs, commercials, feature films, or educational documentaries. The multiplicity of audiences' interpretive positions, the various things people do in consuming these texts through dominant, contested, or oppositional readings (Morley 1989), and the various imagined identities that grow out of these acts (Appadurai 1990) are therefore constrained from the start by the way producers prefigure those acts of consumption. The consequences of these processes of encoding become quite complex in material that crosses cultural and national borders (Michaels 1994; Liebes and Katz 1990; Feld 1994b), raising questions about the role played by media forms in the formation of cultural and national identities.

A reconceptualization of the production process, or the process of encoding, as a multiple and richly contested one encourages a greater unity between unnecessarily divided, incongruent theoretical discourses about production and consumption and provides a fruitful engagement with the study of media production. This realization, applicable to diverse contexts of media production and circulation, illuminates how certain pressures on the public broadcasting system in the United States encourage the system to construct, seek, and address its audience through particular program formats and topics. I argue for an understanding of those elusive audiences (Bird 1992) as a kind of invented but quite real (though loosely defined) community of consumption, constituted by class and culture, whose future presence is inscribed in many practices undertaken during production. The very separation made between "audience members" and "producers" is an artifact of the history of mass communications scholarship tied to an industrial model of communications research. As such, it has become an ideological distinction that, when transcended, offers the richer conceptualization that production and consumption processes are intertwined.

Producers of documentary television, just like authors of other texts or performances, engage in a complex, multifaceted process of interpretation, evaluation, and anticipation based on conventional practices available within that genre. Recent "poststructuralist" theoretical perspectives have, however, argued for a view of communication that has greatly deemphasized or "decentered" the "author" of texts, and relegated the "author function" to a set of ideologically bound practices, privileging instead the moment of reception.[16] This argument opened the work of consumption to more complex analyses, shifting the focus in communication studies to an agent-centered view of audiences, an important break from the limitations of the producer-dominated sender-receiver model. However, as several writers have noted (i.e., Tulloch 1990), the swing has at times gone too far toward the audience. The focus on reception as the site where meanings are created can obscure the analysis of the production of media forms, segregating theory and research on mediated communication into studies of production and studies of consumption.

In opposition, some theorists have called for a new emphasis on the production of texts, one which rethinks notions of authorship and revives interest in the text's producers.[17] Indeed, I hope this book demonstrates the value of pursuing a more nuanced view of the critical role of authors/producers and the encoding process, both recognizing their agency in the communication process and situating the constraints on their work of cultural production in relevant historical and social contexts. This approach addresses the shortcomings of work in media studies of cultural production (often of mass media forms) in complex societies, called "the production of culture" approach, which suffers from considerable theoretical and methodological limitations.[18] In Jensen's critique, the "production of culture" approach failed to take culture seriously, regarding it as a subsidiary product, a particular type of commodity—"reflecting only the structure and process of its production" (Jensen 1984:107)—rather than as the "means through which people construct meaningful worlds in which to live" (1984:108). The capacity to work between producers' interpretations of their behavior, observations of the work process itself, and the texts (and artifacts) produced offers the researcher a rich, multileveled approach to a given communicative form. Rather than seeing meaning as determined by "the moment of enunciation" (Radway 1988a:362), this view would consider production as a process of negotiation through which textual meanings emerge into public cultural form.

DOCUMENTARY MEDIA PRODUCTION AS SOCIAL PRACTICE

Scholarship in cultural approaches to communication has been stuck with a theoretical and methodological division between analyzing the structures of production for various kinds of texts, and the analysis of their reception. As researchers and theorists we seem bound within the economic metaphors we live by. The recent development of work on the reception and interpretation of media texts has risen up against a now less vital tradition of research about their production, and the divide between these two regions of inquiry segments the study of communicative processes in unnecessary and detrimental ways. Writers within audience studies have commented on this divide. The editors of the influential collection *Remote Control*, for instance, suggest that "we might do better to rethink the usefulness of the production/consumption dichotomy" (Seiter et al. 1989:8). Similarly, Grossberg calls attention to "the problem of the gap between productive interests, textual practices, and consumption effects or, in simpler terms, the gap between encoding and decoding" (Grossberg 1987:33). As Caughie maintains, there is some difficulty in escaping from "the economic problematic of production and consumption." "Consumption reverses the terms," he writes, "but it remains within the same discourse" (Caughie 1986:167).

I contend that this problematic is propelled by *disjunctive*, even hostile "discourses" regarding production and consumption, which we can attribute, in part, to divergent theoretical foundations and research agendas, particularly concerning the allocation of "agency" in the communication process. While production studies addressed new areas, they did not develop a great deal of theoretical momentum. Audience researchers, on the other hand, were propelled by theory, drawing on, most prominently, Stuart Hall's model of communication (i.e., 1980), which aspired toward a holistic view of the communication process,[19] and recast traditional understandings of the relationship between texts and viewers. Much of this work foregrounds viewers as agents themselves rather than as passive receptors of cultural products. Audience work turned to a form of ethnographic method to move out and apply this theoretical foundation to study actual reception processes, resulting in a growing body of research and theory. Unfortunately, we have abandoned the situated study of production in the process. This shift in focus leaves us with a shallow view of texts that arrive in the home preencoded with the dominant ideology of an institution or class segment, awaiting decoding by the subjected or oppositional viewer.

The consolidation of audience and production studies offers benefits: we can apply research models grounded in socially based theories of communication to the study of both production and reception, recognize a convergence instead of a divide in these social actions, and attempt to further a holistic theoretical framework encompassing these moments. Toward this end, we can use insights from audience studies to reinvigorate research on production.[20] In a counterreversal of the characterization of "the viewer as producer," we can see *television producers as viewers,* and more generally, *cultural producers as consumers* in the broad sense: as interpreting, active agents, who decode "texts" (both material they generate in their production work and a variety of material they consume outside the work context) within their own complex of tastes, preferences, and practices.

In saying this, I do not want to deny the obvious—that the makers of television texts, just as the creators of any communicative product or event, employ conventionalized and specialized occupational practices and practical knowledge, work within an institutional context with its own inherent cultural logic, and produce a tangible text, product, or performance; none of these acts are attributable to a conventional audience member. Clearly, these conventions and practices, and their experience and training, invest them with an insider's competence and perspective, and a unique stake in the process. These investments inflect all their interpretive acts, making them audiences in a special sense.

What this view highlights is the abundance of acts of evaluation and interpretation that cultural producers engage in as a necessary and formative dimension of their productive work and as a self-defining activity in other dimensions of their lives. It allows us to see producers, not only in their specialized institutions, but as agents grounded in the same types of interpretive worlds in which their audiences are, and to see how, as a group of interpreting individuals, they negotiate the production of a text. Envisioning producers as working through an interlocking series of evaluative and interpretive actions, an evaluative framework, or expressive ideology (Feld 1994a) illuminates the forms of communication they engage in, the contexts for these actions, and how the texts they produce come to bear the meanings they have. Most important, this reorientation in theory allows us to consider authorship as a grounded, empirically assessable dimension of cultural production, to attribute some definable forms of agency to authors, and to investigate how authorship operates in a particular setting or domain.

Although much of the work in film studies diverges so far from the grounded ethnographic perspective outlined here to be of little help, devoted more to psychological and critical paradigms of analysis and theory, some scholars have developed a practice-oriented perspective that incorporates a concern with production, consumption, and the text. Bordwell, Thompson, and Staiger's detailed historical work on industrial and aesthetic practices in dramatic cinema illustrates this concern with production as a social practice: "A mode of film practice, then, consists of a set of widely held stylistic norms sustained by and sustaining an integral mode of film production. These norms constitute a determinant set of assumptions about how a movie should behave, about what stories it properly tells and how it should tell them, about the range and functions of film technique, and about the activities of the spectator" (Bordwell, Staiger, and Thompson 1985:xiv). Their attention centers on fictional modes. Compared with other film genres, documentary has, over time, received less attention from scholars. Though a significant and growing body of literature on documentary film and video now exists, research on production and reception, and the consequences of institutional constraints on these processes, has been of marginal concern in documentary scholarship.[21]

This study shares the view of documentary as a highly constructed and manufactured media form that operates with a historically shifting set of conventional codes and formats, but simultaneously relies on the viewers' perception of its transparency and truth value. Producers and viewers of these works seem to "encode" and "decode" them in a frame markedly different from that employed in the production and reception of fictional works. The level of attention, the types of inference made from narrative structure and from a receiver's sense of the "real" world, and the very circumstances and purposes of watching these works are as well formed and separable from fictional film as are the specific elements of practice and production through which they are made. In Nichols's phrase, documentary is "a fiction (un)like any other" (Nichols 1991). Despite the theoretical insights of this recent work on documentary, the grounded, practical life of these forms has not been sufficiently addressed. The conventions and construction of its code— structures of composition and editing, of narrative and authorial voice and point of view, of pacing, rhythm, exposition, and a myriad of other meaningful features—and the way these conventions are regarded by makers operating in particular institutional and cultural settings have not been studied in great depth. This book explores these features within documentary practice, using a grounded ethnographic approach.

The theoretical frameworks that I have found most useful to the anthropology of media forms come from more culturally and socially oriented paradigms of scholarship. We need models that regard the production and consumption of texts as interpretive practices embedded in complex cultural processes. Michaels, in a study of the use of television in Australian aboriginal communities, proposes "a model of the intrinsic structures of the TV medium as a negotiation of texts between producers, technology and audiences, a model which intends to identify some significant features of the social organization of meanings involved in this signifying activity" (Michaels 1991:305). His analysis, influenced by Worth's anthropology of visual communication, argues for the application of a "hermeneutic model" that posits a cyclical process in the social life of television texts, "a systems conceptualization of television as a socially organized message transmission system" (Michaels 1991:306). Michaels calls for the investigation of the diverse ways that communities and cultures perceive, interpret, and produce television texts (Michaels 1994).

Michaels's work resonates with the larger framework advanced by Appadurai for the exploration of public culture. In his discussion of the dimensions of global culture flows, Appadurai coins the term "mediascapes" to

> refer both to the distribution of the electronic capabilities to produce and disseminate information (newspapers, magazines, television stations, film production studios, etc.), which are now available to a growing number of private and public interests throughout the world; and to the images of the world created by these media.
>
> "Mediascapes," whether produced by private or state interests, tend to be image-centered, narrative-based accounts of strips of reality, and what they offer to those who experience and transform them is a series of elements (such as characters, plots and textual forms) out of which scripts can be formed of imagined lives, their own as well as those of others living in other places. (Appadurai 1990:299)

Appadurai emphasizes the complex and interconnected qualities of these "mediascapes," their trafficking in narratives of self and other, and the way they are enlisted in constructions of identity, community, and nation.[22] While it is beyond the scope of this book to connect with empirical satisfaction the grounded work of *Childhood*'s production with global flows of culture, some suggestive insights can be drawn from the fact that this was an international coproduction between British and American television entities, with "strips of reality" and "narratives of the other" produced in a variety of cultural and national settings, then encoded in televisual form. Appadurai's work offers an appropriately multilayered, culturally centered theoretical framework for understanding media practices in which to place my own work. In summary, the theoretical stance I take regarding documentary television is to see it as a constructive act of social communication and cultural production. The texts that are documentary television programs emerge from the variety of social interactions that occur in its making, guided through all production stages by interpretive and evaluative acts, constrained and steered by the field of production within which the work is embedded, and articulated and interpreted through conventional codes. In Michaels's sense, television production is a form of cultural mediation based on negotiations between powerful social agents that shape a text, presented in the context of a hybrid public culture. Through these mediations the complexities of production and reception become part of the many processes by which cultural identity, the way individuals regard and "know" themselves and cultural others, get produced and reproduced. The cultural authority that American society places in both the documentary form and in public television contributes to the importance of these identity-producing processes.

THE FIELDWORK SITUATION: MEDIA POWER AND "STUDYING UP"

I began this research project with the naive assumption that I would not have great difficulty finding a producer working on a documentary program or series intended for public television who would be willing to be scrutinized by an ethnographer. Film and television makers working within the "public" sector, I reasoned, would be committed to opening up channels of information and would therefore be sympathetic to the kind of study I was proposing—and be interested in participating as subject. Perhaps my offer of free labor in exchange for access would even add an incentive. I narrowed my pool of choices by seeking a production whose subject focused in some way on the representation of culture, though within broadly inclusive parameters. I hoped to gain access to much of the project's ongoing, day-to-day work— to observe planning sessions, location shoots, the screening of footage, and editing sessions—and have access to proposals, correspondence, and the project's pool of film footage.

My presumption was that an independent production geared for public television broadcast would be less concerned about its public image and more interested in free assistance than a project produced completely "in house" by a PBS station, and therefore would be more likely to grant me access. After telephoning a network of independent and staff producers in the spring of 1989, I came to realize that the PBS system operated as a much more closed world with more restricted working practices than I had assumed. I found it ironic that documentary producers who relied on their subjects' willingness to expose aspects of their life to an observer with a camera and recorder were unwilling to expose their own work practices to an observer with a notebook. In retrospect, I think this might have been predictable.[23] Though I received many interested and sympathetic responses to my queries, few people were interested enough to consider agreeing to this type of investigation.

The story of my failure with one potential site is instructive. I learned of an executive producer at a PBS affiliate station beginning to coproduce a short series of documentaries on Asia through a complex, delicate, and, for my research purposes, extremely interesting partnership with overseas television companies. He expressed enthusiasm for my project and a willingness to provide access to the series, and he even offered to arrange for some financial support for my project. However, the week before I was to begin observing their preplanning sessions, I received an apologetic early-morning call from this executive producer informing me of the acute resistance of the public information office at his station, dooming my participation with the series. My appeals to various station administrators remained fruitless. An administrator had become concerned about protecting both the station's public reputation and its relationship to its production partners during a potentially difficult coproduction. Participation in my study could risk embarrassment for any of the partners. With sincere apologies from the producer, the group withdrew its participation.

After this disappointment, I became elated when Geoff Haines-Stiles at The *Childhood* Project expressed some interest in my research. *Childhood* promised to be an impressive series and a rich site for my research, and I had nearly run out of other possibilities and patience. Beginning with my first telephone call, the fieldwork situation that evolved presented significant challenges.[24] After reviewing my research proposal, Haines-Stiles invited me to *Childhood*'s office for an interview (during which he thoroughly critiqued my proposal). About one month later, WNET's administration gave me permission to conduct my research. I began visiting The *Childhood* Project office in early December 1989 as they were ramping up into production. Their willingness to participate in my study stemmed, I presume, from a combination of factors, including Haines-Stiles's past association with the Annenberg School, his interest in the research material I might contribute to the series from the field of communication, and WNET's secure position in the PBS system.

Social scientists, particularly anthropologists and sociologists, have written at some length about the complexities both of conducting ethnographic studies of one's own culture (Moffat 1992) and of "studying up" (Nader 1974), choosing as research subjects individuals and institutions that occupy a higher status in the social structure than the typical ethnographic subject (who is usually of lower class and status than the researcher) and, occasionally, than the researcher himself or herself. These dynamics of social power are relevant here, since PBS producers and staff, although they are not elites in an economic or class sense, do hold significant cultural power and status through their privileged position in the field of public television production, and they are generally well educated. Radway discusses the degree of subject self-consciousness that obtains when one studies elites: "They know, after all, what academics 'do,' and they can quite adequately imagine how they might be represented in an academic discourse that would take them as its subject" (Radway 1989:9). She writes that subjects' knowledge of what academics do is powerful and can influence the ethnographic process. This form of subject knowledge can assist the researcher in obtaining information through situations where participants willingly include the ethnographer in the project's networks of oral and written communications. At the same time, self-consciousness about the research process and the anticipation of the value of specific pieces of information as "data" can also induce participants to conceal certain kinds of information and occasionally deny access. These issues were particularly relevant in my own work, in which participants, especially Haines-Stiles, had a clear notion of the academic work I was undertaking[25] and influenced my access and participation.

More unusual in this field situation were the complexities of studying a group whose work has such reflexive correspondence with the doing of ethnography. Both The *Childhood* Project and my research on it were engaged in the nonfictional representation of the lives of others. My study focused on the work lives of subjects whose occupation centers on finding willing subjects to interview, observe, and document, and whose representation they control. While I was aware of this situation much of the time, it became especially obvious to me during the odd and not infrequent moments in the field when the subject of my research was brought to the foreground. Often this took the form of questions and humorous remarks about my field notes, which I had incessantly scribbled into a composition book (I received occasional requests from staff for those notes as a resource for remembering references); statements made in my presence that qualified or explained an action or incident; and teasing about whether these statements would end up in my report. For instance, producer/director Gene Marner, while directing a shoot in a day care center in suburban New York, decided to use more rolls of film than the budget had allotted. He made a wisecrack about my registering this excessive expenditure in my field notes. With this joke Marner revealed both a clear understanding of my work, an acknowledgment of the self-consciousness resulting from my presence, and the confidence to feel immune to any potential damage resulting from it.

Haines-Stiles and I negotiated an initial arrangement—what he called our "quid pro quo"—where he would grant me access to the project in return for my services of conducting research on children and media and searching for ethnographic film material. He agreed to allow me to attend meetings and go to the office for day-to-day work, and he consented to be interviewed. I had to work out arrangements with other staff members to gain similar access, and we drew up a contract allowing them a degree of editorial approval over my writing. Our formal written agreement granted the producers the right to review and comment on the manuscript I submitted, as well as on any forms of academic publication. I would not be bound to incorporate their comments, but if contested points of fact remained, the producers could contact my advisors or editors to express their disagreement. For any popular publication that would result from this research, though, they reserved more editorial authority, specifically the prerogative to edit my text before publication. Although it took a bit of uneasy negotiation to arrive at this agreement, I felt comfortable with what it offered me, and felt that the constraints they demanded were fair. Haines-Stiles did respond to drafts of this book with extensive commentary and some requests for editorial changes, and I complied with many of these. I feel that his reflections improved the text without compromising my authorial objectives, and the sincerity and seriousness of his responses convinced me of the relevance of my analysis.

The producers and staff were generous with their time and attention throughout the research process, and Geoff Haines-Stiles surprised me with his willingness to allow me some access to confidential situations. He directed my attention to documents and anecdotes he considered useful to my work, placed my name on the office routing list, through which I received a substantive amount of office correspondence, and kept me fairly well informed of project occurrences. I was also granted access to many document files and all the film footage, and had no restrictions on whom I might talk to about the project. Still, I did not have complete access to all the meetings and correspondence that I wanted. Because of convenience or confidentiality, I was excluded from certain meetings and flows of information that I think would have served me well. For instance, I was excluded from an important advisors' meeting that focused on the role of the "on-camera hosts" and from business meetings with WNET officials. I state this not to complain about my treatment, but to point out the limitations of any study in which subjects with a certain amount of power allow themselves to undergo this degree of scrutiny and oversight.

RESEARCH STANCE: FROM OBSERVATION TO PARTICIPATION

My research situation carried with it a double edge of identity conflict and, consequently, a complex interpersonal role for me to fill. Besides being an academic, I also have training as a filmmaker and continue to work on independent and freelance documentary productions. At more than one point in my career, I saw myself on a vocational trajectory in film and video production, and pursued employment in public television, and have worked on programs that have aired on PBS.[26] My professional background influenced my participation in *Childhood*, a PBS production with a great deal of professional prestige. I came to the project with preformed opinions about, and competencies in documentary production, and my ambivalence about how much of these to reveal presented me with a dilemma both strategic and ethical. Ethnomusicologist Henry Kingsbury writes about a similar dilemma during his fieldwork in a musical conservatory (1988:23), where he debated revealing his extensive musical background because he was concerned with the effect this revelation would have on his ability to participate as a researcher. He worked out what he thought was an optimal mix of honesty and research efficacy, revealing something of his training, but not the full extent of his competence, a stance similar to the one I employed.

My initial role as academic researcher limited my participation in *Childhood* and made visits to their floor at WNET somewhat awkward. The producer/directors seemed hesitant to invite me along on location shoots, since from their point of view I would be of little help and something of an obstacle in a setting that called for unobtrusiveness. The ethnography of office work, in which subjects' primary activities are speaking on the phone and typing on computer keyboards, leaves little room for productive observation without conspicuously disturbing their work. This I did to some degree. As the project and my relationship to it evolved, I offered more services to the series, and the staff recognized additional skills I had to offer. My revised stance as participant *and* observer afforded me a role in the production that made my visits to the office much more purposeful, provided me greater access to information, and resolved what sometimes felt like a duplicitous presentation of self.

As Radway relates, conducting research with accomplished practitioners in a field one is, at the least, sympathetic to, and who also have a certain amount of cultural power, confronts issues not easily resolved: "In developing the relationships necessary to any ethnography with members of a powerful elite, the ethnographer runs the risk of compromising his or her willingness and ability to critique the practices of that elite. Relativism may be the unavoidable result of getting to know well-intentioned people who are nonetheless caught up within institutional practices that the ethnographer would otherwise want to critique or even oppose" (Radway 1989:10). I willingly embrace a certain degree of relativism if it is the result of an analysis with more empirical depth and theoretical grounding than an explicitly critical approach. Also, following Radway's distinction between practitioners' intentions and institutional practices, the ethnographer can maintain a critical attitude toward institutional structures rather than against the individuals who work within them.

The traditions of interpretive social science and fieldwork approaches to communication bolster my approach in this study. These paradigms see ethnographic knowledge as the product of an encounter between interpreting researcher and thinking, acting subjects, propelled by the objective of portraying and analyzing "native" frameworks of understanding and action. As I show in the next chapter, many have argued that interpretive research needs to move beyond these native conceptualizations to consider as well how these frameworks are put into productive practice. This tension between "native" theory and practice is central to the work of Bourdieu, and other ethnographers have described and built upon it.[27] The ethnographic model employed here seeks to move between, on the one hand, native understandings, conceptualizations, and theories and, on the other, real-life practices and institutional constraints, to consider the relation between the symbolic and the practical.

POSITIONING THE ETHNOGRAPHY OF MEDIA PRODUCTION

Although I became more autonomous as my participation expanded in reflecting on the fieldwork I realize how my initial positioning close to the executive producer and the producer/directors constrained my research. Although this constraint was in some ways appropriate—I approached the study to analyze the producers' ideological framework as it is put into practice—it is worthwhile to consider how my situation might have limited the research I did and the expression of that work in this written form.

One way to assess how my association with the producers limited my participation in the series is to hypothesize how my research would have differed had I taken the role of a technical staff worker, perhaps as an editing assistant, occupying a place on the opposite side of a well-institutionalized divide in media production between production personnel and technical staff, management and labor (a divide that does not exist to the same extent within the independent production tradition in which I had worked previously). My view of the project would have been a bottom-up perspective, concerned more with portraying the day-to-day labor of program construction rather than the larger issues of series conceptualization. I might have focused more on an understanding of editing practices, and how the material for *Childhood* differed from that of other series or programs, and emphasized the authorial role of the technical staff in shaping the programs. I would have had easier access to work in the editing room, but would not have been invited to higher-level meetings. In sum, I would have encountered a different set of constraints and possibilities.

Another aspect of this constraint is captured well by what Charles Bosk described as the problems inherent in "a gift relationship":

> The problem of objective description and analysis is in itself formidable if one were only observing a television program, for example. In fieldwork, the problem is made more complex because of the deep relationships and attachments one builds over time to one's subjects. As Charles Lidz (1977) has correctly pointed out, the right and privilege of being an observer is a gift presented to the researcher by his host and subjects. So the observer has, in addition to whatever the other problems that becloud his structured role-relations with his subjects, the very special problems that attend the giving and receiving of gifts. (Bosk 1979:203)

Bosk talks about the feelings of solidarity and obligation that often result from the fieldwork situation, and warns against three associated dangers that the gift of access exercises as a tyranny over the ethnographer:

> (1) The danger of overrapport, so thoroughly merging with the subject's point of view that one cannot achieve the critical distance necessary for analysis; (2) the danger of overindebtedness, so thoroughly feeling a sense of diffuse obligation that one can no longer assess what one does and does not properly owe his subjects; and (3) the danger of overgeneralization, so thoroughly idealizing one's subjects that one sees their behavior as representative of all persons in a class. (Bosk 1979:204)

My perspective in this study admittedly flirts with the dangers of overrapport to some extent. As an ethnographer, I was positioned by the conditions of my research and my interest in understanding and representing the producers' point of view into the producers' camp. As a documentary filmmaker, I confess to feelings of respect for and identification with the producers and their work and realize the potential inhibition of my critical impulses. Yet my identification with and occupation of other roles in the production simultaneously protected me from overrapport with the producers. My work as both an academic researcher and scholar and as a paid freelance crew member allowed me to view the project and the producers' perspectives from these other positions as well. My eventual staff position, low within the hierarchy of The *Childhood* Project, also protected me from overrapport, since I shared some of the production's grunt work with the staff, enabling me to identify with their roles.

Perhaps more important, I identify myself as an independent filmmaker outside, and to some extent denied access to the circles of power through which these producers work. I share the independent media community's frustration with the insularity of American public television, and feel critical of the direction into which this institution has been moving as it attempts to reshape itself. This ongoing critique, observable in the alternative media press (*The Independent, Afterimage*), is not at issue here, however. Although I do not fault *Childhood*'s producers for maintaining this exclusionary system—the fault lies at other levels of decision making within organizations like WNET, PBS, and CPB, which control the funding and staffing of these projects—I do view that system with a fair amount of cynicism, tempered with a sense of envy for the producers' place within it.

I was also prey to what Bosk categorizes as "overindebtedness," since I felt I owed the producers a great deal for the access I received. The difficulty I had locating a site for my research project is evidence of the unique opportunity the project afforded me. My vocational identification as a filmmaker also intensified this feeling of indebtedness: not only was I given the gift of fieldwork access, but also that of association with an impressive television production, an addition to my own reserves of symbolic career capital: the key players in this project could potentially help my own career as a filmmaker. In addition, I felt the constraints of knowing that Geoff Haines-Stiles (and perhaps others) would eventually read this text. I would have to justify to him any critical interpretations and would feel guilty over any potential transgressions of the trust we developed. I tried to guard against this sense of overindebtedness as best I could, knowing the importance to my research of maintaining some appropriate amount of critical distance.

My experience with other contexts of film and television production helped me avoid the problem of "overgeneralizing," extending my analysis of the actions of these producers to all forms of documentary production, or even to public television documentary more specifically. For instance, during this research period I was hired for several days as a production assistant for a network documentary on children's health care, which provided an enlightening contrast to *Childhood*. This production was shot on videotape rather than film. It devoted much less time to research and preparation than was typical for a comparable shoot with *Childhood*, and tended to intervene much more directly in the pro-filmic behavior than was done in *Childhood*. This kind of comparative view continually led me to consider the particular configuration of personnel and circumstances that characterized The *Childhood* Project.

In sum, if I have sacrificed a certain degree of critical distance in exchange for a more deeply textured understanding of the work of production, I feel that such a trade-off is justified, especially in light of the critical armchair writing so prevalent in media studies. This last point deserves some emphasis, for I envision this study as both an argument for ethnographic studies of the media as well as a statement encouraging the positive aspects of public broadcasting. In much the same way as grounded ethnographic research on audiences and on viewing practices has opened up media research in a number of directions, field-based studies and analyses of production processes can move us past what are fairly flat and pedestrian conceptualizations of how meaning is mediated in television production—and in other genres. In its potential for a progressive form of intersubjectivity, ethnographic work on documentary media production can provide the same reflexive engagement and self-critical knowledge available through public television documentary.

LIMITATIONS TO THE ETHNOGRAPHY OF MEDIA PRODUCTION

After a few months of research, I became convinced that, even if I had total access to The *Childhood* Project and unlimited resources of time and money, I could never adequately account for all of the important events in the production and for all the perspectives that key individuals brought to bear on this work. Too many people were doing too many things at too fast a pace for me to track them all. It became clear that I could only represent in my writing a portion of the day-to-day work of the series, an overview of the project's design and objectives, and the perspective of the New York–based producers and the academic advisors. I rely on the fact that as an ethnography, this case study allows me to see the general in the particular, and to portray that particular instance with as much interpretive depth and explanatory breadth as is manageable: this is both the power and limitation of ethnographic work. As the research project progressed, I saw that a high level of redundancy occurred in The *Childhood* Project's day-to-day work, particularly concerning the more important issues in the series. Although I would miss many data-rich instances, anecdotes, and exchanges, I still witnessed the important structural and conceptual tensions in the series repeatedly in different forms and contexts. In conducting this study, I relied on observations, field notes, formal audiotaped interviews and group meetings, written documents circulated by staff, including program treatments and scripts from various stages of production, and correspondence, research reports, and proposals from the project's files. Many file documents came from the earlier developmental stages of the series, which I reconstructed through these records and through interviews.

Many authors of situated field studies choose to obscure the identities of their informants, using either pseudonyms or generic titles for individuals and institutions. This strategy seemed both unnecessary and detrimental to my approach—and unavailable as well. Since I was empathetic to the views and situation of the producers, I felt it was unnecessary to obscure the identities of the principal subjects. This effort would probably have been futile anyway, since the names of the members of the production team would be clear to those potential readers for whom this information mattered most, that is, other public television practitioners. Awkward attributions like "a producer/director said . . . ," would limit the possibilities of identification to three people at most. In addition, influenced by arguments in favor of a dialogical anthropology (D. Tedlock 1983), I have attempted to include much of the transcribed speech of the production staff in this report. Given my interests in exploring aspects of agency and power, to avoid revealing identities would have been hypocritical. I would gain more by identifying the work of specific individuals in the series and being held responsible for accurately and sensitively portraying their attitudes and efforts.[28]

THEMATIC OVERVIEW AND ORGANIZATION

Like the *Childhood* series itself, this book evolved into a dual structure based on both chronology and theme. The study focuses on a project with a discrete life that unfolded in time, presenting an obvious processual scheme, which would follow the *Childhood* production from planning through shooting and postproduction to the final text and its reception. This is a common structure in writings on cultural production. Though I have attempted to present the chronology clearly, the book's chapters are thematically organized. Since the production stages typical of most television and film projects were not as discretely segmented in The *Childhood* Project—the planning stage overlapped well into the time when footage was already arriving, and the editors worked on constructing the programs while a fair amount of shooting still remained—a chronological scheme would have presented an inconveniently complex storyline around which to work. More critically, though, I believe that a thematic organization will highlight the conceptual issues this study addresses and will allow the analysis to trace these issues through the progressive production stages, rather than detail the procedures themselves.

Chapter Two addresses how the social and professional setting of the series—its place within the public television system and its internal organization and history—situates *Childhood* in a field of production possibilities and constraints. Contemporary pressures on American public television, including financial shortfalls, conservative political attacks, and stresses from changes in broadcasting make it a system perpetually in flux if not in actual crisis, and represent the broadest social forces affecting the program. The public television system looks to "blockbuster" series like *Childhood* as a strategic solution to its present predicament. WNET's stake in the production, the producers' standing within the system, the role the advisors played, and the institutional and financial history of the series are all important dimensions for understanding *Childhood*'s production. The series' producers had to respond to these pressures in both direct and indirect ways, and the material environment shaped the production from conception to maturity.

After the discussion of setting and organization, I consider the nature of

authorship and authority within documentary production. Based on my observations of the negotiations over authorial responsibility and control in the
series, I argue for a more intricate, interactive, and socially grounded understanding of documentary television authorship. Chapter Three begins by exploring the intertwined issues of authorship and authority in light of theories
of evaluation and representation, contesting poststructuralist arguments about
the "death of the author" with a more grounded sense of agency. Drawing on
reception theory and audience research, I develop the analogy of the
producer as consumer and suggest a rethinking of the divide between production and reception, and a more complex and socially situated view of
"authorship" and production. This view sets the work of documentary filmmaking within the social structure and social life of cultural production.

The analysis in Chapter Three draws primarily on observations of meetings for planning, script writing, and editing, and of the discourse employed
in making evaluative decisions. I describe the variety of frameworks and
textual strategies that different members of the production team employ in
sifting through the extensive written and audiovisual material gathered in the
preproduction and writing stages, and the voluminous footage they assembled and had to appraise during production. In particular, I focus on differences in how the producers and academic advisors approach the material to
be included in the series, and the tensions between their varying conceptions
of how to articulate scientific ideas and human experience in television form.
The producers and scholars are dedicated to different frameworks for the
establishment of authority, credibility, and interest, based in part on the different audiences they imagine viewing the series (general versus professional), the multiple uses of this text (parental advice, classroom exposition,
general interest), and the varied textual structures they deem effective (narrative versus expository, "cinematic sequences" versus "good science"). I contend that much of the process of media production involves the theorizing of
reception, and examine the ways in which producers anticipate and accommodate the audiences they presume will see the series (prefiguring a PBS
audience that shares many of their demographic and cultural characteristics),
and act as audiences themselves within and outside the production process.
This analysis reveals a great deal about the structures of pedagogy and pleasure that are self-consciously balanced in this genre of public television documentary.

An examination of genres of public television begins Chapter Four, situating *Childhood* in relation to the lineage of educational programs on public
television. The chapter begins with a critical exploration of theories of genre
in media studies and anthropology. I argue for a broad, socially grounded
conception of genre borrowed from sociolinguistics and performance theory
that examines how social actors negotiate between their expectations of a
text and their experience with it—when either producing or consuming it or

doing both—and which looks at the genre historically, discursively, and practically. Building on this discussion, I trace the history of the genre and how the producers distinguish their work from that in other series (i.e., *The Civil War* [Burns 1990], *Cosmos* [Sagan 1980]) and programs produced by them and their colleagues. This leads to an analysis of how the series' program formats developed and evolved through the production, allowing me to portray both the innovative and conventional aspects of the series. The producers assert specific rationales for which conventional formats do and do not "work" given their series' objectives. *Childhood*'s producers attempted to depart from certain conventional approaches in public television documentary, but wound up relying more than they had hoped on formulaic structures. I conclude that genres change as practitioners work through their aesthetic and topical constraints, and that their generic understandings are multiple, differentially held, and often contested in production.

Chapter Four continues by applying an ethnographic analysis to the formal dimensions of the series, working through the evaluative and classificatory language producers employ in negotiating and developing scenes, sequences, and structures. I maintain that textual analysis should derive from both production practices and the theoretical frameworks that steer producers, illustrating and explicating the aspects of the text that the producers focus on in discourse about and practical attention within the production process. This approach draws on the study of "poetics" or "ethnotheory" from anthropology, folklore, and linguistics, working into the text from producers' conceptualizations of and debates about formal features of the text. In particular, I explore how producers structured individual programs and the series as a whole. These were complex decisions, since the series was organized both chronologically and topically, following children's development from birth into adolescence, and introducing thematic foci where they were age appropriate (for instance, education is presented in "Life's Lessons"/ Program Five, which roughly covers the age span from five to seven years).

The producers operated within specific parameters of time and exposition and were constantly juggling, substituting, and eventually cutting down the visual and verbal material as they moved from script to rough cut to final shows. Simultaneously, the staff had to struggle with the rhetorical needs of the series: connections of themes, characters, and aesthetic style between episodes, and introductions and conclusions for the series itself and for the episodes within. They also had to balance the requirements of both regular and intermittent viewers. Material limitations of both budget and labor costs constrained all these production decisions. The result involved a lengthy, complex, and pressured editorial process throughout all stages of production. A central tension emerged between using documentary scenes of families as dramatic narrative versus using them as scientific illustration, raising the general problem of exposition in documentary form and its relation to audience attention and fulfillment. *Childhood*'s producers were determined to ground the elements of the series in relevant research literature and "cutting-edge" scientific knowledge while producing a series that avoided being didactic or pedantic and was enjoyable for a general audience member to watch. They constantly searched for dramatic, experiential visual material to illustrate intellectual points and combined expository and narrative modes of articulation. In the end, tensions were played out, more or less successfully, between the "magic" of realism and the edification of expository explanation, between the programs as experience and as scholarly knowledge, mediated by the producers' practical logic and theories of program production.

Chapter Five focuses on the representation of other cultural worlds in *Childhood*, drawing on recent critiques within anthropology, media studies, and cultural studies regarding "discourses of the other." However, I situate these debates around the representation of culture in public discourses. This chapter examines how *Childhood*'s producers worked through issues in the representation of culture, selecting, structuring, and framing the film material used of the several cultures represented in the series. I concentrate on the frameworks they employed while negotiating and constructing these cross-cultural representations, describing two particular modes of cultural representation—extended sequences showing a single culture, typical of contemporary documentary, and what I term "cross-cultural tropes," which articulate an explicit comparison between the producers' and/or viewers' cultural practices and those of another culture, an explication of cultural difference.

Childhood's producers structured both the portrayal and comparison of child-rearing practices and children's behavior into the program's basic design and narrative structure, illustrated through scenes of families at home and children at school and play in a variety of cultures. These comparisons raised several thorny issues, resulting in disagreements between the series' producers and academic advisors, who voiced objections to framing this type of intercutting for comparisons between cultures. Indeed, the initial rationale for choosing "representative" families was to allow the producers to employ a kind of televisual shorthand, highlighting cultural differences between what were essentially national cultures without having to explain a great deal about cultural or class differences within a country. Several people associated with the project objected to this strategy.

I argue that this type of comparative analogy is a common structure of understanding in public discourses about other cultures. The producers did not feel uncomfortable taking a certain amount of social scientific license, defending the value of scenes or sequences on different grounds than that of the social sciences. Their justifications emerge from a liberal, humanistic rationale. The producers felt that the Baka rainforest society footage, for instance, evokes a primal human quality in an emotive, poetic way, and were less concerned with its validity (questioned by one advisor) in social scientific terms. I regard this as a case where two systems of authority conflict, and where the producers assert a televisual logic to supersede arguments bolstered by social scientific reasoning. The tension here is between scholarly arguments and strategies for articulation, and what I term an ideology of "televisual humanism," a logic and strategy of articulation that shifts authority to the presumed, predicted, and observed response of the audience. This televisual humanism appeals to a sense of equality and empathy by seeing universalism within difference, drawing on both the social scientific and sociobiological positions, but positing these arguments in relation to an ideology of articulation for its particular audience. Lutz and Collins interpret this same sort of humanism (they call it "classical") in their reading of the motivations behind *National Geographic* magazine (Lutz and Collins 1993). In fact, the overlap between public television and *National Geographic* is not incidental, since *National Geographic*'s documentaries comprise the most popular television programs broadcast on PBS for many years (until they recently left public television), and one might presume that the audiences for these two sets of texts have a great deal of overlap in membership and orientation.

Childhood's producers sincerely hope to convince the viewer of the shared burden of all families, despite cultural differences, and thereby draw the viewer in to "experience" the worlds of these families. Often there were compromises to be made between these two frameworks of authority. The series' rhetorical form pulls simultaneously in both directions; the expository dimensions of the text move to generalize and distance while the observational character draws the viewer to particularize and participate, "to respond to these characters," as executive producer Geoff Haines-Stiles argued. The hybrid text that *Childhood* became contains both these complexes of meaning, yet what emerges is a strong allegorical tendency in which representations of cultural others are constituted as much by how the producers project a version of "ourselves" than how "we" see "others." In Benedict Anderson's sense (1991), programs like *Childhood* and other PBS shows create a sense of imagined community through the projection of commonality and difference, seeing the world as what Barthes characterized as universalist humanism in his essay "The Great Family of Man" (Barthes 1972).

The conclusive Chapter Six begins to synthesize these analytical threads by considering how what Bourdieu terms "financial and symbolic capital" constrains the kind of agency available to producers and the practical strategies they employ. The larger context involves the configuration of this series within the present moment of agitation and adjustment in the PBS system, within the life history of WNET, perhaps the highest profile station within PBS, and in relation to the history of this genre of educational programming. *Childhood* is a big-budget multipart series, a form that distinguishes programming on the PBS schedule, undertaken when the system is searching for its identity in the ecology of broadcast television and grappling for a greater share of certain audiences. Relationships between PBS, WNET, and The *Childhood* Project emerge out of this context: the series exists as an object with a range of value for these different institutions, which assert their stake in the series, and their commitment to it, in different ways and at different times. The hierarchical organization of the production itself provides a second, more local context for understanding production frameworks and practices. By judging how the financial constraints of the project (as one public television producer put it, "You are never out from under the budget") interrelate with aesthetic means and intellectual objectives, I argue for a thicker description of cultural production that posits a complex interaction between agents, institutions, and texts.

By stepping back from *Childhood* and considering the social location of the series and of public television in the broader landscape of American cultural production, we can rethink current debates and conflicts over the value and mission of public broadcasting, the place of television in American public culture, and the articulation and reception of knowledge and information from these media. At various points in this study, I characterize the producers' point of view as lodged in tensions between education and entertainment, pedagogical accuracy and audience pleasure, and between social scientific relativism and "televisual humanism." I argue that these tensions locate this production (and similar material on public television) between highbrow and middlebrow culture. A PBS show like *Childhood* strives to bridge the gap between the popular sensibility we have come to expect of television, characterized by dramatic satisfaction, character identification, and a specific visual and aural aesthetic, and the demands of enlightened educational enrichment, with its scientific authenticity, verbal exposition, and extractable intellectual conclusions. Of course, the popular sensibility it seeks is not that of the mass audience (left to network television), but of the educated, demographically advantaged lay person. In a sense, this tension is a central dilemma operative in the current crisis of public television and speaks to the problematic place that such media forms have in the American public sphere. Critics of the PBS/CPB system from both the political right and left feel that public television does not operate effectively as either educational television or entertainment enterprise. Many of the system's difficulties can be traced to this tension, one that is central to other dimensions of public culture in contemporary America.

By examining how this tension plays out in creating a specific form of cultural production, I make an argument as well for an approach to theorizing the relationship between media texts and social processes that roots itself in the interpretive activities of agents involved in their production, rather than fixing on the work of critics and analysts. The result is an approach to analyzing media as cultural process that neither reifies those texts and practices nor limits them to a venue through which culture is produced, but rather situates media as an integral part of public culture in contemporary life. Although I do not intend here to suggest a program for reforming public television, I do feel that by rethinking the institutional arrangements that further this tension, a new vision for public television could emerge, preserving much that is positive about programs like *Childhood* while relieving the pressures that lead producers to compromise their more innovative objectives. In short, I believe that public television does hold incredible potential for acting as a more democratic and participatory public sphere. A series like *Childhood* represents one model for activating this objective, but there are other models as well. My position is that public broadcasting has to facilitate and make possible a much greater diversity of approaches, voices, and subjects, and to allow access to a wider selection of authors and participants from diverse and independent backgrounds than it does now. But much will have to change about the system and its financial, organizational, and political structures for this potential to emerge. I hope this book contributes to a better understanding of that system and of working within it.

CHAPTER TWO

Childhood on the Contested Territory of Public Television in the United States

THE *Childhood* series was developed, produced, and broadcast at a time of great change within public broadcasting in the United States.[1] Although, as I explain below, *Childhood*'s producers maintained a certain amount of autonomy from higher systemic forces and tensions, the project still was enmeshed in and a product of the public broadcasting system itself, which provided most of the funding, a certain degree of oversight, and the broadcast venue. This chapter situates *Childhood* on the contested terrain of cultural production that characterizes public television at this time, and provides an overview of the workings of the series from development into production. By examining the contours of public television broadcasting, *Childhood*'s place within it, and the logistical workings of The *Childhood* Project, this chapter provides a context for understanding how the series was both constrained by and transcended the possibilities this field circumscribes, and describes the overlapping organizational, economic, and political contexts within which public television programs are produced. Structurally, we must consider these contextual frameworks in analyzing how producers as agents are both limited and enabled by their place in a complex social field. How does this field shape and influence the texts they produce? How do these institutional and organizational forces reproduce the cultural context in which television programs are produced and received? Can we understand how media forms and practices are embedded in the same public cultural forces, flows, and tensions they in turn produce and reproduce?

The debates within and around the public broadcasting system address fundamental questions about the purpose and mission of public television: What stake do different segments of our society have in public broadcasting? What role does PBS's programming, and by extension governmental institutions, play in our national practices of entertainment, education, and democracy? How should public television differentiate its mission from the services offered through commercial television and cable systems? The CPB and PBS have constantly been pressured—particularly during yearly congressional appropriation meetings—to defend their existence as valuable public entities deserving of federal financial support. To complicate matters for public television, cable television and home video outlets now successfully market both the genre of programs that once distinguished public television from other broadcast possibilities and remain its most popular fare—science, nature, and history series, classical and operatic perfor-mances, imported (mostly British) dramatic and comedic serials—and, in some instances, the actual programs themselves. "After twenty years of striving for acceptability, rather than experimenting on the cutting edge, public television is simply one of many alternatives in the media mar-ketplace of the 1980's. Where once its cultural offerings might have made it the only 'oasis' in television's vast wasteland, it is now at best the leader of the pack, one choice in a world of choices" (Shorenstein and Veraldi 1989:237). Imagined media futures of either increased format choices or greater commercial concentration leave public broadcasting supporters with even less optimism.

Perhaps a high point for public broadcasting occurred in September 1990, when PBS broadcast *The Civil War* (Burns 1990), an eleven-hour historical documentary series produced by Ken Burns, a young, much-acclaimed pro-ducer who specializes in historical documentaries about American culture. Well funded by both federal agencies and private corporations, including principal sponsor General Motors, PBS gave the series an unprecedented slot in its prime-time schedule, and unprecedented promotion through commer-cials on network and public television, coverage in the popular press, and ample subsidiary product offerings. *The Civil War* achieved record viewer ratings for public television—an average audience share of 13 to 14 percent[2] —and has resulted in a series of spin-off products (soundtrack recordings, books, a documentary about the music used in the series, and so on), repeat broadcasts, often during fund-raising drives, and a sharp rise in attendance at Civil War historical sites (Leerhsen 1990). Indeed, the success of this se-ries—an extended, multiple, and prosperous life highly unusual for a PBS offering—has galvanized programmers and producers within the public tele-vision system and reshaped certain production and broadcasting practices.[3] The discourse within and around public broadcasting reflects the conviction, at least as articulated by many *within* the system, that a new era in public television had been sighted, perhaps even reached. A speech made by the CPB's vice chairman, Daniel Brenner, soon after *The Civil War*'s broadcast attested to this: "What seems most amazing is that for once in a very blue moon, the public television family put down their six-shooters, joined hands, and made a hit for Burns and *The Civil War*. Now that *The Civil War* is over, we can refer to the current era as reconstruction" (Brenner 1990:31).

The current era for public broadcasting, into which *Childhood* was born, may be looked back on as an era of reconstruction, and the long-term suc-cess of programs like *Childhood* will strongly influence its evolution, but it would not be the first such era. In fact, a critical history of American public broadcasting posits an ongoing narrative of crisis and reconstruction, with crises taking on different shapes at various points in the system's brief but turbulent history. From this critical view, the problems endemic to the system have never been completely solved and manifest themselves as different crises in different periods.[4]

Public discourse over the last decade, reflected in the popular press, describes public broadcasting either as a valuable institution mired in problems (i.e., "PBS: The Best—And Room to Grow" [Bunce 1990]), as an institution that would have something valuable to contribute if it could transcend its difficulties ("Why It's Time for Public Television to Go Private" [Corry 1987]), or as a system so overburdened with problems that it is not worth saving ("Adieu, Big Bird: On the Terminal Irrelevance of Public Television" [Lapham 1993]). All three views recognize that public broadcasting is politically embattled, enmeshed in detrimental controversy, and failing to live up to its mission, however defined.[5] Depending on their political inclinations, commentators blame the system's principal failures either on those who control power within public television (the conservative view) or those who exert pressure from outside (the liberal view). The fault can be placed, on the one hand, with the liberal media elite, who manipulate the system to promote its left-leaning, critical agenda, and, on the other, conservative politicians who constrain programming put out by the system, hoping to limit broadcasting to safe, conservative points of view. This battle has heated up during periods of fissure in public television's history, and increases in significance during congressional negotiations over the appropriation of funds for the system.

An inside history of the system[6] perceives rehabilitation resulting from this discord regarding the current conditions for public broadcasting, including the success of *The Civil War*, as a healthy adult adjusting to its new circumstances after a difficult childhood and youth. On the other hand, critical history regards the difficulties the system has undergone as endemic to its political nature and attributable to the vague definition of and mandate for the notion of public broadcasting itself. By the early 1990s, some significant reform would clearly be necessary for public broadcasting to remain vital through the shifting conditions created by new technologies and old politics. For the third time in the system's recent history, a committee of nationally recognized experts and officials was gathered to study, comment on, and provide strategic recommendations for the system's reform, sponsored by the Twentieth Century Fund. The Task Force on Public Television's Report, titled *Quality Time?*, begins with an executive summary outlining its mandate—"to reexamine and possibly redefine its mission, to critique its structure and the process by which it produces programming, and to develop proposals for meeting its financial requirements and for building public confidence"—and summarizing its rationale for recommending change:

The majority of Task Force members are convinced that only by reinventing itself can public television meet the needs of the American public in the twenty-first century.

Indeed, driven by an immense increase in the menu of programming available, the fragmentation of the overall television audience is likely to continue. In
this context, the broad national values, the linkages among educational experiences, the in-depth coverage of public issues, and the common cultural experience that the best of public television can offer seem of greater value than ever.
The Task Force does not believe, however, that these lofty goals are attainable
without substantial revision in the existing system. (Somerset-Ward 1993:3)

The valuation of public television's mandate in *Quality Time?* reflects a
moderate liberal defense of the system's existence and a counterargument to
the free-market ideology driving the attack on public broadcasting in the
United States and in other industrialized countries. Beyond the discrepant
readings taken by the left and the right, most historical readings of public
broadcasting's ongoing crises tend to agree on the following chronology:
after a nascent period of productive but disorganized broadcasting by educational stations, the Carnegie Commission convened to assess and comment
on the state of educational television and proposed a plan for its future.
Public broadcasting was officially born in 1967, when President Johnson,
following the Commission's recommendations, signed the Public Broadcasting Act. A dual structure was devised: the government would approve funds
to be dispersed to the Corporation for Public Broadcasting (CPB), a nonprofit private entity, set up to oversee the system, fund original programming, and direct money to a network of member television stations, which
became the Public Broadcasting Service (PBS). This complex structure was
designed to cushion the network itself from direct political interference and
influence and has remained in place since then. Through the system's history, advocates have both made proposals to Congress and placed pressure
on it for more permanent, nonfluctuating sources of funding for the system
such as the British Broadcasting Corporation (BBC) enjoys—what one
writer described as "the holy grail of [a] dedicated tax source" (Public
Broadcasting Report 1991:5)[7]—and counterproposals to eliminate, or at least
greatly decrease, the present level of funding. The result has been neither of
the two, but a continuing process of authorization and appropriation that has
kept the system running at relatively constant levels of funding, though without the financial stability, political shelter, and autonomy those within the
system have always coveted.[8]

In the current period, pressures on public television have been building.
Rowland and Tracey (1990) point to ideological, economic, and technological tensions that reached a high point in public broadcasting internationally
in the late 1980s and have continued to increase in the 1990s. Ideologically,
the New Right criticized what they saw as a liberal bias within public broadcasting, while the New Left denounced the national broadcasters as elitist,
unaccountable, exclusive, and divisive. Economically, diminishing support

from federal funds began to erode the system's financial base, increasing disparities in income between public and commercially funded broadcasters, and increasing financial pressures on organizations that produce and distribute programs. Technologically, new forms of distribution via cable, satellite, and videotape heralded the fragmentation of the public audience (Rowland and Tracey 1990:8–9). The forces that Rowland and Tracey outline have converged on public television in the United States in the present period, combining with fears of an even more hostile technological environment in the near future, to cause the recurring tensions that many commentators have recognized. Ideologically, indirect political pressure through the process of funding the CPB itself, jurisdictional discord between autonomy-seeking stations and the CPB/PBS administration (which recently instituted a more centralized structure for production and programming decisions), disputes over public broadcasting's mission, and a graying of the boundaries between programming on PBS, network, and cable television have all plagued public television. The programming function of the system—the choice of what programs to produce and air, and when—has remained relatively unhampered by direct political pressure, although the recurring congressional appropriations that determine the amount of funding for the system as a whole exert pressure on PBS and CPB at higher bureaucratic levels.[9]

Analysts of public broadcasting blame the appropriation process for insufficient and unreliable funding, which they believe has generated recurring problems and led to a redefinition of the intents and boundaries of public television.

> Public television's major problems stem from the harsh economic facts of patchwork funding, but there's truth in Bill McCarter's tough talk: "Congress just isn't going to build a BBC." Even if Congress is willing to buck Presidential displeasure and restore a few million dollars to CPB's budget, it isn't about to quadruple or quintuple the appropriation. And this is what it would take to make public television a taxpayer-funded—and, therefore, taxpayer-accountable—alternative. (Aufderheide 1984:36)

Both affiliate stations and independent program producers have had to look for nonfederal sources of financing, increasingly turning to corporations and private foundations for production funds, and to private donors and members for operating funds. As Hoynes (1994) has illustrated, the search for these sources of money has had a direct effect on programming, steering producers and station administrators toward programs more likely to garner increased financial support, higher ratings, and additional memberships.

The attack on the system is evident in headlines such as "Is PBS Really Worth It?" (Lewyn 1990), "Not with My Money" (Ferguson 1990), and "Give Up on Public Broadcasting" (Irvine 1986). Critics suggest that if PBS is offering the same fare broadcast by the networks and cable television, there is little justification for funding the system through federal resources. Thus the system finds itself caught between the need to offer an alternative to the networks and cable, based on the original mandate for public service, and the attempt to avoid ratings obscurity.

AUDIENCES, MISSION, AND PUBLIC TELEVISION'S IDENTITY CRISIS

> Public television's dilemma is that if it cannot attract large enough audiences, many of its funding sources—corporations, foundations, and the federal government, not to mention the audience itself—may dry up. If it gears its programming to the ratings game, it will betray the principles on which it was founded (and may not increase its ratings anyway). (Shorenstein and Veraldi 1989:236)

It remains for PBS to try to refine its programming philosophy without fundamentally altering public perception of its programming objectives,[10] and simultaneously to garner greater interest and financial support for those programs and for the operation of the system as a whole. PBS has experimented with, and begun to implement, marketing strategies as a remedy, once considered inappropriate and, in some cases, even illegal for public television to employ, such as the advertising campaign designed with General Motors for *The Civil War* (Burns 1990). Other programming strategies at this time included a drive to achieve a common national schedule and experimentation with novel program formats (i.e., a successful multicultural game show for teenagers, *Where in the World Is Carmen San Diego*, and a fast-paced but short-lived magazine program on popular culture, *The Edge*).

PBS's experiments with alternative venues for distribution represent another tactical response to both economic needs and technological changes. The service seeks to expand the boundaries of its field into both cable television (through the formation of PBS Distribution Services, a nonprofit corporation that will explore postbroadcast markets for PBS programs, and the proposed establishment of a cable television station called *Horizons* dedicated to interview and lecture-based programming) and home video distribution (through the initially successful PBS Video), though these projects are pending. PBS's embrace of more noticeable alliances with commercial, corporate entities, which have historically underwritten a portion of costs for major public television programs for the sake of public visibility, has also affected their programming. One result is a less and less restricted form of advertising that differs from commercial advertising in style and format, but not in the pressures placed on the producing organization. The solicitation of major corporate sponsors and the fear of offending them steer PBS producers and broadcasters away from controversial programs and issues—a form of self-censorship—and result, some have argued, in an overall reduction in public affairs programming, once regarded as a strength of public television. Even Bill Moyers, one of PBS's most prolific, highest rated, and seemingly most autonomous producers, noted the pressures of indirect censorship on his own program development, delineating the direct role Chevron Oil played in developing his series *Creativity* (Grubin and Mayers 1982).[11] In more blatant incidents in the recent past, programs on controversial subjects were blocked from or shuffled within the schedule to protect the interests of major corporate funders,[12] or to avoid offending station contributors.

In their pursuit of corporate and private support, local public television stations and the national PBS system itself now compete with other networks and stations for higher viewer ratings (in specific categories) and project the system's value as a corporate underwriting investment. As the costs of production have risen along with an increase in competition from what some within the system refer to as "look-alikes"—cable stations such as The Discovery Channel, Arts and Entertainment, The Disney Channel, Bravo, and Cable News Network, that produce and carry comparable programming— PBS has had to search out more viewers (particularly from a demographic stratum with excess disposable income) as well as more contributors, members, and corporate underwriters for their programs. Overall viewer ratings during the prime-time hours have slipped over the past few years (Colford 1990) from a high in 1986–87, although with a slight rise in the summer of 1990. Perhaps more important, public perception about public broadcasting increasingly questions its social value and purpose.

PBS IN THE PROCESS OF REFORMING
ITS IDENTITY AND STRUCTURE

PBS's attempts to market itself reveal a central rift within the system's self-image and mission, and therefore its place on the American cultural landscape. While PBS is going to great lengths to distinguish its programming from material on the networks and cable television, to define that which public television alone does well it often relies on a definition by exclusion. As Brenner explained, "For the 40 percent of Americans today who can't or won't subscribe to cable television, public television is the sole source for non-marketplace driven programming choices" (Brenner 1990:31). The phrase "non-marketplace driven" is misleading, since decisions made by public television organizations reflect a drive toward increased audience ratings, appealing to the kinds of support mentioned previously, and defining an alternative market. Hoynes draws an analogy between the logics of the economic marketplace that drive commercial television and both the funding and public marketplaces that support public television (Hoynes 1994, chapters 5 and 6). As he and other scholars have pointed out, PBS is being driven into more of a marketplace orientation (experiments with advertising and a cable subscription service exemplify this trend), and its response is to see its programming as a viable commodity and to broaden its audience base. These shifts affect how the system chooses the programs it funds and broadcasts, and how it schedules and promotes those broadcasts. The tension between the market and the "nonmarket," the hybrid space that public television occupies in the United States, must be considered central in analyzing the system. It is refracted throughout the production process, from funding through broadcast, and at all levels, from institutional structure to television form.

THE LONG-FORM DOCUMENTARY SERIES: "SOMETHING WHICH PBS ALONE DOES"

Public television's support of *The Civil War* series revealed its stake in both the type of subject matter the series covered and, more important here, in the program format—the long-form documentary—for reforming the system's identity. Commentators on public television regard the long-form documentary series, exemplified by *The Civil War* and by other recent popular series such as *Eyes on the Prize* (Hampton 1986) and *Making Sense of the Sixties* (Green and Hoffman 1991), as one program genre distinguishing PBS's offerings from those of its competitors. The Twentieth Century Task Force's report refers to these series as "the icing on the cake" that separates public television's programs from those of its competitors, and argues that PBS alone is willing to commit the funds necessary to produce major series (Somerset-Ward 1993:140). Along with the major ongoing PBS programs such as *The Newshour with Jim Lehrer* (formerly *The MacNeil-Lehrer Newshow*), *Frontline*, and *Great Performances*, they account for a major portion of the public broadcasting programming budget. The roots of the multipart series go back to the beginnings of public and educational television here and in England, and the form itself resonates with earlier models of pedagogy. These include the classroom lecture series, the illustrated lecture that Musser (1991) describes as a precedent for modern cinema, and the textbook (on which early series were partially modeled, and later programs, such as those funded by the Annenberg/CPB Fund,[13] were designed to replace). *Civilisation* (1969) with Kenneth Clark, *The Ascent of Man* (1973) with Jacob Bronowski, and Alistair Cooke's *America* (1973), landmark series produced by the BBC, pioneered this form for educational broadcasting. The BBC was initially the prime mover in originating documentary series, and British funding and production entities have since cosponsored and coproduced many productions housed at American PBS stations, as they did with *Child-*

hood. The CPB created its Challenge Fund to develop several series each year, importing the BBC model.

I take up what I term a "folk history" of this genre of programming in greater detail in Chapter Four, but here I want to stress the prominence given this genre within the field of public television programming. Interestingly, a relatively small pool of producers and personnel, a limited number of organizations, and fairly continuous streams of federal, private, and corporate funding have been responsible for the production of multipart documentary series. The resources and capabilities a major series requires make it difficult for any producer or production entity without the proper credentials and connections to obtain the necessary funding, station support, and guarantee of placement on the national PBS schedule. And it is revealing that producers working within this programming genre have a sense of being part of a tradition that goes back to these early series.

During my research on *Childhood*, I heard *Childhood*'s producers and WNET's administrators make frequent reference to past highly regarded documentary series, often reiterating their claim that *Childhood* fits within *tradition* this production tradition. I take as meaningful their interest in invoking that tradition when describing the series. For instance, promotional literature described the series as in the vein of these other landmark PBS shows ("Like such past PBS landmarks as *Cosmos* and *The Mind* (Hutton 1988), it is a series on the cutting edge of knowledge." [*Childhood* Corporate Solicitation brochure, 1990]) and was sure to mention the pedigree this series inherited from its ancestors.[14] An article in the *Los Angeles Times* reported on the early stages of the series:

> Haines-Stiles, an independent producer who served as senior producer and director for KCET's "Cosmos" science series, said that he and David Loxton, head of drama at WNET, originated the idea for the series because they were aware of the emergence of new ideas and information about childhood as "a mirror of society," and because of the success of other broad-ranging public-television series such as "The Ascent of Man" and "The Brain."
>
> "We've been encouraged by the audience response to these kinds of series, which raise significant issues, but which deal in subject matter that is not usually seen on commercial television," he explained. (Taylor 1987:9)

WNET and *Childhood*'s key production staff all benefited from their association with past productions. Both *The Brain* (Sameth 1984) and *The Mind* (Hutton 1988) were highly regarded series recently coproduced by WNET and the BBC. Geoff Haines-Stiles worked as senior producer for the series *Cosmos*, which producer/director Erna Akuginow worked on as well. Gene Marner produced several episodes for WNET's *Heritage: Civilization and the Jews* (Labaton and Siegel 1984) and *Art of the Western World* (Adato 1989), a series on which Ann Troise, Geoff Haines-Stiles's assistant for

Childhood, also worked. Haines-Stiles brought Peter Montagnon, the British executive producer, on to *Childhood* largely because of his extensive experience with this form.

Geoff Haines-Stiles discussed the series *Cosmos* in relation to the genre of long-form educational series:

> [*Cosmos*] was a great big successful series. [. . .] I'm incredibly proud to have worked on it. It really was the first home grown American big series. It was a co-production with the BBC, and it was the first time the BBC was brought in as a minority partner to an American project. And I worked with Adrian Malone, who has many oddnesses, strangenesses, but also has a set of rather grandiose ambitions that you can use television to truly do things that books can't—you can do some things that books can do and some things that books can't do, and that it's an art form of its own kind. And he came up with, I guess he must have come up with it or borrowed it from somebody, a phrase called creative documentary, which is really a good way of describing the sort of thing that we are doing here. It's not a cinéma vérité documentary. It's not *CBS News Reports*. It's not drama or fiction on the other hand, but it's doing things that they did in *Ascent of Man* and it's carrying that further, and it's saying that it's a form of communication that's just different from other forms of communication. And I think that the big series like *Civilisation*, which Montagnon did, or *The Ascent of Man*, which Malone did, are really something which PBS alone does. (Interview with Geoff Haines-Stiles, March 2, 1990)

In a letter to a staff member at PBS, David Loxton described *Childhood* with a humorous reference to Bronowski's *The Ascent of Man*: "The implicit— and often explicit—message of the series is so vast and all-encompassing that perhaps a more appropriate title would be 'The Ascent of the Child'" (letter from David Loxton to Cathy Wyler, PBS, July 25, 1991).

As I elaborate in the next chapter, the long-form documentary series carries with it certain formal and presentational conventions—historical practices judged as successful in the past and therefore having a degree of inertia about them. *Childhood*'s producers deliberately and explicitly chose to go against some of these aesthetic norms and accept others, decisions that both opened possibilities for the series and constrained the producers in certain stylistic ways.

CHILDHOOD'S DEVELOPMENT: "THE SYSTEM WANTS THE SERIES"

Geoff Haines-Stiles and David Loxton gave birth to The *Childhood* Project in 1985 through a series of conversations. According to Haines-Stiles:

> I had previously worked with David Loxton who was then at WNET trying to develop a series of science fiction dramas for public television *Playhouse*. We

had one of those produced. It was a hard project—it ended up with co-financing from Canada, and back and forth, deals are always complicated but, David Loxton and I got on with each other and he said, "You know I've been asked by WNET to think about whether there's any big series that might be worthwhile to think about undertaking following along from *The Brain* and *The Mind*." And he said, "I've been developing more dramatic projects recently, but you did *Cosmos*." [. . .] So, I said, "Well actually I have been thinking of something ever since *Cosmos*, which convinced me that big series could do things that were more like books, and I'll tell you what's been on my mind if you tell me what's been on your mind, and we'll see what's going on." And I said that I'd been thinking about, since university back in England, about where people get their ideas from, specifically where kids get their ideas from of the world. That's education in the very broadest sense, not just school but things outside school. He said, "That's interesting because I've been thinking about development and the way kids grow up." So we said it seems like we're thinking about the same project so we should try and put something together. And we did. We spent a couple of days, I was in town for like three days, and we very quickly said this would be something which we thought the PBS audience would be particularly receptive to—a look at the way in which children grew up, different ideas about children, looking historically, and how children get their ideas about the world. And we pushed it to George Page, who's the host of *Nature* and was then the senior science person, and he basically on the spot said, "It sounds like a great idea." So we then went about a very short but intense development period. (Interview with Geoff Haines-Stiles, March 2, 1990)

The collaboration united an experienced executive producer (Loxton), who was within the WNET hierarchy (director of drama and senior executive producer of specials); an independent producer (Haines-Stiles) with a growing track record within the public television system, and a major producing station; WNET. The direct access Loxton and Haines-Stiles had to George Page, a senior administrator, reveals their position of power and influence within the system. This arrangement set up the beginnings of an administrative structure for the production that, after a few transformations, would guide its trajectory during the following years.

In April 1986, Haines-Stiles and Loxton submitted their initial proposal to WNET and the work of fundraising began. In June, WNET requested and later received $100,000 from the PBS Program Development Fund,[15] made proposals to the National Science Foundation (NSF) ($500,000 requested) and the CPB Open Solicitation Fund ($150,000 requested), and began negotiations for coproduction arrangements with several British television companies. By the middle of 1987, the project received commitments of $150,000 for research and development from the CPB Open Solicitation Fund, $400,000 in production support from the NSF, and between $750,000 and $1,000,000 in coproduction funds from Britain's Channel Four. These funds were designated to administer fundamental research for the series, to fund the writing of initial series treatments that drew extensively on that research, and to begin to assemble the advisory board for the series. Peter Montagnon of Antelope Films in England was invited to join the project as co-executive producer, with Antelope Films the conduit for the funds from Channel Four. Haines-Stiles and Loxton formed The *Childhood* Project, the production entity that actually produced the programs, in association with Antelope Films. After several years of planning and development, the formal, eight-month preproduction period began in July 1987, with both the upper-level administrative staff and a core group of advisors in place.[16]

Later, the CPB Challenge Fund, a new funding mechanism (at that time), supplied the bulk of the production budget.[17] *Childhood* requested $2,500,000 from this fund and was granted $2,000,000 late in 1987. Childhood also received $400,000 from the NSF and $300,000 from the National Institute of Mental Health, which was funneled through, but in addition to, the money from the NSF. The series also received $226,000 from the CPB Open Solicitation Fund. At this point in the development period, the following funds had been committed:

$100,000 from PBS Program Development Fund (Committed in August of 1986)

$150,000 from CPB (December 1986)

$400,000 from the National Science Foundation (July 1987)

$2,000,000 from the CPB Challenge Fund (October 1987)

$750,000 from Channel Four for R & D and development and production

$250,000 from the National Institute of Child Health and Development

$300,000 from National Institute of Mental Health

(Figures from "Thirteen Memorandum" from Anne Gorfinkel to David Loxton, June 21, 1989, re: Quarterly Status Report Update)

The series had been condensed, though, from a ten-part treatment to six one-hour episodes—Geoff Haines-Stiles hoped to expand it back to eight programs when additional funds, anticipated from corporate sponsors, became available.

Going into preproduction, *Childhood* was conceived of as an eight-episode series that would explore child development from a multiplicity of cultures and through history, with insights from a variety of scholarly and scientific disciplines. A series proposal from this period describes *Childhood*'s content and approach:

Childhood will present for a general audience the ways parents and societies have raised their children throughout history and across cultures. It will reach back in history to hear a Sumerian schoolboy's lament about harsh teachers and excessive homework, study contemporary "hunter-gatherer" societies like the

African !Kung or the North American Cree of Paint Hills, for clues to our remote ancestor's childhoods, and spend time with the children of the "hunter-
gatherers in pin-stripe suits" of today's American suburbs.

[. . .]

Childhood will not present one single man or woman's point of view. The
approach will be cross-cultural and interdisciplinary, featuring the insights of the
world's leading anthropologists, sociologists, historians, educators, developmental psychologists, pediatricians and biologists.

Childhood will be filmed on location around the world. It will consciously
strive for ethnic, sexual, geographic, political and economic diversity.

Childhood will be an informational series. The study of Childhood is now a
part of many traditional disciplines and is revealing startling and unexpected
observations—new facts that revolutionize many assumptions about children
and parents. *Childhood* will present the new interest in childhood and report
recent findings.

Childhood will be dynamic and entertaining television. It will use the full
range of documentary and dramatic presentation techniques. (From *Childhood*:
A Proposal for an 8-part Television Series)

Like other documentary series before it (*Civilisation*, *Cosmos*), this proposal
is ambitious in topical expanse and intended method. The promotional copy-
writers take a certain amount of rhetorical license ("the world's leading anthropologists . . . "; "the full range of . . . techniques"), and highlight objectives for the series that are clearly attractive to funding agencies ("general
audiences," "diversity," and "new facts"), while providing sketchy details
about the program-to-be. Most importantly, the producers have the kind of
authority and organizational support required to convert this proposal into
the funding needed to produce the series.

WNET provided the institutional umbrella for developing, funding, and
producing *Childhood*. One of the first educational television stations in the
United States, WNET played a critical role in the development of the National Education Television Network (NET), which later evolved into the
Public Broadcasting Service. Today, it produces more program material, with
the possible exception of WGBH in Boston, than any other PBS station, and
has supplied the system with what public television practitioners regard as
some of its most memorable and widely shown programs and series. The
station underwent a great deal of financial difficulty during *Childhood*'s life
in production, and toward the end of that period had to lay off 10 percent of
management, including administrators involved with the *Childhood* series.[18]
Still, it is important to keep in mind both the national profile and influential
power of the station and the legacy of major series production it established.

The *Childhood* Project occupied an institutional space mostly within but
partly outside WNET.[19] The station was the conduit for all the funds raised

from American sources, applying station staff to this task, and housed the production facilities for the series. This type of organization for a major production—the sponsoring of an otherwise independent production at a producing station—is not unusual. By doing so, the station can sponsor, originate, and distribute television programs without having all of the production personnel on the permanent payroll, avoiding the cost and uncertainty of the long development periods typical for these series. This arrangement allows independent producers to have a great deal of control over their productions, but with the financial backing, administrative fortitude, and national stature of one of the highest-profile PBS stations. But this configuration raises an important question about how much and what kind of influence the station might have over the life of the series. From my vantage point, WNET's control over the series was limited in overall scope, and exerted only periodically,[20] less with issues pertaining to series content and form, and more around institutional concerns.[21]

As a result, WNET had a general influence over the series, not a determining one. The station intervened into actual production decisions (not including the role they played in corporate fundraising, public relations, and the production of the *Childhood* companion book) mainly in the planning process, when the station responded to the initial treatments, in the presentation of the work in progress at a national PBS meeting, at key points during editing, and in decisions and negotiations over scheduling for national broadcast. In many cases, though, *Childhood*'s producers weighed what they knew about or could anticipate as WNET's opinions in making difficult series decisions. As far as I observed, they never considered WNET's wishes as paramount or unmovable—even though WNET had rights of review—always weighing the station's requests against the possible benefit to the series. This much autonomy for a production at this high level of funding and visibility is unusual and attests to the staff's qualifications, the value WNET felt the series had, and their confidence in the producers and the series' subject matter.

From early in the life of The *Childhood* Project, Haines-Stiles and Loxton had been looking for coproduction partners. Coproduction arrangements are common for major public television series, often with British and American partnership, offering a method of sharing costs and resources in return for broadcast rights.[22] The actual contribution of partners (financial and logistical) and the agreements for broadcast vary depending on the specific arrangement. "For public television, co-production is 'the nature of the beast,'" says Suzanne Weill, senior vice president, programming, of the Public Broadcasting Service. At least three quarters of the programs that make up the PBS schedule have more than one party involved, she said, ranging from public television stations to independent production companies to foreign broadcasting services" ("Co-productions Now Dominate Public Television,"

1986:68). In a typical arrangement between overseas public television entities, one partner will take a majority role, raising most of the money, hiring
personnel, and housing most of the work, with the other partner contributing
some lesser amount of funds and services in exchange for the right to offer
this program through its system. Given the expense of these ambitious series
and the limitations on funding, coproduction arrangements provide an advantageous, perhaps even essential way of stretching the available money.[23]

For *Childhood*, the consummation of this relationship would be tricky,
since much of the principal funding was not yet in place for the series.
Loxton described early progress in this search in a letter to officers at CPB
and PBS:

> *Co-Production*—While in London and Japan, Geoff and I will be continuing to
> work the co-production fronts. Strongest possibilities right now include Channel
> 4 (which will be even stronger if further discussions with the excellent Peter
> Montagnon—"Ascent of Man"[24] and "Heart of the Dragon"—as our British line
> co-producer continues to be fruitful—he is very well-liked by Channel 4). We
> will also have further discussion with both the BBC and Thames as alternatives.
>
> In Japan, we are focusing our energies on Asahi and a couple of very strong
> corporate possibilities. (Letter from David Loxton to Ron Hull at CPB and Suz-
> anne Weill at PBS, November 25, 1986)

Despite having a strong Japanese presence in the content of the series,
Childhood did not succeed in working out an arrangement with a Japanese
production partner, nor did their proposals to the Canadian Broadcasting
Corporation and Brazilian Television meet with success. *Childhood*'s approach to Peter Montagnon, though, resulted in a coproduction arrangement
with Channel Four in England. Montagnon came to play a critical role in the
series. He took charge of the filming of families in Japan, Brazil, and Russia,
was present at the WNET office for most of the executive meetings and
important occasions, had a close relationship with a few of the advisors, and
generally contributed his expertise with documentary series.

At this point, The *Childhood* Project had most of its expected grant funding in place, but had not yet succeeded in securing any of the corporate
underwriting it was counting on, presenting the executive producers with a
dilemma. Would it be best to begin the series underfunded, hoping to raise
additional money during the production period, or to wait until all the funding was in place?

PETER MONTAGNON: Then we had to realize, because the awful truth was that
the fund raising looked as if it was sort of dying on the vine.

DORNFELD: On the American side.

MONTAGNON: I got Channel Four in, but that's only for a relatively small proportion of the budget, say about a million out of three. And, we then had, the

next big problem was whether to stick out for doing the full series, which was more, say about twelve, or whether to use the money that was on the table. My advice was that I thought if you don't do it now, it probably would just die on you, because it had taken about two days to get to that point. And you get all the problems within a network of getting the controllers to keep their money committed over one financial year, if it can't be used, and it screws things up for the planners in a fairly largish sort of way. And also for the fund givers [. . .] and I think it was possibly me that was more instrumental in saying "do it" than anybody else. I think Geoff just pinned his flag to the mast that he wanted to do twelve episodes because he spent so long thinking about this and planning and dreaming about it, that—and it has this shape—he had a commitment to it and knowledge of it, and he couldn't see quite how in the hell he could do what he had in mind in a lesser number. I got Channel Four to carry their money over to the next financial period, but it was fairly dodgey because the BBC right then had gotten its own series on childhood, which turned out to be an absolute paper tiger, nothing really, but it was making the Channel Four people run scared. It was getting progressively more difficult, and it was also getting more [risky] with the funds, because one would have one fund in and then another one would dribble out, some other minor fund would dribble out, as you try to keep it in. My sense of it was that there actually was a degree of real grave danger of it not happening if one stuck out for it [. . .] and we took that decision. We said, "Are we going to do it or are we not?" We decided to do it, so we pressed the button. It was then that Channel Thirteen also came in and said that they would make up the difference until such time as they got the other sponsor. And so that's how it went, and it wasn't ideal, but it hardly ever is. (Interview with Peter Montagnon, August 1, 1990)[25]

CORPORATE FUNDING AND ANCILLARY MARKETS

Given the nature of the *Childhood* series and WNET's reputation and success with past programs, WNET's struggle to obtain corporate support for the series through the development stages and much of its production period came as a surprise. It was not for a lack of effort, though, since from the early stages the executive producers, with significant assistance from WNET development staff, sought out support from major corporations in the United States and Japan, and counted this support in their budget projections. Before these corporate funds were committed, WNET felt more anxiety about corporate support than The *Childhood* Project did. WNET was obliged to make up the remainder of the budget not supplied by federal and public television funds, whether or not they obtained corporate funds, and the series progressed under these terms. *Childhood*'s producers helped WNET's corporate fundraisers in their efforts (i.e., in developing promotional material, meeting on occasion with corporate officers), but the bulk of this responsibility fell on WNET's shoulders. It was not until well into production that Nabisco agreed to contribute one million dollars to the series.

The early stages of corporate fundraising revealed some flexibility on the part of the producers in planning elements of the series in ways that would encourage corporate support. For example, during development, through a complex series of contacts, Haines-Stiles, Loxton, and Montagnon came close to working out a sponsorship arrangement with Toyota Motors Corporation in Japan. In conjunction with these discussions, the producers raised the possibility of casting the families of one or two Toyota factory workers as the Japanese on-camera representatives for the series. After seriously considering their support of the series, Toyota declined both the involvement of their employees, explaining their concerns about a perceived conflict of interest, and their series sponsorship. There were other examples where approaches were made to production entities in other countries, with the offer to tailor the series to the needs and desires of that host country (i.e., by changing the series host or including families native to that corporation's country), but none came to fruition.

Along with scheduled broadcasts on PBS in the United States and Channel Four in England, The *Childhood* Project had contracted for both a companion book to the series and educational distribution in the United States and Canada, and had explored distribution to overseas markets. The sale of the rights to the series' companion book—to be written by anthropologist Melvin Konner and also called *Childhood* (Konner 1991)—to Little, Brown, a well-established publishing house, paid WNET an advance of $500,000. The producers regarded that sort of advance as higher than expected, testifying both to the past sales successes of PBS companion books and to the broad audience that *Childhood* and Little, Brown expected to reach. Unlike most companion books for PBS or BBC-distributed series, which closely match the text of the programs they accompany, the *Childhood* book would be autonomous from the series, both in the writing process and in content. Although Konner, well known and well published in the academic and popular press, worked closely with the series as one of its key advisors, providing research articles and academic contacts, contributing greatly during group meetings, and appearing on camera as an "observer," *Childhood*'s executive producers encouraged him to depart from the series content and form in writing the companion book. Still, Geoff Haines-Stiles provided substantive input into Konner's writing, and the two texts are clearly connected. The *Childhood* book reached bookstore shelves during the fall 1991 airing of the series.

With British coproduction in place, the series was guaranteed some overseas distribution. Beyond this, the producers discussed and explored other likely broadcast markets, including Japan, India, and South America.[26] During the middle stages of production, the executive producers contracted with Ambrose Video in New York for nonbroadcast distribution in the United States. Ambrose distributes several other PBS series to schools and libraries and for individual purchase. What is instructive about these business arrangements, and representative of major PBS series like *Childhood*, is the anticipated strength and breadth of these ancillary markets, and the importance of building them into the series through the production period.

THE PRODUCERS' PLACE IN THE SYSTEM

The reputations of The *Childhood* Project's three executive producers assured that the series could operate at its high level of funding, visibility, and access to public broadcasting institutions. As mentioned above, *Childhood* originated with David Loxton and Geoff Haines-Stiles as executive producers and Peter Montagnon as co-executive producer. When Loxton died of cancer in 1989, just before the start of production, Montagnon's credit was upgraded to executive producer along with Haines-Stiles. Loxton had had a long, impressive career in public broadcasting and occupied a place of prominence in WNET and the national public television system before beginning work on *Childhood*. The first director of The Television Laboratory at WNET, an innovative forum for programs started in 1972, he was named the director of special projects for the National Program Division at WNET in 1982. He executive-produced a nationally broadcast series, *Non-Fiction Television*, which won several prestigious awards,[27] and WNET appointed him director of drama for their National Program Division in 1985. During his career he commissioned and produced some highly regarded drama programs for public television, including a pioneering production of Ursula Le-Guin's science fiction novel, *The Lathe of Heaven* (1971; Barzyk and Loxton 1980), which Haines-Stiles coproduced with him.

The initial stages of work on *Childhood* found David Loxton at or near the top of his career trajectory, while Geoff Haines-Stiles was on the steep part of his upward curve. Haines-Stiles was born in England and educated at Cambridge University (B.A. and First Class Honors in History, M.A. in History), in addition to his graduate work at the Annenberg School of Communications. After leaving graduate school he worked on a local television news magazine show in Philadelphia, then on the national PBS series *Cosmos*, featuring Carl Sagan, considered a landmark PBS series (although it received critical reviews)—an important step in his career. Because of personnel shifts on *Cosmos*, Haines-Stiles's responsibilities grew during the production, and he took over directorial responsibility for two of the episodes, along with being the senior producer. After *Cosmos*, he worked on

Figure 2.1 Executive producer Geoff Haines-Stiles in discussion with cinematographer Richard Chisolm while directing a scene with "observer" and advisor Urie Bronfenbrenner. Associate producer Rudy Gaskins looks on. (Photograph © Lawrence Ivy.)

several other science programs for public television, including *Nova* shows and the well received *The Creation of the Universe* (Ferris and Haines-Stiles 1985). He was also director of national productions for KCET in Los Angeles and worked on dramatic adaptations of science fiction stories, including *The Lathe of Heaven* with Loxton.

Geoff Haines-Stiles's responsibilities as executive producer of *Childhood* exceeded those he had assumed on previous productions. When Loxton died, Haines-Stiles took over more administrative responsibility for the series than he had anticipated, adding the upper-level contacts with WNET officers that had been Loxton's responsibilities to his work with developing the series treatments and production plans. Later, after the project released one of three producer/directors, Haines-Stiles took over that staff member's production responsibilities (the writing, producing, and directing of what evolved into three programs), leaving him with both extensive administrative and production responsibilities. His willingness to shoulder such a burden impressed many people involved with the project, who were amazed by his seemingly endless energy and ability to juggle the overwhelming details involved in the series' production.

Peter Montagnon has an extensive list of credits and positions within public television in England. After producing the landmark series *Civilisation* with Kenneth Clark, he became the first head of television and radio at England's Open University. Later, forming his own company, Antelope Films, he developed and executive-produced *Heart of the Dragon* (1983), a well-regarded series on Chinese culture, and *The Long Search* (Eyre and Montagnon 1978), about religion. Montagnon brought extensive overseas production experience to the project, along with his proficiency in vérité-style documentary, and a well-developed understanding of how to pull a major series together.

THE ORGANIZATIONAL STRUCTURE OF *CHILDHOOD*

Childhood was organized as a coproduction of Thirteen-WNET and The *Childhood* Project in association with Channel Four/London and Antelope Films, Ltd, with WNET as the principal corporate entity. Peter Montagnon described how decisions were made in splitting up responsibilities between Antelope and the New York-based *Childhood* staff:

> DORNFELD: Is that how coproductions are often done, where one of the entities will deliver a couple of programs?
>
> MONTAGNON: It can be, but it depends an awful lot on the material that's going in. If you've got a common gene pool of materials, so to speak, as it looks as though we were likely to have, it might end up in either, any of the programs, then you can see the dangers of actually, or the complications of splitting that pool up half on one side half on the other. So, then we looked at the pros and cons of whether it would be cheaper and better to do the postproduction in London or in New York, and there were quite a lot of arguments for London and quite a lot of counterarguments for New York. If you could say that largely in terms of film editors it might be easier in London, because at any one time you've got more people in the business of making documentaries, so you have a larger pool of talent to draw, and I think that's also true in part of cameramen within this specific area, because there are just more people doing it, by the special nature of British television. More money gets spent making documentary programs here probably than in the USA. But we batted that around and the problem obviously was the relocation of directors and pro-ducers. We thought in the end, no, when you added the pros and cons up, it didn't really quite make sense. It made more sense to do it here than to do it in London. I think that was the right decision. [. . .] Then we had to work out roles, and it seemed to me that one of the things where we might score, was just enough the roots, the links we've got with people overseas, because we just tend to do an awful lot more overseas shooting, again, (there's a lot more to do), so we can call on, we've certainly got the cameramen. (Interview with Peter Montagnon, August 1, 1990)

Haines-Stiles and Montagnon worked out an arrangement putting Antelope in charge of scouting and administering the filming of the overseas families (the New York office supervised filming the U.S. families), and assisted the New York staff in compiling scholarly research and archival footage.[28] Montagnon acted as the primary conduit of requests and advice to those crew members the project hired in Russia, Brazil, and Japan (though he arranged to have footage shipped directly to the New York office), and he made at least one trip to each of these countries to check on their progress. The fax machine and telephone kept a steady flow of contact and messages between the *Childhood* office in New York and Antelope in London, and Peter Montagnon made trips over to the United States every few months. As the partners had designed, Antelope's intense involvement waned toward the final editing stages.

The executive producers assembled an ongoing production staff with substantial documentary and public television production experience. The New York–based staff, housed on the tenth floor of WNET's building on West 58th Street in Manhattan, fluctuated in size between fifteen and twenty people, growing in number once postproduction began and the editing staff joined the office (see the figure in Appendix A for the series organization). By design, the New York staff represented an unusually diverse set of cultural backgrounds and a balance in gender. While organized and managed by two white male executive producers, under the oversight of mostly male, mostly white administrators at WNET, the series relied on two Asian women in key positions, an African American male as associate producer, two female cinematographers, and other women and people of color. Through the preproduction and into the production stages of the project, *Childhood*'s producers spent an unusual amount of time and energy searching out, meeting with, and evaluating the work of the freelance production personnel who worked on the series. They solicited sample reels from many cinematographers and resumes from potential support personnel (assistant camera operators, sound recordists, etc.). The producers were intent on hiring the best freelancers they could arrange to work with, and went to great effort evaluating, contacting, meeting with, and assessing the work of cinematographers in particular. It was surprising that most staffing decisions were made independently of the WNET hierarchy,[29] a level of autonomy that is probably atypical of major PBS series.

CHOOSING SERIES ADVISORS AND "OBSERVERS"

Childhood's advisors and on-camera hosts, called "observers," were chosen over the course of the project's development and early production (a process that preceded my involvement with the series). A brochure for fund-raising lists the advisors involved in the series and describes them as "prominent experts in the many fields that touch on childhood" (see table 1).

During preproduction, the executive producers requested that each advisor respond to a series of research-based programmatic questions (i.e., "What key thinkers must be in the series?"), and consulted with some of the advisors on a range of topics, including research literature in their fields, other scholarly contacts, collections of archival film, stills, and visual art, and logistical issues pertaining to the series (choice of locations, families, etc.). Later in the production process, the producers brought several new advisors in to speak and respond to questions at meetings: Ray Hiner, a history professor at the University of Kansas, an expert in the emerging area of family history (Hawes and Hiner 1991); John Demos, a historian of Colonial New England, who had written a study of family life in that place and time

---

TABLE 1

Developmental Psychology
Elizabeth Bates, Professor of Psychology, University of California/San Diego
Urie Bronfenbrenner, Professor of Human Development, Emeritus, Cornell University
Robert Hinde, Professor, Medical Research Council on the Development and Integration of Behavior, Cambridge University and Master of St. John's College
Jerome Kagan, Professor of Developmental Psychology, Harvard University
Lewis Lipsitt, Director, Child Study Center, Brown University
Alvin Poussaint, Child Psychiatrist, Judge Baker Guidance Clinic, Boston
Sandra Scarr, Professor and Chair, Psychology Department, University of Virginia
Julius Segal, author and former Director of Public Information, National Institute of Mental Health

History
Henry Steele Commager, Professor Emeritus, Amherst University
N. Ray Hiner, Professor of History and Education, University of Kansas
Harriet Rosenberg, Professor of History and Sociology, York University

Anthropology and Sociology
Melvin Konner, Professor of Anthropology, Emory University
Richard B. Lee, Professor of Anthropology, University of Toronto
Jay Ruby, Professor of Anthropology, Temple University; Director, Center for Visual Communication
Thomas Weisner, professor of Anthropology and Psychology, UCLA

(Demos 1986); and Robert Wozniak, professor of psychology at Bryn Mawr and a historian in the field of developmental psychology.

A subset of the initial advisors—Urie Bronfenbrenner, Robert Hinde, Jerome Kagan, Melvin Konner—played more prominent roles throughout the project, remaining in close contact with the production staff and leading the producers to other scholars, to research literature, and to locations for shooting. These four, along with the later addition of psychologist Sandra Scarr and the director of the Children's Defense Fund, Marian Wright Edelman, were designated as "on-camera observers," the visible hosts for the series.[30]

- Urie Bronfenbrenner, professor emeritus of human development at Cornell, is well known both for his theoretical writing on what he terms an "ecological" model of development (Bronfenbrenner 1979), and for an earlier study he conducted comparing childhood experience in the United States and Russia (Bronfenbrenner 1970). Bronfenbrenner's work stressed the importance of the interactional context of family and culture in human development and deemphasized biology.

- Robert Hinde, professor at Cambridge University and master of St. John's College, has done extensive work studying animal behavior in addition to human development. His pioneering work in ethology included studies of bird communication and primate behavior (Hinde 1982). Hinde has applied research with animals, particularly primates, to theories of human development and relationships. His perspective seeks out the integration of biology and culture in individual development (Hinde 1987).

- Jerome Kagan, professor of developmental psychology, Harvard University, comes from an orientation more strictly rooted in cognitive and developmental psychology. He researches issues concerning personality and cognition, looking at attachment, maturation, and resilience, and argues that normal children progress at universal stages of development, despite the interactional and cultural context in which they are raised.

- Melvin Konner, professor of anthropology and psychiatry at Emory University, is a prominent sociobiological anthropologist who has conducted research on childbirth and rearing practices with the San people in southern Africa (1972). He has also written several popular texts focusing on the biological basis of human behavior, including *The Tangled Wing: Biological Constraints on the Human Spirit* (1982) and *Why the Reckless Survive, and Other Secrets of Human Nature* (1990), and frequently writes columns and articles in scientific and popular publications.

- Sandra Scarr, professor and chair of the Psychology Department at the University of Virginia, is best known for her book *Mother Care, Other Care* (Scarr

Figure 2.2 *Clockwise from upper left*: *Childhood*'s "observers" Robert Hinde, Melvin Konner, Sandra Scarr, and Jerome Kagan. (Frame enlargements from the series.)

1984), a consideration of the effects of day care on mother and child. She also collaborated on the writing of a well-respected textbook in psychology (Scarr, Weinberg, and Levine 1986) under the general editorship of Jerome Kagan.

• Marian Wright Edelman, director of the Children's Defense Fund in Washington, D.C., was the last observer brought into the series. Edelman is an African American activist who is a nationally known spokesperson on issues about family life in low-income, urban settings. She argues for a greater emphasis in government policy to the devotion of resources to solve problems such as infant mortality and health, articulated in her well-known book, *Families in Peril: An Agenda for Social Change* (Edelman 1987).

I return throughout this study to consider the role that particular advisors/observers played in the series, both on and off camera, for it is revealing of both the production process of educational documentaries like *Childhood*, and of the intellectual, aesthetic, and formal conventions and positioning of these programs.

Figure 2.3 "Observer" Marian Wright Edelman in West Virginia with a mother and child. Geoff Haines-Stiles looks on. (Photograph © Rudy Gaskins.)

PUBLIC TELEVISION AS A HYBRID FIELD

The *Childhood* Project, a well-funded public television documentary series, needs to be located in a field of cultural production in a particular historical period. We can consider the value of the production for all the relevant and invested agencies—federal funding sources, corporations, the PBS system, WNET as a sponsoring station, Channel Four in England, the two companies originally developing production (Geoff Haines-Stiles Productions and Antelope Films)—as well as agents: the various individuals to whom *Childhood* represented a variety of moments in their career trajectories, the legitimated and willing consultants who came from their positions of power in the academic world, and the variety of viewers who watched the series in its various distribution formats. By embedding the production within this complex field, we deemphasize the specific moments of production and consumption, both of which are difficult to define: When does production begin? At conception of the idea? Receipt of first development funding? Agreement on the final scripts? And when does consumption start? At the first broadcast of the series? Viewing with funding agencies? We view all these processes within larger social fields and social structures and can extend the metaphor to consumption, looking at the "field" of consumption as a complex of individuals, agencies, and forces. In a conceptual sense, we can see these fields mapped on top of each other rather than as processual stages, thereby synthesizing our analysis of production and consumption.[31] For example, PBS's search for a stable audience can be located at points of tension between productive institutions (PBS and its stations, cable stations), financial forces (government spending, corporate support), and specific demographic groups of viewers (primarily higher-income audiences), all of which consume the very programs that are in question and interpret these programs through their own social perspectives.

This metaphor also allows us to look for central tensions within a field of production/consumption and view those tensions within smaller moments of interpretation and evaluation. The field of educational, nonfiction public television, as I argue, is situated first within specific social locations of privilege and power (urban, educated, middle to upper-middle class) and also within broader tensions in American culture between entertainment and pedagogy, pleasure and progress, diversion and edification. Both these categories of social location simultaneously inflect practices of production and consumption. They represent what Bourdieu might call a "structured space" for public television—a terrain constrained by certain obstacles and specific possibilities and always inflected within the cultural worlds its agents occupy. This terrain provides the contours within which the production of *Childhood* had to navigate.

CHAPTER THREE

Negotiating Documentary Production

AUTHORSHIP AND IMAGINED AUDIENCES

IN WHAT IT HOPES is a strategic response to its vulnerability in the shifting media landscape, the Public Broadcasting System and, particularly, its affiliate stations are attempting to construct a new public profile for themselves. Critical to this profile is the projection of a loosely defined community of viewers, identifiable in certain demographic slices, loosely sharing an identity based on this community's consumption of like programs that appeal to its base of interests and knowledge. With this image established, the system might demonstrate to underwriters and politicians the value of that audience as both a financial resource and as a political bloc while continuing to pursue this "community" for membership pledges and donations. In Ien Ang's terms (1991), the construction of this audience would be "institutionally enabling," both for the crucial rhetorical weight it could provide in debates over the system's existence, and in a less abstract sense for the direct income it would furnish the affiliate stations through paying memberships. This construction shares a great deal with processes that Benedict Anderson (1991) identified when describing nations as "imagined communities" formed through communication media, but with public television we are speaking of a limited slice of the national pie.

The system uses the slogan "Viewers Like You" in program credits to acknowledge the financial support it receives, an address to the audience that attempts to position viewers as participants in the system. However, we can read that phrase in several ways. One is as tautologically defining any potential viewer—a viewer like me can be anybody watching a particular show, a statement of gratitude to paying members and an encouragement for nonmembers to join. More critically though, it is a statement of distinction. PBS thinks it knows who its viewers are, or at least who its donors are, and addresses them to separate them out from the chaff of people who watch prime-time television. In doing so, they imagine a community of like-minded audience members, sharing an educated, urban, middle- to upper-middle-class background and orientation, interested in certain programs and the kinds of products, often program tie-ins, marketed as membership "premiums" during station fundraisers. We could turn their slogan back on itself by shifting from "Viewers Like You" to "Viewers Like Us," positing an

isn't this geographically + class biased against the democratic ideals of PBS?

identification between producers and viewers implied in the way stations solicit potential members. Station executives in shirt-sleeves pitch direct-address testimonials to their shared belief in the value of public broadcasting, and hype the enjoyment to be had in consuming programs (and companion merchandise) the system offers. However, something of a contradiction remains in the system's conception of its viewers; PBS simultaneously appeals to and claims the patronage of viewers with a demographic profile attractive for program underwriters while professing a broader, more populist audience than the system's critics acknowledge. This tension between the system's simultaneous appeals for both the top and the middle rungs of the demographic spectrum reveals the system's conflicted position in what Bourdieu (1984) would call the "social spaces" of cultural production and consumption.

PREFIGURING AND PROJECTING *CHILDHOOD*'S AUDIENCE

Many of the issues concerning the larger landscapes of media production circle back on producers' presumptions about audience composition and their anticipation of audience response. Barbara Herrnstein Smith's description of writing captures this process well:

> The reader's experience of the work is prefigured—that is, both calculated and pre-enacted—by the author in other ways as well: for, in selecting this word, adjusting that turn of phrase, preferring this rhyme to that, she is all the while testing the local and global effectiveness of each decision by impersonating in advance her various presumptive audiences, who thereby themselves participate in shaping the work they will later read. Every literary work—and, more generally, artwork—is thus the product of a complex evaluative feedback loop. (Smith 1988:45)

Discussions throughout the production process for *Childhood* provided many examples of the "prefiguring" of reception and of the audience, which I group into three overlapping areas: producers' concerns about audience composition, strategies for maintaining audience attention, and the prefiguring of audience response to specific program elements.

First, *Childhood*'s producers operated with and debated preconceptions of the makeup of the series' intended audience—which demographic segments (gender, class, level of education) will watch the series, and what knowledge and interests these groups bring to the program.[1] The potential for multiple markets for broadcast and distribution—the initial and primary U.S. market, but also England, Japan, Brazil, and elsewhere—complicated these predictions, which were not consistently held among the production staff. For instance, the British coproduction partners raised concerns about British viewers' potential reactions and spoke out against program elements that seemed too explicitly American-centered.[2] Given WNET's role as the majority partner for the series, CPB money providing most of the funding, and broadcast on PBS to precede release in the United Kingdom and elsewhere, the American audience was the primary concern throughout. But the producers had to consider how audiences in other countries would respond to the series. Complex questions remained about how viewers in Europe and the Third World would interpret images of "typical" American families and how American viewers might react to footage of families from other cultures.

The producers assumed that American viewers would have lived fairly sheltered, middle-class lives which would color the way they see the world, and they would be unaware of the difficult conditions in which many children are raised. In a discussion over the series' treatment of infant mortality and the associated mourning performed by different cultures after the death of a child, a dramatic and historically relevant topic, Marner referred to their potential audiences' class position and ability to relate to circumstances of impoverishment beyond their experience: "In general, the PBS audience is an elite audience, and privileged people whose kids probably have pretty high survival rates, and this is going to be, I think, striking, this point" (History Advisors Meeting, February 19, 1990). Though the public broadcasting system generates a fair amount of empirical audience data, some of it questioning these assumptions,[3] this conception of the audience still holds weight. It exerts an impact on programming decisions throughout the life of a production, from judgments about what series and programs to propose and fund to the choices made in designing and producing sequences for a specific show.

These assumptions guide producers concerned with the pragmatics of articulation through the strategies they employ to maintain viewers' attention over a program hour and from week to week, and they aid in digesting the core of information the series offers. It is on this pragmatic level that tensions existed between opposed intentions of pedagogy and pleasure, conflicts that would emerge through the working relationships between producers and academic advisors. *Childhood*'s British executive producer, Peter Montagnon, articulated a strategy for balancing these rhetorical tensions:

Television like this works best when it's a Trojan horse. You have to say, "I want to do something deadly serious for the public. I want to give them knowledge, information that they haven't got—in this case, in an area which is immensely important, it's about bringing up their young. And I've got to do it in such a way that they can take it in and remain oblivious and be consistently interested." So it mustn't be pedantic, it mustn't be academic on the surface. It can be truly, truly like that at its heart, but you've got to conceal that in an envelope which makes it sufficiently attractive for people just to watch it, otherwise it doesn't work. The exercise is a useless exercise. (Interview with Peter Montagnon, August 1, 1990)[4]

The producers agreed that an elite, educated strata, not representative of the general American or British population, makes up the core public television audience in the United States, and that these viewers should be addressed in a way that both respected and engaged their intelligence while not assuming they held much subject-relevant knowledge. Montagnon said he assumed

> that the person who is listening to the broadcast is intelligent, really quite reasonably intelligent, but because they are being asked, no matter how you sympathize, to take on more concepts and things which require thought and effort, you've got to reduce the effort to as little as possible; but the requirement of thought will always remain. So they've got the intelligence, but it's only innate intelligence; you mustn't assume that it's trained intelligence. . . . You must never use words that cut them out. You must never refer to experiences that cut them out, because they can't know about it. So it's got to be accessible to someone who absolutely, certainly doesn't know, but is clever enough and motivated enough to want to understand you. So you have to organize it in such a way that you don't cut them out, because that's infinitely condescending. (Interview with Peter Montagnon, August 1, 1990)[5]

Assumptions about the level of complexity that audience members could handle guided difficult pragmatic decisions about program content: what subjects to include, how much expository material to introduce, and how much time to spend on these topics. For instance, early in the production period the producers debated whether to include sequences about both abnormal development and the onerous social conditions for child rearing in impoverished regions of the world. Much of the staff regarded this material as powerful subject matter, politically important, and relevant to their audience, and therefore argued for its inclusion in the series. Yet, the producers simultaneously gauged their audience's level of understanding and potential reactions to this less pleasurable material, and tried to predict the kind of topical information about child development—both normal and pathological—the audience would have been exposed to through other sources. They also considered what viewers would like to see explored.

> PETER MONTAGNON: I suppose that we could easily underestimate just the sheer volume of information there is to get over, before we get into these issues. We're not even off first base.
> MELVIN KONNER: [. . .] You have to ask yourselves about what you want the viewer to feel about watching the next episode of *Childhood*. Is it going to be the feeling of a warm cozy experience of normal development that the viewer

can identify with to some extent—childhood at its best, parenting at its best, and the family as it's supposed to be functioning in all its varieties around the world—a pleasurable experience? Or is it going to have a little bit of that edge of guilt and fear that comes from watching something that's a deviation or pathology? How big a dose of that do you want? (Advisors Meeting, December 12, 1989.)

The producers wound up including less of this difficult material than initially planned for several reasons: because of the economy of program time, the effort to avoid a current-events format, and the desire to produce what they felt would be an enjoyable show. They anticipated that *Childhood*'s viewers would expect a substantive amount of parental advice and information that would credibly support or oppose specific parenting practices, but resisted tilting the material too much in that direction. They argued that the series was designed to portray a range of views about child rearing and experience, and to suggest that the specific practices that parents employ are not as important as the presence of a strong base of responsive interaction. Yet the producers and advisors expressed some reservations about failing to satisfy what parents might expect in the series. Konner saw "a serious conflict because the audience is aiming to get something out of this that is useful in terms of their own parenting, their own teaching, their own interactions with children, in the situation that most of us find ourselves" (Melvin Konner at Advisors Meeting, February 19, 1990). They attempted to resolve this tension by being explicit about the role of parental "advice" and the psychology of child development through history, and noting the changing, contradictory nature of this advice while avoiding explicit recommendations. In retrospect, Haines-Stiles felt that "we tried to make the series 'reflexive' . . . and did not take the audience with us. Hence too clever by half" (Haines-Stiles's comments on this manuscript, December, 24, 1995).

Although the producers and advisors shared a view of PBS viewers as elite and sheltered, they also realized their audience was not monolithic, that there were different viewer segments to appeal to, and that these differences obliged the producers in different ways. Along with its reception by a general upper-middle-class audience, Geoff Haines-Stiles felt strongly that the series would have a place on the national agenda and would be viewed by people with social status and influence. This projected audience, he felt, obliged the production to articulate a political position regarding the state of children's lives. Gauging the interest and intelligence of this potential audience and the place of the series on the "national agenda" challenged the producers and advisors throughout the production. During the middle production stages, the producers hoped to devote an entire program to the problematic circumstances of children's lives around the world, but this program never materialized, because of pressures of time and budget. Some of this social consciousness about childhood problems made its way into other program sequences, and into a follow-up to the series called *Childhood in America*. Yet the series' avoidance of an explicit political agenda reflects public television's general ideological orientation toward being what Erik Barnouw termed "safely splendid" (Barnouw 1978:150).

The producers grappled with program structure by attempting to predict audiences' responses to specific sequences and program formats, and debating their senses of how long specific types of sequences would hold the attention of what Turton (1992) called the "unknown and uncommitted" audience. As Geoff Haines-Stiles put it, they based these decisions on "art, gut, hunch—not focus groups." This is the level at which the broader forms of "prefiguring the audience"—which audiences and which program strategies—are applied in the evaluative work of program construction, and feature prominently in the work of editing. They sought to balance didacticism with cinematic pleasure, which, they postulated, took the form of revealing, dramatic, humorous, and humane family sequences and otherwise "cinematic" images. Staff discussions opposed these pleasurable sequences against more directly lecture-based, scientific material, which the academic advisors deemed more significant and valid in scholarly terms. The academic advisors, in retort, discredited the merely "cinematic" material, labeling it as "pretty pictures" and by that denying its scholarly value. The producers showed a great deal of concern about employing strategies that would maintain the audiences' attention: projecting which forms of televisual articulation would satisfy the audience and, conversely, which forms might bore them, confuse them, or drive them away?[6] This level of anticipation also involved the subjective qualities mentioned earlier, but here these assessments are projected onto audience members. Gene Marner explained the value of a sequence portraying different family structures by referring to the uniformity of the families of most public television viewers: "But then we're going to get into a discussion of what are the variety of family structures, because most of our audience is going to have families more or less like ours, which for all their peculiarity are fairly predictable. And I think we [the audience] want to find out something about what families have been" (Advisors Meeting, February 20, 1990). Note here the assumption that the producers share a great deal of cultural knowledge, concern, and interest with their audience, even on the level of social organization—that the phrase "viewers like you" also refers, from the producers' point of view, to "viewers like us."[7] These presumptions and predictions form a fundamental part of the aesthetics of program production, addressed in the next chapter.

It became clear in these discussions that both sides of this debate defend their positions by invoking audiences, either empirical ("I have not heard that response from anybody that has seen the footage"; "I have") or presumed ("Every parent knows it," but it is "interesting for the audience"; "It's totally familiar knowledge"). The estimation of what has "value" for the audience is an equation embedded in authorial assumptions: it depends on where the scene occurs in the flow of the text, what information viewers bring to that sequence, what constellation of viewers is assumed, and a variety of other factors that make these complex processes difficult to predict. Following the lead of recent audience research, it is illuminating to consider how the social and personal backgrounds of various staff members might condition their interpretive frameworks. Although most of the staff members came from a similar class segment—middle to upper-middle class, college educated—significant variations existed in cultural background, advanced degrees, and types of production experience that influenced their work. This is not a line of inquiry I directly pursued, but it represents the holistic view of authors to which I return in this chapter's conclusions.

(What is The status of difference in The imagined audience?)

DISCOURSES OF EVALUATION IN TELEVISION PRODUCTION

It is important to note that much of the work of authorship, even in an effort as collaborative as a documentary television series, gets conducted with either referentially vague or minimal verbalizations. A significant amount of evaluation in the work of assembling television programs involves intellectual, subjective, and cognitive processes that are difficult to put into words. Feld models the variety of kinds of "speech about music" as how one (musician, listener, or analyst) "engages and places an item or event in meaningful social space through ongoing interpretive moves" (Feld 1994a: 93). Becker reflected on these inarticulable or difficult-to-articulate processes, and the vague language associated with them, referring to the creation of art works. He speaks generally about processes of editing as centered around "choices" as "alternatives more or less consciously chosen between." Becker described the difficulty of gaining access to those choices:

> Artists make the choices with reference to the organization they work in; that, at least, is the assumption of the analysis that follows. It is not easy to find out about these matters and thus prove the assumption, because artists find it difficult to verbalize the general principles on which they make their choices, or even to give any reasons at all. They often resort to such non-communicative statements as "it sounds better that way," "it looked good to me," or "it works."
>
> That inarticulateness frustrates the researcher. But every art's practitioners use words whose meaning they cannot define exactly which are nonetheless intelligible to all knowledgeable members of their world. (Becker 1982:199)

These reflections were borne out in my research on *Childhood*, where I encountered formulations similar to those Becker cites. I would argue, though, that the terms practitioners employ, although referentially vague, still represent a rich and valuable domain of metaphoric, reflexive language, giving voice to a lexical domain theorizing evaluation, classification, and aesthetic ideology.[8]

On beginning the fieldwork, I was immediately struck and overwhelmed by how much material The *Childhood* Project staff processed and I would have to sift through to become conversant with the series' subject matter. First, there was a large body of research in child development, psychology, sociology, anthropology, and history, along with popular-press literature, assembled during the extended development stage of the project, which continued to accrue during the production and postproduction stages. The producers also screened many relevant programs, historical and ethnographic archival footage, and technical sample reels from candidates for key freelance positions. They pored through collections of photographs and artworks while simultaneously reworking program treatments and initial scripts. Geoff Haines-Stiles had command of an impressive amount of this material, as did *Childhood*'s principal researcher, Victor Balaban; the other producer/directors and staff mastered smaller subsets of the scholarly corpus.

Soon after the principal staff was installed in the WNET offices, the initial "families footage" began to stream in from Brazil, Russia, and Japan shot by camera crews the project hired to track *Childhood*'s families over the project's year and a half. As discussed earlier, this material, which made up close to half the finished program's screen time, was unusual in that the producers did not go out on location to direct this shooting but commissioned locally based crews to follow and film families the producers chose, directed in part by producers' lists of necessary material. At the same time, staff researchers brought in a variety of documentary, educational, and artistic motion picture material and stills (tape dubs and xeroxes) to scrutinize for potential use. In a heightened sense here, the producers were in the position of audience members, waiting with anticipation as footage or archival material arrived, then evaluating its quality and considering how it could be employed in constructing sequences for the series.[9] Along with this families footage, the three producer/directors planned and directed more than fifty days of documentary and observer shooting (for which they were present), both in the United States and overseas, to assemble much of the rest of the material for the seven episodes.

As the logging and editing process began, producers and editors honed raw footage (already translated, transcribed, and catalogued) down to "selects," the usable shots pulled out of the picture and sound reels. Then, adding some preliminary narration where appropriate, they began to build sequences out of these selects and "rough assemblies" out of the sequences. The audience for these intermediate stages was primarily a producer/editor/assistant editor team. They worked through these rough assemblies—adding and rewriting scratch narration, juggling scene sequences—until they became "rough cuts" (a more coherent and refined, but still preliminary form), which were shown to and critiqued by the advisors and key staff at WNET. Also, Haines-Stiles oversaw the assembly of a demonstration reel early in the postproduction stage, which he showed at a national PBS meeting, screened for potential donors, and sent to others associated with the project. The response to this "demo reel," mostly positive, was taken quite seriously as the first review of the project. These intermediate stages of textual production, during which producers and others viewed the program, had significant evaluative consequences and helped shape the series as it moved from proposal to product. In a condensed period, the producers finished the fine cuts of the episodes. I present this brief postproduction chronology to illustrate the density of moments for evaluation and interpretation, and the centrality of these processes for shaping the emerging text. A textual analysis that fails to access these moments loses a great deal of richness in understanding the ideological and conceptual forces brought to bear on the text's constructions.

THE SOCIAL ORGANIZATION OF AUTHORSHIP

Reception theory in communication has built on the important insight that audiences are not monolithic, and that one can distinguish their interpretations along certain social structural dimensions, usually of gender, class, and race. This realization is germane to processes of media production as well, arguing against common assumptions of a single dominant ideological message embedded in television or film texts. It is rather the case that media productions, even documentary programs, are more often collaborative enterprises, in which decisions over content and structure are dispersed throughout an institutional organization. Though one individual may hold primary authorial responsibility and power, several agents influence the shaping of a text. As Tulloch put it: "Because of its complexity of production practices, a television work must always remain polysemic despite its quest for a preferred meaning" (Tulloch 1990:200). That polysemy is locatable in the negotiations around production practices.

Although I argue throughout this chapter that *Childhood* was characterized by a shared form of authorship, responsibility and control were not shared equally. The social organization of production distributed authorial agency along a hierarchy of responsibility and power (Appendix A), beginning at the level of executive producer, in complex and somewhat flexible structures amenable to empirical investigation. Personnel operated both with a sense of their authorial role and through the negotiation of certain tensions between individuals sharing authorial responsibility. Whether this structure left "spaces for resistance to dominant ideologies" to operate, as Tulloch argues in his work on television drama, remains a complicated question. Perhaps this is not the most relevant framework for considering the diversity of views negotiated through the production process. Yet, both the full-time staff and freelance production personnel noted the project's collegial and collaborative working environment, the sense that although hierarchies existed, boundaries between levels could be transgressed and participation was welcomed beyond what was traditionally expected from specific job categories. Geoff Haines-Stiles described how David Loxton, Peter Montagnon, and he built this mode of collegiality into the organizational process for the series:

> What we said from the beginning was that we wanted to have a situation in which we had a lot of round-table meetings in which people said, "This is what my show is going to be doing," and other people said, "Oh, if you're doing that then what I can do is make my show respond to that." And Gene I think came up with the phrase "collegial," and I'm not sure if collegial was really the best phrase, but it was good. I remember with great satisfaction lots of the meetings we had on *Cosmos* in which we sort of went into the room in the morning and said, "Program Five really sucks. What are we going to do about Program Five?" And the back and forth between people was extremely good. That's the kind of feeling I wanted to recapture, on this project, and it is different from any of the others. And again that results in more talk, maybe, than just, "OK, I've got a script" or "I've got my idea and I'll go out and do it." (Interview with Geoff Haines-Stiles, March 2, 1990)

Other multipart public television series operate by having executive producers contract episodes out to individual producers who, with administrative review and approval, work independently on their shows. The executive producers package the completed shows together as a series. Gene Marner remarked on the process at *Childhood* in comparison to other series he had worked on:

> I think it's, the process here, for me, it's different from other series in that there is a process, and it's been very well done, I think. Other series that I've worked on have not either had the luxury or foresight to do this, and so producers would tend to work in isolation from one another, and only relate to one another through the executive producer, and there was no, the atmosphere of collegiality which Geoff has tried to encourage and which I think is very wise and useful and bound to improve the prospects for the series, has been a lot of fun. It's interesting. Not only fun, but I think it's been very productive. One, you know, you can very easily lose sight of the thrust of the whole series, unless you are kind of involved in talking about it and thinking about it at every stage, and pretty soon, in fact just about now, I am sort of getting severed from other programs than my own, but I've already internalized enough of the other stuff to

have a feeling that it's all part of one big project. Also, the fact that we'll be out shooting materials for one another is inevitably going to color our attitudes, let's say, of the other materials and our awareness of how things relate to, how programs relate to one another. (Interview with Gene Marner, March 6, 1990)

The type of interchange that Haines-Stiles and Marner describe did take place with *Childhood*, particularly among the producer/directors. There were frequent script and staff meetings during the preproduction stage and well into production, allowing collaboration on improving program elements and keeping departments informed about one another's activities and concerns. Haines-Stiles, Akuginow, and Marner embraced input from staff members and from principal freelancers. Richard Chisolm, a freelance camera operator who became the principal director of photography for all of the domestic shooting, echoed this view of collegiality:

I feel very integrated in the meat of this project in a way that's unusual for me, totally unusual, and that even when I go to their office and hang around, I feel like I'm part of a team thing, and this is no accident I think. Part of it has to do with a very egalitarian and open way of managing this production, which a lot of times in a big corporate kind of production setup, there's a very strict hierarchy and you can't even talk to the executives, and the executives are in another city, and the directors are aloof and opinionated and nobody ever questions what they think and say, and the underlings are hidden in a separate room and doing a separate thing and there's a whole bunch of separations within a system. And in *Childhood*, in New York, in the production office there is this incredible delicate kind of consortium feeling. In fact, there is a hierarchy; in fact, the salaries are not, you know, communistically set up; in fact, there's a huge hierarchy, but out of the twenty or thirty people that work in and out of that office, some freelancers but mostly staff kind of contract people, there's an amazing kind of openness and receptiveness from one to the other, and that Geoff, this is no accident, that Geoff and Erna [Akuginow] are kind of running the show and leaving all the doors open. I've never seen their door closed in their offices. I mean literally and figuratively, the doors are open to new ideas. But you go to some of these other series that are being made, or have been made in public television, and you just don't find this kind of cooperation and ethnic diversity and age distribution. (Interview with Richard Chisolm, September 22, 1990)

Although Chisolm's depiction of the open door exaggerates a bit (I did encounter some closed doors), the figurative implication conforms to convictions others expressed about The *Childhood* Project's ethos, particularly in contrast to more commercial kinds of productions.

From my observations, this form of collegiality, combined with the staff's sense of working on a series with a national profile, created an environment that encouraged staff commitment and enthusiasm. The staff acted as if they

Figure 3.1 Producer/director Eugene Marner discusses a scene with "observer" Sandra Scarr. (Photograph © Lawrence Ivy.)

Figure 3.2 Producer/director Erna Akuginow directs a historical sequence in Colonial Williamsburg, Virginia. (Photograph © Barry Dornfeld.)

were part of an important project, a feeling probably shared in other PBS productions. I wondered if a tension existed between this collaborative mode of work and the feeling of authorial control that producer/directors might seek to retain, so I asked Gene Marner if he felt a loss of authorial autonomy, to which he responded:

> No, I mean, first of all, this is a job. I don't say that meaning that I don't care about it. I've accepted a commission to work on a project. I didn't invent it, it's not mine, and it's been presented to me as one in which we're all going to share and do it together, so I have no problem about that at all. And I'm very well aware, especially in the documentary world, of the degree to which all these things are collegial anyway, and collaborative enterprises, that just, it doesn't happen any other way. Including feature films as well, are also, there's an awful lot of [. . .] I mean it's really such a collaborative business that even if you're writing and directing, writing and producing, as we are here, the fact is there's so many people feeding us materials, feeding stuff in to us, and there's so much research that has been done, to base this on, that to talk about authorship is inappropriate, I think. (Interview with Gene Marner, March 6, 1990)

Marner has produced and directed independent documentaries and feature films himself and has worked as part of a team of directors, so I view with authority his acknowledgment of distance from that role ("it's not mine") and of the collegial quality of *Childhood*'s organizational structure. Marner's comments resonate with Becker's observations on the collaborative nature of artistic production, even in situations where a single artist is credited with authorship. My views differ from Marner's only in that I see authorship as potentially divisible and collaborative, not an either/or phenomenon; perhaps he would agree that despite this collaborative ethos, hierarchies still existed. The closing series credits reflect these hierarchies as well, since they represent the division of responsibilities in typographical distinctions, assign an order of importance to job categories, and ascribe to single producer/directors the authorship of the shows for which they had primary responsibility. All this occurs despite the collaborative mode of production.

Within this collegial environment of shared authorship, some tensions or struggles over responsibility were inevitable. One of the more revealing tensions existed between the producers (executive producers and producer/directors) and the academic advisors, particularly those who were also on-camera observers. *Childhood*'s on-camera host format contributed to this tension, since the observers, the scholarly guardians of the series, had a stake as authors of the program that went beyond their advisory role. The producers derived the notion of "observers" from the "Society of Observers of Man," the French scientific association that in 1800 took custody of and studied the "Wild Boy of Aveyron," a feral child made famous in François Truffaut's 1970 film, *The Wild Child* (*L'Enfant Sauvage*). (See Shattuck

1980 for further discussion.) The tension between the producers and observers surfaced at different points in the series but peaked during a meeting when the observers responded to the rough cuts of several episodes. Here the Observers raised objections about the quality and design of the episodes at that point, to which the producers responded by articulating their position in defense. The following exchange reflects the stake the observers, here represented by Urie Bronfenbrenner (providing opening comments following those of two of his colleagues), as claimed in the production process, and Geoff Haines-Stiles's reassertion of authorial hierarchy.

> URIE BRONFENBRENNER: I guess I wanted to underscore the same concern which my colleagues have expressed, that at the present time there's a tremendous job to be done, and if I may say so it is a job, the job that remains to be done is one that has to fall on our shoulders, because we're talking about things that are missing that we know something about—we the observers. And that brings me to a final dilemma, because it seems to me, *it's very hard for someone else to tell our story.* And while we may not be the best tellers, I'm not saying that we have to be the voice-over, but *I'm saying that the text has to be ours,* and, where it's appropriate, in our voices as well, but that's a separate question. I hate to say this because the clear implications are more work for the four of us, but I think that's what we contracted to do. I feel somewhat frustrated, because I think we have been trying to do that job, and the results of our efforts are not yet reflected in the way in which the material is presented. And instead, some other constructions are imposed, which are difficult for—I'll speak for myself—me to understand in the light of what we have been saying about what is known and what isn't known.
>
> GEOFF HAINES-STILES: We all have spent a lot of time getting up to speed in your area, and now you're getting up to speed in our area, and we're trying to make this thing go forward together. A fundamental premise where it's reasonable to assume that you as academic observers are coming from a different perspective from ours, and yet where we're seeking to get a synergistic, not just a buzz word, but a meaningful word, relationship—I think that we feel the family scenes are on the edge of both being interesting and informative and human and leading us to see the scientific nuggets in a clearer light. We do not see it as one thing or the other thing; we do not see it as either entertainment or information. We still feel, and you can make your own judgments about whether we have the abilities to pull it together, that the two are beginning to gel, and it's obscured by the length of the sequences, obscured by the inadequacy of the script, but it's not made impossible by the nature of the sequences. (Advisors Meeting, February 3, 1991; emphasis added)

Here Bronfenbrenner, representing the observers, described what he viewed as the academics' crucial role in the completion of the series and sought to claim responsibility for "our story." Geoff Haines-Stiles's response was diplomatic but forceful and defensive. He recognized their collaborative, "synergistic" role ("you're getting up to speed in our area"), but asserted the producers' authority "to pull it together." I would characterize their relationship as the producers telling the observers' stories for them, along with other stories as well. They are in a sense the ghostwriters for these author/observers, drawing on their images and words while remaining invisible as authors. The producers "quote" the observers, and they stage those quotations as they see fit, within the limits constrained by the actual observers' performances that they film and how the observers are willing to represent themselves. The result is a polyphonic text ultimately controlled by the producers.

Although the observers were not formally given copyright or editorial veto as authors of the series, an obligatory relationship developed between the executive producers and a few key advisors. Correspondence indicated that Haines-Stiles and Montagnon felt obliged to check with Jerome Kagan and Robert Hinde on decisions about the choice of other observers and advisors, the choice of writer for the companion book, and the inclusion of scientific material for the series. It is important to consider the observers' contribution as advisors to the project in its earlier, formative stages. They played a role in directing the producer/directors to areas of research and evaluating the value and validity of scholarly material, and they felt that their involvement allowed them some oversight.

Earlier in the production process, I had asked Gene Marner to describe the academics' role in helping form the episodes, a relationship he saw as less shared and "synergistic" than what Geoff Haines-Stiles described in the advisors' meetings:

> DORNFELD: What about the kind of academic, the amount of academic stuff. I remember when I think we first talked in your office here, I was just telling you what my general plans were, and you said something to the effect that, "Well, if you just come up for the big meetings you're not really getting the meat of the work."
>
> GENE MARNER: Yeah. Did I say that? Well, it's because, I mean, the academic meetings tend to be academic. And they're about, tend to be about limited areas of the project, and they're mostly very informative, and they, more than anything else, they help us. Well, let me tell you what they help me to do. They help me to internalize some of this material. [. . .] So, in October, were the first meetings. So, when those meetings started, I didn't know anything, I just hadn't read anything, except the outlines, the treatments, you know. I just had no background at all, except being a father, and those meetings were very important to me because they let me understand the kind of interests and focuses that people who really do know about this material have, what they care about, what's important. And, from that point of view it was very useful.

It was also very useful to, I found that at those meetings, I learned what, really, what not to say, what not to do. It doesn't tell you what to do, because you have this huge universe of things that you have to cover, and you have to be selective. But, what I think I do find out from those meetings what you really should not say, do, or even think about, and that does save a lot of time and trouble, and I hope embarrassment later on when we send our scripts out later on to the advisors. But the idea is just not to get off, you know, on the wrong track, by pursuing some bad leads. Those meetings have been very useful from that point of view.

On the other hand, they don't generate television programs, I mean they, you know, the people who attend those meetings know about their fields, they don't know about, they know about information, they don't know about how that information is conveyed by television, and how an audience, what an audience can sit and watch and—I'm not sure we know that either, but we at least have experiences doing programs that people either have watched or others have praised, and so, we have some handle on it. It's a big mystery anyway, but the people who come to those advisory sessions don't know, don't have experience of that at all. So, somehow, we have to take what they tell us and translate it into what would be useful for making a television program. (Interview with Gene Marner, March 6, 1990)

Childhood's authorial dilemma is somewhat unusual. With series like *Cosmos*, *Civilisation*, and *The Africans* (Mazrui 1986), it was clear that the story the series represented was the host's, whose personality drove the formative ideas and who contributed substantively from script writing to final cuts. Those series designed without a host (*Eyes on the Prize* [Hampton 1986], *Making Sense of the Sixties* [Green and Hoffman 1991]) do not have this inherent negotiation over authorship.

In my view, The *Childhood* Project distributed authorial responsibility between producers and observers, or possibly from the producers to the observers, with a specific protocol. The academic advisors and observers operated in two ways; as a resource, providing scholarly information and cases for the producers to select from in developing programs, reviewing and refining scripts, co-writing their own "on camera" scenes, and choosing locations (though the academics are not the only source of this information), and as a certifying authority, holding the right and responsibility to approve the intellectual and factual content of the episodes at various stages. But the producers maintain the authority to "generate television programs," as Marner said, to structure the intellectual concepts ("scientific nuggets") into visual and sound images as they see fit. They claim an expertise in this authorial work, an ability to understand how audiences interpret television form, which the observers concede to, while exercising the prerogative to comment on stylistic elements of the programs.[10]

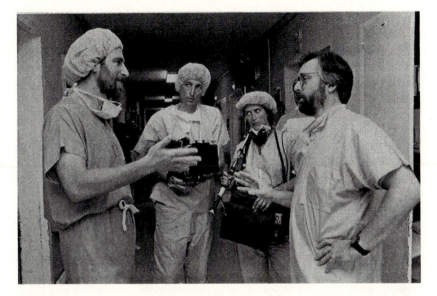

Figure 3.3 Observer Melvin Konner (*right*) and Geoff Haines-Stiles discuss a scene shot with a newborn baby in a New York City Hospital. Cinematographer Richard Chisolm and Sound Recordist Brenda Ray look on. (Photograph © Lawrence Ivy.)

Authorship is also shared and negotiated between the producers and the staff and freelance personnel working under them. The occupational procedures the series employed—and are shared in the documentary film and video industry more generally—mandated this sharing of responsibilities. Haines-Stiles, Akuginow, and Marner assigned tasks to the associate producers, researchers, and production assistants working under them and worked closely directing freelance and staff crew members—particularly cinematographers and editors—during production and postproduction. The producer/directors wrote all the material for their episodes, sifting through research literature, film footage, and budgets. The associate producers, along with production assistants, were responsible for researching subject areas, scouting locations, calculating financial expenditures, and implementing logistical arrangements. These supporting tasks greatly influenced the rendering of particular scenes. For example, in my role as researcher I worked on the development of the "Drum School Sequence" shot in Ghana, West Africa. I was able to direct Gene Marner and Rudy Gaskins to David Locke, an ethnomusicologist who had worked extensively with a Dagomba master drummer who became the focus of that sequence. Typically, the associate producers followed a scene from start to finish, and *Childhood*'s producer/

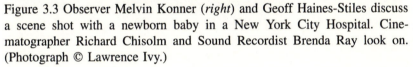

directors gave their staff considerable license to develop and steer scenes as they researched them.

Technical staff—production and postproduction crew members—played a critical authorial role as well. During shooting, for instance, the cinematographer greatly influences the rendering of any given scene. The series commitment to an observational mode of documentary shooting and recording dictated a passive role for the producer/director during the actual shooting events. *Childhood*'s producer/directors would plan these documentary shoots and prepare the camera and sound operators for what they hoped to get out of a scene, but once the event began, they would mostly let events unfold spontaneously. The cinematographer, therefore, became something of an on-site "director" for that scene, deciding what to focus on and how much to shoot, conferring with the producer/director during breaks in the action. Richard Chisolm described this shared role of authorship for the cinematographer, the nature of his preparation by the staff, and how this relationship unfolds:

> RICHARD CHISOLM: Somebody will call me in advance of the shoot, they'll say, "What we're hoping to get is a sense of this kid's jealousy toward his sister. And we're hoping also to get the real life situation of what it's like when he gets together with other boys, or the real thing with his mother and how his sister's treated differently than he is by the mother." Or the fact that the father is not around much and there's certain kind of ideas and content things that they plant with me in advance so that once I'm on the shoot, I haven't just had ten phone calls about logistics, I haven't just had three or four memos and long conversations about content, I've had the whole works and I've had it so redundantly exposed to me that by the time the shoot comes along the producers and directors don't have to say anything out loud. They don't even have to be there. This is a controversial issue, but, in fact, a couple of times they haven't been able to be with me after this information's been planted with me. I've gone out and shot whole documentary sequences for a whole day with some of their staff people as helpers and with other freelancers, where I become surrogate director for the day or something, and to me there's no problem with that. It's just a question of thinking in synch with them.
>
> DORNFELD: Why do you say it's controversial?
>
> CHISOLM: It's controversial in terms of, "Gee, I'm director but you're saying I don't need to be there on location?" For some people it's an ego issue, for some people it might even be an economic worry that, you know, that they're into doing their job or not earning their money or something. But with this kind of real-time, real-life filmmaking, a lot of it does rest on the camera and sound department as to how what moments are going to be captured and how they're going to be captured. There's not a lot of opportunity to step aside and have a major dialogue or argument about what's going to

happen or what you're going to shoot next, because it's actually happened and you either get it or you don't. (Interview with Richard Chisolm, September 22, 1990)

Chisolm's comments have to be considered in light of the fact that he is a cinematographer who appreciates working with a fair amount of authorial autonomy. However, I think the producer/directors would agree that this style of documentary shooting requires shifting significant responsibility to the cinematographer, though Haines-Stiles, Akuginow, and Marner did a substantial amount of preproduction work to set the scene and reclaimed that authorial control in the editing stage.[11]

The editors also worked closely with the producer/directors and were given a great deal of responsibility in determining both the footage that wound up in the final programs and the structure of that material. Haines-Stiles, Akuginow, and Marner each had their own editor, and that editor's assistants, assigned to their two or three shows. They each had a major voice in hiring that editor, in recognition of the intimate working relationship required, and thought carefully about how that editor's stylistic tendencies and experience configured with their own and with the needs of the series. To-

Figure 3.4 Producer/director Erna Akuginow directs a shot for the "Budding Babies" sequence, in a New York City studio. Cinematographer Nancy Shreiber operates the camera rig. (Photograph © Barry Dornfeld.)

Figure 3.5 Producer/director Erna Akuginow watches a video monitor as crew members set up another shot for the "Budding Babies" sequence. (Photograph © Barry Dornfeld.)

gether, the producer/directors and editors screened all the material relevant to the episodes they were working on, commenting on, and noting which "takes" were the most useful for a given sequence. The producer/director would typically suggest how she or he felt a sequence would best be assembled, and then leave the editor to construct a first draft of that sequence, returning to comment and suggest changes. The editor's role was to implement, suggest versions and variations, work through problems, and generally render the producer/director's objectives into appropriate form. Doing so clearly involves an estimation of the viewers' reactions, a prefiguring of the audiences' response, which the editors felt particularly attuned to do.

I asked Larry Silk, the supervising editor for the series, and the editor for Programs One, Two, and Seven, produced and directed by Geoff Haines-Stiles, how he gauged the audience's response, what kind of feedback he received. He talked about having an instinctive sense of audience, an ability that he felt editors obtained from watching many films. "Editors are really proxies for an audience," Silk said. They "love to see how real people respond to what they cut." It was interesting that he was privileging the place of the editor as more in tune than the producer to an audience sensibility, and saw the editor as an important buffer between the producer and the viewer.

Silk's views mesh with the industrial folk wisdom of film production that the input of an editor, who arrives on a project after the shooting stages and therefore brings fresh eyes and different concerns to the viewing process, can be critical. Editors reinforce this wisdom, telling stories about how they "saved" a given program from the director's failings on location.[12] As Haines-Stiles pointed out, Larry Silk comes from an independent filmmaking background, an orientation that is both populist and elitist in its own ways.

This complex portrait of the sharing of authorial responsibility throughout the production team exposes as inadequate typically monolithic descriptions of directorial intention and decision-making in media production. Not surprisingly, the various members of *Childhood*'s large, intentionally multicultural staff will differ in their judgments about program material, often in substantive ways. Authorship for this kind of production then involves a negotiation of interpretation and authorial power.

SHARED AUTHORSHIP AND POLYSEMY

Following audience theory, we can call the interpretations of the executive producers, or for certain material, the expert advisors, the *dominant* readings or evaluations, and posit other conflicting or *oppositional* interpretations, and assess the roles these play in the formation of the final text. Interpretive or evaluative disagreements are often resolved through the assertion of authority by the person higher in the evaluative hierarchy. However, in a work as collaborative as a multipart television series, there will be scenes, sequences, statements, and nuances that go against the dominant framework. These might be the result of several things: negotiation and compromise among production staff, slippages of meaning which those at the higher rungs of the interpretive hierarchy let pass, either consciously or not, or the potential ambiguity of certain textual structures, which are able, at times, to contain conflicting articulations.

Morley suggested that "insufficient allowance is made for the fact that the meanings of a text frequently escape the conscious mind of its author" (Morley 1981:4). In a discussion with Akuginow about my research, she articulated a similar formulation, raising what she sees as the subjective nature of many production decisions as a potential problem for my analysis. The producers rely on reactions to material that are subjective, emotional, and often difficult to rationalize or articulate, although they pursue confirmation of their personal reactions through interaction built into the production process. In a discussion during an advisors' meeting, Marner related his positive response to a scene shot in the kitchen of a Russian family, in which a young girl chops cabbage as her father cooks, as having a "virtually magical quality" that the audience can feel (Advisors Meeting, December 14, 1989). Similarly, Geoff Haines-Stiles would describe certain sequences he liked in terms of their "cinematic" or visual appeal, a term used to attest to the subjective enjoyment of a sequence and its power to evoke an emotive and revealing aspect of family life with which an audience can identify. The pleasure experienced and attached to this material would differ from the intellectual value to be gained from expository, narration-driven, and possibly scientific sequences, and arguments lodged in its favor would project this experience. With the consideration of the multifaceted, collaborative production process for a series like *Childhood*, and the range of interpretive frameworks individuals bring to this work, the possibility for the text to contain ambiguity and polysemy multiplies, questioning the complete power of determination that ideology-based theories of media production attribute to media producers.

SHOOTING STRATEGIES

The producers associated the variety of materials they employed in the series with a variety of shooting styles and production strategies, each requiring definite investments of effort and expense. In planning scenes, they had to consider both the practical constraints and the aesthetic benefits involved in making a particular point through the use of a particular strategy, and weigh them against other strategies or other scenes. Peter Montagnon described this decision-making process early in the production period:

> I was thinking that actually, really, there's an awful lot of information there, and that the main problem is how to make that information into celluloid. By what means and through what examples. And it only comes when one actually takes it program by program. [. . .] Let's assume that we try and make all the points that are there and don't argue about how many we can make right now. If we try to make those points, how are they best made. Is it best to get at it through very, very controlled setups,[13] and not worry about going around to various countries or anything like that, but just say we want the most controlled setups we can get, and we've then got to re-create that, and stay and observe it and get it clear, and then say that the point really shines through. Or does one travel around and try and get it in a more anecdotal way and hope, or hope that it's going to emerge as we shoot it? I don't know the answer, but you, I was just wondering how you feel and how you thought about it. (Advisors Meeting, December 14, 1989)

In this passage, Montagnon does not explicate the value the producers have invested in scenes obtained in an "anecdotal way" and seems to favor the efficiency of controlled setups. Haines-Stiles, Akuginow, and Marner, on the other hand, favored sequences that could be rendered by using their pool of observational "family footage." These sequences allow them to make the intellectual points they intended using a more realistic, documentary design.

From a strategic point of view, this family material was more difficult to control and predict. The producer/directors would compile lists of the kind of footage they wanted (which were forwarded through the Antelope office in London to the overseas crews), but they were dependent on the abilities of the camera crews and on fortuity to obtain these "moments" on film. The degree of control the producer/directors hoped to exert in "directing" these sequences from afar is evident in the level of detail in the producers' "shopping lists" for the family footage, which specified material needed from specific families and from all the families more generally. Haines-Stiles, Akuginow, and Marner developed these lists based on their early scripts, attempting to obtain the footage necessary for specific sequences as envisioned at that time. After the meetings above, Akuginow sent Antelope Films a two-and-a-half-page memo describing the scenes she needed for Program One:

> Don't need full-blown birthing sequence, but would like evidence of:
>
> whether delivery is in recumbent or upright position
> technologically loaded delivery or simple natural procedure
> is father of or apart from the procedure
> whether newborn is delivered to mother or medical attendant
> and if at all possible, would love to see newborn's first reaction to its new world
>   as the head appears and the rest of body is still in canal.
>
> After birth . . . In delivery area, would like the camera to push past all other distractions and move in tight on newborn to record in detail the characteristics and behavior of the "biological organism"—I don't think it's necessary for me to prep a list . . . We should simply document the reality in close-up mode. (Memo from Erna Akuginow to Peter Montagnon, December 1989)

One can imagine a "controlled setup" strategy for filming those same details, but such a strategy might sacrifice the documentary feeling of the scenes and the cultural context in which these events took place. Both strategies were employed at different times, but overall the producers employed the "observational" documentary approach whenever possible, which was also the approach the advisors favored. Because the family footage involved spontaneous uncontrolled shooting, it was considered a more expensive strategy than using controlled scenes. Vérité shooting is notorious for the amount of film footage it uses. The high shooting ratios typical of this form of observational shooting result from a strategy that avoids intervention and requires extensive filming of behavior, waiting to capture on camera and sound recorder illustrative moments of interaction. The vérité approach is unwilling

Figure 3.6 Observer Jerome Kagan in Hino, Japan, performing a test of child development based on Piaget's model. (Photograph © Nancy Tong.)

to risk the loss of a sense of spontaneous, authentic realism in favor of the efficiencies of time and film stock that can result from exerting control over the action.

As opposed to the spontaneity necessary for the filming of families, the observer material was much more controlled in approach. Haines-Stiles, Akuginow, and Marner directed and rehearsed these scenes, which were carefully written and located and shot with multiple takes. The observers collaborated on the writing of this material, which purports to present an observer's views on subjects in which she or he has some expertise. Most of the observer sequences were shot late in the production process, reserved for a stage when many of the editing decisions had been made and the producer/directors could define which observers they needed to speak on specific topics in a given program.

This discussion of shooting strategies raises a more general point about the exploratory processes of documentary production. In a sense, the dilemma for this form of documentary production is that it strives for a high level of spontaneity, with the producer/directors hoping to obtain revealing moments on film while working through a complex production process that requires predictability as well as the ability to anticipate and write in script form the spontaneous things they hope to record. The practical logic to this theoretical dilemma involves an extended process of working between plans and products, reformulating intentions while confronting the reality of their execution, and rescripting programs while evaluating what "works" and what does not in the footage being compiled. The following excerpted discussion captures that practical logic, spurred on by advisor/observer Mel Konner's inquiries and sense of uneasiness about this documentary process:

MEL KONNER: Well, I thought about this a lot, since the last meeting, and I'd just say my impression is that you're sort of going about it backwards when you get the experts in and you listen to all they have to say, and list all these things that you have to cover, and then go and film to try to cover all those points. I could see doing a little bit of this strategy, but in my ideal world, as the author of the book and maybe getting involved in the production, would be to let you go and film, and I know the timetable is not going to allow this anymore, but go and film these families and bring back . . . . How many feet of film will you be able to have, total?

PETER MONTAGNON: I think we've got perhaps one hundred and fifty rolls per family.

KONNER: Then you go through that and you find the best television, and when you get to a ratio of ten to one or five to one, then you bring in a bunch of experts to watch the film. And then they tell you what's in the films that they see, that you might not see. You've already selected the best film, then we look at the film and we see this great thing happening in cognitive development, this last piece of film where the baby is playing, the Russian kid, then we tell you the story, you know, the expert story, and then you write the narration, because you've started with the ethnographic data in the form of high-quality film, and you know you've got that problem licked. Of course you need to know where to point the camera and what to film and so on, but certainly you know enough to do that. . . .

GEOFF HAINES-STILES: The thing which is unusual about this process is that it is ongoing, it is iterative. We shoot film, we look at the film, we talk about what we see, we say "more of that, less of that." So that it's not as if it's either or, it's an ongoing process in which we figure out what it is we want to say. And we say things as mundane as, "This is too much lighting in the Japanese situation," and "Oh, wouldn't it be nice to update Margaret Mead and have babies being bathed in four cultures, because the Japanese bathtime is going to look totally different from the U.S." So it's by knowing what we're doing rather than knowing less.

KONNER: And I said the problem here is that the fundamental television principle behind this series is documentary, the fundamental principle is "let's escape the *Nova* format, the didactic *Nova* format," but then you have scripts, and you're trying to write scripts and outlines before you do the documentary shooting, which pretends that they're doing the shows. . . .

HAINES-STILES: What we have here is a new form of documentary. It is not your everyday documentary. It is not your father's PBS.[14] (Advisors Meeting, December 12, 1989)

Some other PBS producers would consider this indeterminate process too luxurious and wasteful and approach their research, development, and production in a more linear fashion—a different practical logic locked into different circumstances. For *Childhood*, shooting strategy is tied to authorial stance through the desire to be extremely accurate in scholarship and science, and to include the advisors in this production process. The budget allowed this process to unfold with less pressure than is present in many other documentary projects.

PRODUCERS AS AUTHORS AND AUDIENCE MEMBERS

Producers, while engaging in the constant process of evaluation and interpretation in their work, are also audience members in a more conventional sense. They, too, consume media forms (PBS shows, NPR newscasts) in their leisure lives, and live a lifestyle not too distant from that of their audience. The potential impact of subjective domains of experience and interpretation leaves open the influence of producers' own viewing practices, preferences, and structures of understanding on their production work. Bourdieu writes that works "in both style and content . . . bear the marks of their authors' socially constituted dispositions (that is, their social origins, retranslated as a function of the positions in the field of production which these dispositions played a large part in determining)" (Bourdieu 1984:20). The books the production staff spoke about, the news items they debated around the coffee machine, and their own family experiences which they saw reflected or contrasted in the footage they were editing all contributed to their "socially constituted dispositions" and influenced the shape of the series in more or less observable ways.[15] For example, Geoff Haines-Stiles spoke with praise about National Public Radio's (NPR) programs, and talked about how listening to news programs such as those hosted by *Childhood*'s narrators made his long commute from suburban New Jersey to New York City bearable. The literature on cultural production has neglected this social dimension, resulting in shallow views of producers who do not recognize their cultured lives beyond their work, and furthering assumed divisions in competence and knowledge between producers and audiences.

During my work with *Childhood*, the production staff talked about the films and television programs they watched in terms not dissimilar from those used by other members of their class and culture. They might have a vested interest in certain dimensions of the text, be more attuned to technical concerns, more informed about the organization of production in general and of specific programs, and have a particular interest in programs shown on public television.[16] But I would argue that their interests in a program's coverage of a particular topic, assessments of its style and competence, and its relationship to other comparable works do not diverge as much from those of other potential viewers (particularly those of the same class and level of education) as the literature would lead us to believe. This perspective on producers as viewers raises questions about what Morley called "a potential disjunction between the codes of those sending and those receiving messages through the circuit of mass communications. The problem of (non-) complementarity of codes at the production and reception ends of the chain of communications" (Morley 1983).

Studies of media production, in my view, have exaggerated this disjunction; producers are not as privileged nor audience members as impoverished as the divide between production and reception has led us to believe. The process of production requires that the producers act to a large extent as surrogate audience members, putting themselves in the place of their potential audience as they react to the material they are shaping into programs. This is not to imply that the interpretive procedures that producers and viewers employ are identical, but to suggest that producers move in and out of the frame of surrogate audience member. Perhaps the crucial difference is that producers learn (at least partially) to articulate a metatheory of the interpretive frameworks we all employ, and apply this metatheory when making programmatic decisions. But they are able to do this in part because they rely on their own subjectivity in this application, reacting to material they shoot and edit as viewers themselves, and often falling back on their subjective responses to defend these reactions.

These reflections on production can help us rethink the habitual divide between production and consumption, the traditional notions of what producers do, and our conceptions of authorship. Contemporary film and television theory would argue that there is a dominant ideology embedded within media texts, and that the audience member or viewer is always negotiating through and is more or less prey to that ideology. An ethnographic approach widens the perspective to consider how implicit and explicit theories of practice applied by the producers, the social world in which they live, the production apparatus (institutions and practices), and broader cultural tendencies all inflect the text with a complex of meanings (and condition the text's reception). The communicative (aesthetic, evaluative) events that define production and consumption need to be situated in relation to these social, institutional, historical, and biographical contexts.

PBS producers and staff are a group with a great deal of cultural capital. Their backgrounds are largely isomorphic with the demographic profile of much of the PBS audience (as are other domains of production characterized by concentrations of cultural capital, such as academia, book publishing, and the art world). That is, they are educated, come from at least a middle-class background, and are engaged in consuming a conglomeration of products and performances that might be advertised in the back of their public broad-casting station's promotional magazine. At the same time, the PBS system attempts to maintain a balance between a pedagogical mission and a populist one, and to simultaneously assert its role in practices of education/enlighten-ment and leisure/entertainment, spreading them more broadly across social classes. This balance contrasts markedly with that of the BBC's public ser-vice model, which (until the recent privatization) was explicitly oriented to public service and intellectual concerns and, in Frith's words, "first of all, a response to the fear of Americanization" stemming from the dissemination of popular culture from the United States (Frith 1988b:25). The BBC, struc-tured to "keep broadcasting in cultured hands" (Frith 1988b:25), has through-out its history been staffed by members of the upper class, whereas Ameri-can public television has always tried to resist being labeled elitist, recently motivated by the need to demonstrate its populist reach as a defense of its federal support.[17] American producers design programs within these class-related tensions, attempting to distinguish their work from the wasteland of mainstream television without losing its audience to less enlightening chan-nel choices. By studying their, and by extension our, authorial practices we can learn a great deal about the taste, knowledge, and values of sectors of the American middle class in general, and about how these cultural disposi-tions, when put into production practice, work to project and shape a particu-lar description of the world.

CHAPTER FOUR

Public Television Documentary Poetics

A VIEW OF *Childhood*'s producers as active, interpreting agents negotiating the structure of the texts they produce within the complex field of public television enriches our understanding of the process by which they constructed the series. Cultural frameworks of authorship, authority, and interpretation guide the procedures by which meaning is made manifest in aesthetic form. This chapter focuses more closely on the structure of the textual forms themselves, working through the evaluative and aesthetic language producers employ in negotiating and developing scenes, sequences, and programs in the series. My strategy here is to derive textual analysis from both the observation of production practices and the metadiscursive expression of concepts guiding that practice. These expressions offer an illustration and explication of the aspects of the text that the producers focus on in discourse about the production process and practical attention within it, and they reveal the theoretical frameworks that agents employ in the process of textual production.

This approach draws on the discourse-centered study of "poetics" as practiced in anthropology, folklore, and linguistics rather than on paradigms of poetics in media studies.[1] Approaches to poetics in media studies, by which I include an admittedly broad sweep of disciplinary perspectives, tend to treat media texts as separate from the more immediate social contexts in which they are embedded (produced and consumed), and apply "nonnative" (often classical, political economic, ideological, psychoanalytic, or cognitive) analytical frameworks for textual readings of these texts. An ethnographic approach to poetics grounds analysis in the social use and interpretive context of texts, studying formal features as they are discussed and employed in the social life of the text. Bauman and Briggs, in discussing speech performance, identify this approach as "the ethnographic and analytical investigation of form-function-meaning interrelationships within situational contexts of language use" (Bauman and Briggs 1990:79). Adapting this approach to media forms, the analysis in this chapter focuses on the textual features I observed the producers attending to, debating, and negotiating. These features include the narrative structure of individual programs and of the series as a whole, the use of specific program elements, textual conventions and aesthetic strategies within and across individual programs, and the tensions between language and visual images and between modes of exposition and modes of illustration.

THEORIZING AND RESEARCHING GENRE

The consideration of the broader issue of media genres—culturally based constructs for classification—offers a starting point into the "investigation of form-function-meaning interrelationships" in public television documentary. With few exceptions, television genres, like those of other communicative forms (film, popular music, verbal performance), are immediately recognizable to a culturally competent viewer. If one were to turn on the television unprejudiced by expectations about what they might encounter, it would take only moments to recognize that a show such as *Childhood* is an educational documentary program similar to others regularly shown on public television and on some cable stations. Specific cues encoded in visual and audio style and structure (length of scenes, amount of synch-sound material, subtitles, tone of narration, on-camera host format, transitional devices between scenes, etc.) would indicate the broad genre within which to locate the program and guide one's choice of appropriate interpretive strategy.

It is in these specific formal devices that genre is both recognizable and articulate.[2] In his encoding/decoding model, Stuart Hall termed these formal features "meaning structures" (Hall 1980), calling attention to their currency as shared conventions for production and reception. The conventional currency of genres, coupled with the conservatism of television programming, reinforces these interpretive strategies. As Fiske stated: "Television programs appear to fall 'obviously' into clear generic categories—cop shows, soap operas, sitcoms, hospital dramas, quiz and game shows, and so on. Television is a highly 'generic' medium with comparatively few one off programs falling outside established generic categories" (Fiske 1987:109). The predictability and recognizability of genres is reinforced by what Neale, theorizing about dramatic cinema, describes as the systematic nature of genres:

> Genres are not simply bodies of work or groups of films, however classified, labeled and defined. Genres do not consist only of films: they consist also, and equally, of specific systems of expectation and hypothesis which spectators bring with them to the cinema, and which interact with films themselves during the course of the viewing process. These systems provide spectators with means of recognition and understanding. They help render films, and the elements within them, intelligible and therefore explicable. (Neale 1990:46)

Neale includes the "spectator" and the context of viewing, and regards this spectator as an active interpreter, which more traditional approaches to film and television, focused on texts alone, had not done.[3]

Genre has become increasingly important, along with the notion of style, for analyzing artistic, verbal, and ritual performance. Here, genre provides both an entry point and intellectual framework for categorizing a group's expressive forms.[4] The problem of defining a culturally appropriate framework for expressive practices runs through ethnographic and media studies of genre. As Altman describes, film studies has struggled between a "user's" vocabulary of genre, derived from the film industry's self-promotion, and a critical vocabulary based on structuralist and semiotic applications of genre.[5] Altman's position moves much closer to the ethnographic one, which as Urban and Sherzer discuss with regard to the ethnography of speaking, turned toward grounded approaches to genre, "where it has come to mean a way of speaking that is *culturally recognized*, usually through a lexical label" (Urban and Sherzer 1988:286). While film studies has discussed genre primarily within predetermined analytical categories, the ethnography of speaking looks at speech genres as they are performed in social life, deriving generic categories from metacommunicative lexical encodings, the labels that people employ in discussions relating to categorization. This framework can be applied effectively to media production and reception.

However, generic distinctions within educational programming prove more elusive and indistinct than with fictional texts: a horror film or a television soap opera complies with articulable conventional definitions much more easily than a major PBS documentary series (though we seem to know a PBS documentary when we see one). I encountered a shortage of discrete "lexical labels"—both in fieldwork and in the scholarly literature—for both categorizing PBS genres and articulating the specific generic properties of *Childhood* and of PBS programs like it. Still, attention to the categorical language employed by producers, however blurry, is revealing about the intended functions of this form, about audience expectations, and about the specific implication of particular aesthetic elements. In fact, much of the aesthetic discourse I heard throughout the production of *Childhood* pertained to genre, though sometimes through metaphorical or analogical language. Genre is applicable then as both an abstract analytic framework through which to view the communicative practices of production and reception, and as a heterogeneous category historically acted upon (invoked, applied, and negotiated) by practitioners, which warrants investigation in its own right.[6]

Genres consist of a complex of stylistic and formal features historically and conventionally grouped together, employed in both production and reception. Individuals' understandings of genre negotiate between their expectations of a text and their experience with it, whether producing or consuming it, or both. Genres have a currency and import even prior to the work of production, influencing expectations critical for setting in motion structures of production. A program is developed (planned, funded, scripted), shot, edited, and slotted into a station's schedule with continual attention to genre: what type of program it is, how it coheres with others of its type and contrasts with different genres, and what textual and contextual features are appropriate, conventional, and effective within that generic class. We should rethink genre as more than a way of classifying texts, but as a strategic framework, a set of cultural practices that guide, condition, and mediate between communicative production and reception—historically, discursively, practically. Issues of genre connect broad social concerns about the system as a whole to microtextual issues of program design. For instance, ongoing debates and conflicts concerning the funding and role of public television reflect institutional and political stances regarding the nature of programming appropriate for public television and, by extension, the program formats, points of view, and subject matter the system should fund and broadcast, including in what relationship and structure.

Childhood was designed to be both conventional and innovative in its televisual form: conventional in that the producers and, presumably, the viewers, place the series within a traditional, albeit loose and ambiguous, genre of nonfiction television; and innovative in that by both intent and circumstance it departs from those conventions in revealing ways. *Childhood* lies close to the center of the range of generic appropriateness for a public broadcasting documentary, and its legitimation throughout its production life reflects this. It was funded and developed by one of the major producing stations in the PBS system with significant financial capital from public television, and broadcast nationally during PBS's prime-time schedule. That the series coheres with certain generic conventions and expectations for extended format documentary programs attests to the relationship between generic features and this organization of production. The negotiations around these generic features bring to light aspects of the workings of this specific genre and grounds this analysis of the poetics of public television documentary. These negotiations also refract questions of authority, authorship, production strategy, and production practices.

Genres are also emergent. The degree of relative stability of a given genre is a historical and empirical issue, amenable to research. Although my focus here is not the history of major documentary series in public television, I have tried to situate this genre historically and formally. It exists in the minds of the practitioners who produce it and the officials who administer it,[7] and their expectations include specific formal and rhetorical dimensions. What is clear from my work with *Childhood* is that the notion of genre, as applied to a specific series of programs, needs to be seen as developing and transforming through discourse and productive work. Formal elements of *Childhood* changed in significant ways during its production. Other series (especially programs these producers and staff members will work on in the future) will borrow from *Childhood*, just as *Childhood* borrowed from and reworked preexisting structures. Understanding works in terms of genre does not just locate "their value in what they have in common," as Fiske (1987: 110) argues, but in how a given work reproduces and remakes a given genre, operating, as Nichols maintains in his institutional definition of documentary and its makers, "in dialogue with that tradition and with their cohorts" (Nichols 1991:15).

Conceptions of genre are also differentially regarded and held, reflecting the multiple and contested nature of production discussed earlier. My research included an unfolding dialogue over the way this series made use of the formal, televisual resources available to it as a representative of this genre, and how generic conventions operate as a form of currency in the production process. In addition, these negotiations over genre raise overarching issues about the approach to television inherent in this set of programs, about the relationship between producers' intended meanings and audience interpretation, and about cultural stratification. Throughout *Childhood*, the producers negotiated through critical tensions around and made ideologically driven choices between the pedagogical and entertainment purposes of the series and of specific sequences within it, just as these tensions exist throughout the public television system itself (as I discussed in Chapter Two). Documentary forms are more obviously caught within and more prone to reproduce this dichotomy than other television genres (although not exclusively, since other genres, such as "good drama," work through similar tensions). The tension between the aesthetic engagement of popular television and the edifying benefits of educational programming drives much of the viewing and production practices within public television.[8]

A FOLK HISTORY OF MAJOR DOCUMENTARY SERIES

The "major documentary series," the loose genre *Childhood* can be placed in, represents one of the more conspicuous categories of programs broadcast on public television. Public affairs programs, news, drama, comedy, performance, nature, and science programs are all represented during PBS's program week, yet the documentary series remains a principal, "culturally recognized" form we associate with public television and a category of program PBS features in an effort to distinguish itself. The literature in film and television studies has surprisingly neglected the long-form educational documentary, resulting in little academic discussion about this genre. References do exist which associate long form documentary with public broadcasting (although cable television has eroded this exclusivity), and address its salient features. Hammond, for instance, located this genre of programming within the broad category of "theme documentary." He suggested the more specific term "cultural program," and opposed this to journalism, describing public television as "a bountiful haven for the theme documentary. Many of its documentary series, such as *Nova*, *Civilisation*, and *The Ascent of Man*, are some of the best cultural programs ever presented on TV" (Hammond

1981:12). Later, Hammond defined the theme documentary by distinguishing it from both television news and cinema vérité:

> The television theme documentary is more complicated than the news documentary. It provides for more amplitude than the television news documentary and it lacks the haphazard, yet harsh, dreamlike qualities of the vérité approach. Where the television news documentary tends to control the artistic treatment by sticking closely to an analysis of a particular news event, the television theme documentary tries to control the "life." TV theme documentary sets up artistic credos for its subjects, then proceeds to explain them subjectively, even personally. Such programs make no attempts to be objective, as do news shows. The rule dividing the two forms would appear to be: if you build your actualities around a news lead, you end up with a TV news documentary. But if you build your program around a theme—a point of view—then you have created a theme television documentary. (Hammond 1981:25)

Hammond's approach is inconsistent and oversimplified. For one, many so-called "theme documentaries" employ cinema vérité material, a technique also widely used in journalism. His odd characterization of the "harsh, dreamlike" approach of vérité material further obscures the distinction, as does his grouping together of very different kinds of programs. Also, research on television news emphasizes its subjective qualities, and the way in which news attempts to "control the life" it records (Tuchman 1979; Schudson 1991). Still, it is true that "theme documentaries" do share journalism's commitment to an ideology of objectivity, or as Nichols states, "they regard their relation to the real as direct, immediate, transparent" (Nichols 1991:4), relying instead on particular stylistic and expository strategies. In short, the academic literature on documentary does not offer much assistance in characterizing the genre within which *Childhood* fits. Perhaps this is because of the short history of this still emerging genre, and its limited profile in televisual culture.[9]

Still, we can begin to place this series and this genre by considering historical and categorical connections that participants in The *Childhood* Project made with other major series. In developing *Childhood*, Geoff Haines-Stiles and David Loxton intentionally designed programs that would cohere with the conventions and structure of the extended format educational series, a format familiar to these producers. Haines-Stiles's awareness of working within a tradition of program production and exhibition surfaced in discussions and promotional material for the series. Haines-Stiles cited the term "creative documentary," attributing it to Adrian Malone (executive producer of important series including *Cosmos* and *The Ascent of Man*) to distinguish this generic form from news, drama, and cinema vérité, and mark its hybrid nature (located between objective reportage and subjective commentary). However, I have not encountered Malone's phrase "creative documentary" in other places. In proposals for funding the series, written for readers familiar with the history of PBS programs, the producers categorized *Childhood* quite generally. They described it, at various points, as "a major PBS series," an "informational series," and "a documentary series," and referenced the genealogical relationship practitioners recognize between this and other well-known series: "CHILDHOOD is an eight-part television series in the tradition of ASCENT OF MAN, COSMOS, and THE BRAIN. Its subject is as vast, complex, significant and fascinating" (*Childhood*—A Proposal for an 8-part Television Series, 1989:2). Detailed descriptions of the goals for *Childhood* and the content of programs specified the nature of the series. The audience for these proposals, officials within institutions that fund public television programming, would not need much categorical description to understand the design and intent of the series, but they might be impressed by the association between *Childhood*'s producers and the series tradition. A CPB Advisory Panel's comments about the proposal reflected their easy understanding of the design of the series, and its fit within generic expectations. A summary of these comments included: "Good, steady PBS fare," "Meets all criteria," and "Standard and steady PBS." This last response was not a complete endorsement, though, since it continued, "I'm afraid this will be middle of the road, conservative, and sterile on a subject that shouldn't be."[10]

A more widespread awareness of the lineage of this genre emerges in a few telling pieces of testimony from the makers of previous major series. For instance, when Jacob Bronowski was approached to do the series *Ascent of Man*, the producers and he were aware of previous series done by Kenneth Clark and Alistair Cooke, and took these as models. "The invitation to me from the British Broadcasting Corporation was to present the development of science in a series of television programmes to match those of Lord Clark on *Civilisation*" (Bronowski 1973:13). In an interview, Bronowski's wife explained: "Someone from BBC said exciting films were being made on the subject of civilisation [*sic*]. They took him [Dr. Bronowski] to the studio. He went with Aubrey Singer to view them. At the end (of the viewing) he said, 'How dare he [Clark] call them *Civilisation*! They're beautiful and they're History of Art but they *are not civilisation*!' Aubrey replied, 'You could do one on civilisation.' Bruno said, "I could, but I won't'" (Rita Bronowski in Hoachlander 1977:72).

Clark, working with Peter Montagnon, was credited with the innovation of a television series form that other producers imitated: documentary material structured around a monologic commentary delivered by an on-camera host, and a multiprogram expositional approach to a sweepingly large subject, with a basis in extensive, often interdisciplinary research. The type of testimony cited above reinforces the existence of a "folk history" of the form, a history that my work on *Childhood* confirmed.[11] In Chapter Two I described how production staff often marked *Childhood*'s familial relationship to

previous landmark educational documentary series. References to formal and
aesthetic qualities of other programs—a host termed "Bronowskian," a sequence consciously designed to differ from a comparable scene in *The
Mind*—were part of the metadiscourse of the production, including promotional material and proposals that referred to the legacy of *Childhood*. *Childhood*'s production staff made regular comparisons with other related generic
forms—categorical and generic distinctions used to distinguish *Childhood*
from other programming types and to discuss its relevant formal features,
defining the series by contrast.[12]

For instance, in the following discussion about the use of spoken expository material to illustrate a feminist perspective in a sequence about mother-
hood, the producers articulated the stylistic conventions and aesthetic criteria
appropriate for the series:

> MELVIN KONNER: Instead of trying to blend it all into some bland middle
> ground where nobody says anything, put the controversy there, let Barbara
> Ehrenreich or Adrienne Rich stake out the extreme feminist position, let some
> male chauvinist pig like me say the thing about evolution and sex differences,
> and let the viewer . . .
>
> MEG KREUZINGA: But I thought you were against having pop-in experts.
>
> GEOFF HAINES-STILES: I am, so that's not an option as far as this series is
> concerned. That's another series to come up with.
>
> KONNER: Some think, others think. Some experts think, feminists think.
>
> ERNA AKUGINOW: We can do that, Mel, but we have to think of a more clever
> way than talking head debate. What we need are some real bits of situations,
> anecdotes . . .
>
> KONNER: The observers aren't going to come on as talking heads? Sandra Scarr
> can't come on and say something that Adrienne Rich might say?
>
> AKUGINOW: The observers certainly can, but I don't think that . . . I mean there
> will be particular places where debate among the observers will serve us well
> to make points. I don't think that in this particular situation we're going to be
> able to do that with the observers.
>
> HAINES-STILES: There's no doubt about it, that's the argument I want to make
> part of the episode, but that particular convention—the *60 Minutes*, point-
> counterpoint—is not the convention that we have chosen for the aesthetic
> criteria of the series. What Erna's saying correctly is, "What are other ways of
> bringing it to life?" (Advisors Meeting, February 19, 1990)

The television producers here made clear to the advisors that they intended
to avoid the use of "pop-in experts" and a "point-counterpoint" format typical of other genres of nonfiction television.[13] In doing so, they allude to
several different genre formats for educational and journalistic articulation.

In fact, production staff often used television journalism as a point of
negative comparison and made comments to that end: "I don't think we want
to do a CBS news piece on that," or "It will look like an NBC White Paper

or ABC Special." Here, they were referring to the genre of network documentary special that was once a mainstay of prime-time programming but has essentially disappeared in recent times. Other, mostly negative, references to television formats were common—that is, "We want to avoid the feeling of television movie uplift."[14] *Childhood*'s staff regarded this series' format as having greater substance and depth, a more complex rhetorical structure, and a more scholarly grounding than these other television genres. The production staff used these kinds of categorical comparisons to specify, negotiate (where appropriate), and reach agreement about their conceptual approaches to the series and its formal features. This kind of metacommentary is evidence for recognizing what I described in Chapter One as an "ethnotheory" of PBS documentary production and supports the grounding of my analysis of PBS documentary aesthetics in the attitudes and practices of its producers.

"THE AESTHETIC CRITERIA OF THE SERIES"

Like other major public television series before it, *Childhood* is interdisciplinary and covers a broad topical scope. The titles of programs like *Civilisation*, *The Ascent of Man*, *Cosmos*, and *Millennium* speak to the thematic breadth typical of this genre. Peter Montagnon regards being interdisciplinary as a formative feature of the educational series, and the articulation of scholarly work a principal strength:

> One of its great strengths is that it can be, that it goes at the subject laterally, because television tends to bridge disciplines. If you take a rather formal study like this, which goes at childhood, let's say there's a subject "childhood," and then you go to the developmental psychologists. Well normally, within a university, you attempt to narrow this down and to keep it within the enclave of developmental psychologists, if you're doing a study. Television very naturally goes laterally, because you're interested in the other things, you're interested in history, where did it come from, you're interested in anthropology, you're interested in the sociological aspects, and so, without the constraints on you, you naturally tend to go laterally and look for connecting links, and you tend to spread it in terms of your advisors or participants, in a way that you normally wouldn't do if you were studying it as a discipline within a university. That's one of the large differences. (Interview with Peter Montagnon, August 1, 1990)

The proposal for *Childhood* also stressed this integration of academic perspectives:

> We have identified five subject areas: *developmental psychology, anthropology, sociology and family studies, history, education and culture*. However, the unique challenge for CHILDHOOD is that we recognize that in examining real

children in the real world, no one of these factors ever operates alone, but always together with various other forces in a complex dance of interacting influences.

[. . .]

CHILDHOOD aims to spin that sort of web around its great subject, to capture it for a wide audience. The intellectual uniqueness of the series lies in its fertile inter-mixing of academic disciplines normally kept separate. (*Childhood*—A Proposal for an 8-part Television Series, 1989:9)

The advisory board, composed of well-established, high-profile scholars in these disciplines, reflected this broad sweep (see Appendix B). This board, typical for major documentary series, served the series by contributing to the development of content material and theoretical perspectives, providing a resource of experts to review elements of the series, and legitimating the program in the view of funding sources. At the same time, the topical and interdisciplinary breadth articulated in proposals invoked a generic constraint difficult to fulfill. The board and the series failed to represent less legitimated and potentially radical perspectives, and did not give equal emphasis to all the major disciplines represented; the programs evolved toward those sequences and structures that seemed strongest and most realizable, given constraints of time, money, and style.

Childhood employs certain dominant formal features representative of the genre. The producers incorporated a large amount of observational footage (at least thirty minutes per program), mostly of family interactions, rendered with the kind of transparent realism typical of documentary overall, and of many PBS documentary styles. Their intent was to have the programs act as a narrative window on the world the series observes, while effacing the presence of the production crew. On the other hand, extensive and omniscient narration accompanies most of the observational footage, steering audience interpretation of this material, and distinguishing this genre from what is more typically termed cinema vérité documentary style.[15] Narration introducing the first program in the series, accompanying a montage of observational images of the families followed through the series, sets the stage for the realistic representational framework in which the producers employ this material, as illustrated in figure 4.1.

This wedding together of vérité images with expository narration is typical of educational documentary series, although formats vary with regard to who delivers the information—host, narrator, or interview subject—and its density. Other documentary styles (more ethnographic or reflexive and therefore less conventional) might have treated this material differently, perhaps by eliminating the narration and employing minimal identifying captions along with the observational footage. In *Childhood*, two omniscient narrators (one male, one female) deliver more of the expository text than in a series like *The Ascent of Man*, which is carried exclusively by the host.

Narrator (Alex Chadwick): All over the world, our cameras recorded the astonishing transformations that make babies into toddlers, girls into young women, and boys into young men.

In this first program, we witness three contrasting births and see how every life starts with an event that's both universal, and yet very different.

Narrator (Lynn Neary): We meet a Russian family that's on the edge of divorce.

Narrator (Chadwick): We see how a Japanese childhood is structured by the close alliance of family and society.

Narrator (Neary): But how in America, a family sometimes has to fight back against social pressures.

Narrator (Chadwick): In Brazil, we see how parents can change the future by changing the circumstances of their children's lives.

Narrator (Neary): We are about to embark on an expedition of discovery, of our children and our species, and how each of us became who we are. Families are where most children start their lives, and in four families we begin our own journey through childhood.

Figure 4.1 Narration and selected frames from the opening sequence in Program One/"Great Expectations."

The level of production value the producers worked toward also places *Childhood* within the aesthetic criteria of major PBS and BBC documentary series. Production value is a media industry term indexing the markings of quality, stylization, and technical competence favored for a particular production mode. A program is said to have high production value when it manages to employ what are usually expensive (labor and capital-intensive) production techniques, resulting in a show with a polished, professional, and expensive look, even if economically obtained.[16] Producers' shared notions of production value change as stylistic norms change, and specific techniques become fashionable. The producers showed a great deal of concern over the formal qualities of visual images generated for the series. They sought out documentary cinematographers with excellent reputations, and talked at length about visual renderings of the scenes they would shoot. The aesthetics of documentary shooting relies heavily on the cinematographer's success in capturing in usable form the most important events as they unfold. In an internal memo, Geoff Haines-Stiles compared the camera work of the initial Japanese cinematographer with the Russian cinematographer, with whom the producers were much more pleased, illustrating the kinds of concerns the producers articulated:

> I think we are agreed that the Japanese camera work is by no means as superior as the Soviet. You indicated there were several main things you would ask to have happen: 1) more close-ups, and less medium shots; 2) more variety in height, getting down to the level of the kids and shooting less from "outside" and "above" the scenes; 3) more sense of sequence, "process," or in less jargonful terms, more reaction shots, showing kids in context, both with other children and with parents. All these were things which you indicated were in your mind, and I thoroughly agree. However you best think this should be conveyed to the crew/fixer is obviously fine with us. (Memo, Geoff Haines-Stiles to Peter Montagnon, December 19, 1989)

These qualities favored by Haines-Stiles would not be easily quantified but do represent criteria of good "cinema vérité style" documentary camera work. Producers spoke favorably about camera people whose work "reveals in the shooting" the essential characteristics of an interaction and could portray a relationship through the proper choice of composition and angle. In evaluating cinematographers' previous work and footage for *Childhood*, producers looked for fluidity, sensitivity, the ability to follow action unobtrusively, and other more personal variables (flexibility, communication skills, availability to the series, and affordable price).

Most major public television documentary series, particularly international coproductions, work with generous budgets compared with those of independent documentaries, and the look and packaging of these series usually reflects this distinction.[17] *Childhood* was shot on film rather than videotape, for instance, a principal indicator associated with high-budget series, requiring greater expenditures on production equipment, supplies and services, and personnel to get this "film look."[18] *Childhood* also commissioned original music and graphic title design for the series and incorporated extensive original location shooting, particularly in far-off parts of the world, all indicators of a high level of production value.[19] Other less dominant but still recognizable features of major documentary series include the use of still image/art sequences, the inclusion of celebrities (*Childhood* included one celebrity, Dr. Benjamin Spock, along with its largely academic observers), and the production of a companion book for the series.

GENERIC CONVENTIONS:
INNOVATION AND RESISTANCE

Although *Childhood* adhered to conventions fundamental to the loosely defined and malleable genre, its producers sought to stretch the limits of these conventions. Proposals, other written documents, and discussions during the production process posed ways in which the series would depart from normative expectations brought to bear on PBS documentary series, including the mixing of documentary and dramatic modes, an unusual approach to the use of on-camera hosts, and the obtaining and extensive employment of long-term observational footage of specific families. "CHILDHOOD will be a most unusual series, juxtaposing documentary sequences with dramatic vignettes, animation and anthropological film, all seamlessly flowing according to the content and storyline of that particular hour" (*Childhood*—A Proposal for an 8-part Television Series, 1989:9). Geoff Haines-Stiles expressed a desire to depart from conventions set in place by previous series, and concern over WNET's reaction to these departures:

> So, from the beginning, David and I sort of said to each other, "Let's not make this like a boring documentary. We don't want to point fingers at particular documentary programs, but let's not make the mistakes we made on *Cosmos*, let's have something dramatic like the continuity of the family developing over time." That was one of David's main delights in the family sequences, and let's make sure that the subjective experience of being a child is there and therefore the Childhood Minutes concept came in. Peter was very skeptical about that to begin with, but I think since then he's come around. [. . .] And in reality I don't think that any other series has quite put it together this way. And I think that there are a number of people, including some of our staff people, including some of the people at 'NET, who are skeptical about whether it's going to gel. And I don't know if it's going to gel or not, so we're going to see if we can pull a

show together over the summer and see if it works. And what works is, I don't know, because, I think I have a different aesthetic than the people at 'NET, but we have to come to some mutual accommodation, because they have contractually obligated rights of review, so we'll have to see if it works. (Interview with Geoff Haines-Stiles, March 2, 1990)

Correspondence from the series' development period reflects WNET officials' concerns about specific program elements. WNET's concerns exemplify the kind of interaction around genre Neale (1990) posited between expectations and norms, based on the station's recent experience with programs like *Civilisation, Heritage: Civilization and the Jews*, *The Brain*, and *The Mind*. George Page, WNET's senior science editor, who had principal oversight for the series, expressed his apprehension about certain program elements:

As you know, I have always been concerned about the "Families Concept," the "Childhood Minutes" and the dramatic recreations. The latter two simply seem highly contrived and I worry that they won't be effective television. . . .

In short, your basic subject matter is so rich and inherently interesting I don't think you need any risky production innovations to make the most compelling television. You have a wonderful story; why not tell it simply and elegantly? (Thirteen Memorandum from George Page to David Loxton and Geoff Haines-Stiles, June 23, 1988)

WNET's cautiousness exerted a conservative force on the series. WNET administrators hoped *Childhood* would conform to its previous offerings and resisted departures from these successes. Haines-Stiles, aware of this opposition, argued that *Childhood*'s innovative features elevated the work and later felt vindicated by the extremely positive reception the *Childhood* demonstration tape received when screened at a PBS meeting, and by WNET executives' positive response to program rough cuts. Though *Childhood* promoted itself as an innovative series, the programs that resulted raise questions about the powers of conformity that both the genre and this production context assert over a work.

THE MIXING OF TELEVISION MODES

The proposal to combine different modes of documentary and dramatic television represented a principal way the series would depart from generic conventions. The producers identified six principal types of material that would constitute the series, and estimated using these elements in the following proportions (in minutes):

Each hour:

Families cinema vérité film	20:00
Other documentary scenes	18:00
Childhood minutes: "Evocations"	4:00
"Observers" to camera	7:00
Stills animation	2:00
Acquired film footage	5:00
Titles and credits	2:00
Total	58:00

(From draft for "*Childhood* Update," n.d.)

The families footage, other documentary scenes, and stills animation were all designed to include omniscient narration, while *Childhood* Minutes, subjective historical evocations, would be dramatic re-creations and testimonials. It struck me that the combination of these elements, although not unprecedented, represented an unusual hybrid. Producer/director Gene Marner recalled his initial hesitancy about the combination of series elements, the mixing of modes:

> I thought there were too many different kinds of materials. I thought that there wasn't a chance to get involved in anything in a dramatic, in an emotional way, and that a lot of information was being marshaled, one interesting fact after another, but that each hour didn't seem to be a self-contained piece, it didn't have a beginning, middle, and end, didn't have a dramatic story to tell. Each of the hours . . . . It seemed like there was a long line of information, you know, and just hunks had been cut off, and it started and then it stopped, because it's kind of chronological. I'm exaggerating a little bit, you know—but that was the impression I had. [. . .] I still think that in the treatment there are too many different types of materials. I think that perforce, what we will end up with in the shows is fewer different kinds of materials in each program, maybe not in the whole series, but, within each program, I think there will be three, four modes of delivering information, but not eight. (Interview with Gene Marner, March 6, 1990)

In a meeting where advisors (including the writer Jonathan Cott) responded to program treatments and early scripts, Peter Montagnon objected to the mixing of modes on different grounds:

> PETER MONTAGNON: Robert Hinde says, and he's one of our advisors, says that it's a confusion of material. That you can't sort of confabulate one sort of material with the other, and mix them up, because the ordinary viewer, who can't tell the difference between reality and fantasy much anyway, is going to be yet further confused.
>
> JONATHAN COTT: That means, what, *Childhood* Minutes, international families?
>
> MONTAGNON: Well, it's to say the difference between extremely hard-edged bits of data which Jerome Kagan or Robert Hinde would claim are pretty well

established, and hold good all over the world, and those things that are utterly subjective that, even though one gets a tremendous kick out of it, the worth of it is dubious. And whether people can actually evaluate the worth of one piece of information against that of the other. And they would hold that the stuff that is hard, in their terms, should be given priority over this soft stuff, and warn us against confusion on the viewer's part.

COTT: Well, okay, but do they warn you against boredom. [Group laughter]

MONTAGNON: No, that they're probably not so well equipped to do. (Advisors Meeting, December 13, 1989)

The producers expected that the treatments, acting as a kind of resource pool of scenes to be included in the programs, would be boiled down through the production process, eliminating proposed scenes through attrition. In the end, they wound up dropping the dramatic historical re-creations from the series, thereby slightly reducing the number of different "modes of delivering information." The final proportions of modes of documentary in the edited programs included, on average, roughly thirty-three minutes of family material, nine minutes of observers sequences (although most of this was in voice-over, not "to camera"), nine minutes of documentary scenes, and four minutes of archival material for historical sequences.[20]

Still, the impetus for innovation extended to several specific code-features which I consider in detail below: multiple observers, observational family footage, and *Childhood* Minutes. The strategies for structuring these features, and arguments for and against their place within this genre, represent competing aesthetic frameworks for articulating the series' material, characterized in one form in the distinction Peter Montagnon draws in the passage above between hard and soft data. Both his and Geoff Haines-Stiles's anticipation of Hinde's and Kagan's critique of the "softer" material, the scenes and production modes that are less scientifically established, illustrates these competing frameworks, which are refracted through other aspects of *Childhood*'s production.

From Hosts to "Observers"

BBC and PBS documentary series often employ the convention of an on-camera host who guides the viewer through the program's exposition. The roles of Kenneth Clark in *Civilisation*, Jacob Bronowski in *Ascent of Man*, and Carl Sagan in *Cosmos* exemplify "dominant" formal devices for major documentary series, as opposed to the omniscient narration of ongoing programs like *Nova* or *Nature*. One British documentary filmmaker termed this "the coffee-table book approach," where "we would listen to the great men of television—Cooke, Clark, Bronowski, Cameron—telling us about other continents" (Bolton 1992). The format persists as one of the recognizable aesthetic forms on public television.[21]

This generic convention raises two interrelated aesthetic issues, one concerning the presentational format for program making, the "on-screen" role of the host, and the other with the authorial contribution of these hosts, their "off-screen" role (leaving the thematic issues around "telling us about other continents" for the next chapter). These hosts, learned scholars who perform first-person direct-address narration both on camera and off, navigated the expository form of these series, presenting themselves as the authors of the programs they were hosting. Clark, Bronowski, and Sagan were both the primary authors of the verbal information that structured these programs' written scripts and active collaborators in program design. Other series employ on-camera hosts merely as actors, figureheads rendering the producers' prewritten texts. The on-camera host format tends to eschew or deemphasize expert interviews, reserving the presentation of scholarly and interpretive information and authority for the host alone.

With *Childhood*, the producers were the primary authors of these programs, with the observers playing a contributing "off-screen" role through the production process. Loxton and Haines-Stiles chose to depart from the conventional single-host structure in designing the series. According to Haines-Stiles:

> We didn't want it to be like *National Geographic* or *Nova*; we thought there was a real value in having presenters on camera. And yet, in this area, although we thought it would be easier to find one single man or woman who would be our Carl Sagan, we literally didn't find him. We went around the country thinking could it be Jerry Kagan—well, he's incredibly bright, he's certainly charismatic enough, he could be the person, but he represents a very partial point of view, and it's only one of the many points of view that are legitimate about childhood. Could it be Urie Bronfenbrenner? Well maybe it could have been Urie more than anybody else; but even so, he's a man, should we have a male presenting the series? We ended up, because of necessity, saying, there is no one person who we want to invest with—if Freud was alive we still wouldn't want him to host the series, because he's too partial—therefore, we have a unique way of approaching it with the observers.
>
> We're saying, "Let's say that there are a multiplicity of perspectives from which it is legitimate to understand childhood." Let's personify that by having characters on camera who say that, and if in reality Mel Konner and Jerry and Sandy Scarr don't actually agree about something, that's fine. Let's have the audience understand that, because in reality a Japanese family or an American family may have different premises about what's the right form of child care anyway, and let's make sure the audience recognizes that there is no one right way to raise a child, there is not one answer to what a human being is. (Interview with Geoff Haines-Stiles, March 2, 1990)

The multiple-host format was born somewhat out of necessity and seen by Haines-Stiles as embodying an important thematic component of the series, that authority in this broad, interdisciplinary field of knowledge should be regarded as multiple and disputable. It is unclear whether the final programs live up to this objective, partly because the producers utilized observer material less than they had planned, employing more extensive narration instead. The multiple-host format entailed a modified mode of production, both increasing the sharing of authorship and dictating producers' strategies about how and where in the programs to employ the observers, and what perspectives they would each "personify."

Haines-Stiles drew the comparison between his work with Carl Sagan, the host of *Cosmos*, who was involved in most of the production process and the multiple hosts of this series, with its more egalitarian and therefore labor-intensive mode of authorship: "So, *Cosmos* had one person, most of the big series' have had one person. When they've had multiple people, as in *The Brain* series or in *Nova*, they've usually been interviewed as experts responding to the structure of the production staff, rather than as the sort of co-presenters or the storytellers. So we have a unique relationship with the advisors, which is why we've been spending more time b-s-ing and maybe wasting time" (interview with Geoff Haines-Stiles, March 2, 1990). Haines-Stiles located the unique role the advisors played between the strong authorial stance of Clark and Bronowski in those earlier series, and the contributing position experts typically held in other documentary projects. It is instructive to see how producers' concerns over the observers' roles were propelled by their expectations of the multiple audiences for the series and tied to the strategies they employed to best appeal to those audiences. Peter Montagnon reflected on the relationship between the advisors, who appear on camera, and the producers, and how this authorial structure would affect audience understanding:

> PETER MONTAGNON: I think that it's important that the advisors should not seem to be creatures of the filmmakers—adjuncts—even if they are. And when one is actually trying to create this Trojan horse, you have to have magicians around, and the magicians should not be the producers, they should be the guys on the screen, so that cuts seem to be motivated by what they've said, rather than them reluctantly tagging along afterwards to explain the cut you chose to make. I think this makes a great difference to the feel of the program, because the other way around they're just another piece of the mixture.
> DORNFELD: How do you think that affects an audience, if it's the latter?
> MONTAGNON: Well, I think the audience want, I think they tend to put more credence on what the people are saying, and assuming that you want them to do that because you want them to listen hard to what's being said. It's quite difficult to achieve. (Interview with Peter Montagnon August 1, 1990)

The producers devoted much thought to the critical process of choosing the roster of observers for *Childhood*,[22] selecting these eminent representatives from a variety of disciplinary perspectives. Although the producers considered the abilities of these observers to perform on camera, they underestimated the effort they would have to expend with the observers to obtain usable performance sequences competent enough to establish their credibility as both scholarly authorities and authors of the series.

The observers lend credibility and authority to the expository arguments *Childhood* articulates, and given their academic credentials and name recognition, stand as symbols for the series' integrity and level of expertise. Hosts of past major series like Bronowski, Clark, and Sagan had a great deal of status as public intellectuals with wide-ranging knowledge; indeed, these series' originators were considered modern Renaissance men, "great men of television." *Childhood*'s observers might not share their breadth of knowledge or public stature but are still highly esteemed scholars. In addition to knowledge and credentials, public television hosts have conventionally been excellent on-camera performers, capable actors in front of the camera, able to deliver polished and eloquent verbal performances, a combination that Montagnon described as intellectually "formidable" and "having the theatrical quality to put it over." Part of this ability involves reading written texts while looking directly into the camera lens, the accepted convention for a television host, and a much more specialized skill than speaking extemporaneously to an off-camera interviewer. It was in this performative dimension that *Childhood*'s producers struggled with the performances of a few of their observers who, although impressive speakers in person, felt uncomfortable in front of the camera, speaking directly to the lens.

Cinematographer Richard Chisolm spoke at length about the difficulty producer/directors had directing the observer sequences he photographed, and the ability to play on-camera host:

> It's not hard for Carl Sagan or for Walter Cronkite or Dan Rather to talk to a lens or a doorknob or anything else, and Ronald Reagan's a great example, he can look at a prompter, he can look at a doorknob, and completely emote with his eyes. But a lot of these researchers, psychologists, anthropologists were never taught to be on-camera people. Some of them have been to seminars and workshops about how to do public speaking and about how to be interviewed, some of them haven't, and I think it boils down to an ability that you either have or you don't. And it's been very frustrating for me and for producers at *Childhood* to have to sacrifice the integrity of these people because of this technical thing. If they had, from the beginning, had decided to have these people talk off camera, this would not be a problem at all, because those people are easily able to talk off-camera to another face. (Interview with cinematographer Richard Chisolm, September 22, 1990)

The production staff expended significant energy and time worrying about observers' abilities and devising strategies to make them more comfortable and remedy uneven performances.[23]

The multiple-host format obliged the producers to consider which observers could most appropriately speak about specific topics in specific programs, and to devise appropriate locations in which to shoot them. Mel Konner, for instance, delivered scenes in Program Two/"Louder than Words" while dressed in doctor's garb, set in the hospital nursery where the Kauffman family gives birth, describing the newborn's reflexes. Konner's dual identity as both an anthropologist who studies child development and a trained doctor justified this location. The settings and topics of these observer sequences allowed the producers to emphasize their areas of expertise. As the producers scripted scenes, they would consider what information could best be delivered by which observer at a given point in a program. This intermittent and directed use of the observers made them more like conventional interview subjects in the specificity of their appearances, but the tone and voice of their delivery, the summarizing nature of their comments, and their direct address to the camera encoded their role as hosts.

Because the observers contributed to writing the "to camera" scenes they performed and because they remained active advisors throughout the project, the issue of authorship (as discussed in the previous chapter) and the function of this particular program feature became complicated. The commentary alternates between the narrators and the observers, with the narrators delivering much more of the verbal information in the series, even introducing the observers. The on-camera observer format represents an element of *Childhood* that uses generic conventions while deviating from them for reasons specific to the strategies and history of this production. In the end, the producers used less of the observer material than they had initially anticipated, presumably because they were less pleased with these sequences and found it more expedient and effective to rely on narration to accompany documentary material.

The "Families" Concept

Observational scenes portraying the lives of families in Japan, Russia, Brazil, and the United States comprised the bulk of synch sound footage in the series, that is, the illustrative film material that accompanies much of the verbal exposition. Geoff Haines-Stiles described both the early discussions about these sequences, and the role that he envisioned them playing.

> GEOFF HAINES-STILES: Originally, the families weren't part of the approach to it. Erna actually came up with the idea in one of the very early discussions before things were put down on paper, and I said I don't think we'll be able to find families that will get away from *The American Family* problem of seeming, sequences which strive for typicality and then end up not being typical. So we'll get into problems in which people will criticize us for not being

representative enough. And we'll have to shoot so many days and weeks with these families that we won't be able to afford it, it'll break the budget. And how will it go together with the other segments anyway? I don't think it's a good idea. And the more people we talked to, the more people said, "This is a great idea! These families are really going to take us away from. . . ." And the more I thought about it, I said, "Well, I guess they must be right."

DORNFELD: Because of the intimacy that would develop?

HAINES-STILES: One of the things that occurred to David from the beginning was that you had to have a cast of characters. Most documentary programs, if you look at *The Brain* or *The Mind*, they have people, and you get to know people quite intimately, quite quickly, but there's no continuity. So, in this series I see not every family appearing in every program, but the Gholstons will certainly be in the first program and the last program, and Program Two and Program Three. The Kirkpatricks will certainly be in the first program and the last program, and Program Four, Five, and Six, if not just Four and Five. The Kalugins will certainly be in the first program, maybe not in the last program, but in Programs Two and Three. (Interview with Geoff Haines-Stiles, March 2, 1990)

The producers' approach to this "families footage" did generate controversy and disagreement. In their proposals for filming and incorporating family sequences, the producers depended on obtaining footage of a variety of intimate, candid, revealing, and dramatic moments of family behavior that could be used in diverse ways throughout the series. They hoped this material would provide a narrative dimension depicting scenes of characters, particularly children, that viewers would identify with and watch develop over the year or so they would be filmed and interwoven and sometimes combined with expository material. Haines-Stiles characterized this role as a "nonfiction soap opera": "I think that the characters are actually coming to life well enough that you have this kind of dramatic progression" (interview with Geoff Haines-Stiles, March 2, 1990). They arranged to film families in a "cinema vérité" style, denoting hand-held, long-take sequences of undirected, spontaneous behavior. This style of filming is notorious for the amount of time, effort, and film stock (and, consequently, expense) required to achieve intimacy and be fortunate enough to capture the kinds of events and specific moments producers hoped for as they unfold.[24] Most unusual for this series were the devotion of attention and expense to obtaining this documentary footage, and the producers' willingness to plan to use risky material, scenes that they could not script in advance for use in specific sequences. However, the producers incorporated this "family footage" in fairly conventional documentary structures—extended observational sequences within one family and montage structures illustrating behaviors intercut across cultures—usually with extensive narration.

WNET administrators did not concur with the producers' confidence that the family sequences would provide sufficient drama to propel the structure of the programs. For instance, Richard Hutton, a WNET producer responsible for the series *The Mind*, questioned the dramatic engagement that *Childhood*'s executive producers envisioned in creating the family footage:

> This is an entirely personal opinion, but I don't see the drama inherent in the "Families" concept. You may get lucky while you are filming, but it seems to me that the idea puts the cart before the horse; it limits the opportunity for true documentary excitement by limiting the possible range of subjects. I don't understand why the audience should have a commitment to these families; and I suspect that, without a commitment, interest wanes. You may find yourself with huge numbers of exquisitely cute sequences that, over time, pall because they lack the drama of real human stories. (Memo from Richard Hutton to David Loxton and Geoff Haines-Stiles, June 20, 1988)

George Page, WNET's executive-in-charge of *Childhood*, agreed with Hutton, observing that "limiting yourself to a supposedly 'representative group' of families is very risky business from a production point of view. Why limit yourself when the world can be your oyster and you can more easily find compelling families to make any point you wish to make."[25] In retrospect, Haines-Stiles felt the success of this material justified their confidence.

History in Childhood

The producers' treatment of historical sequences in the series illustrates the tensions present between documentary aesthetics, scholarly exposition, and production constraints. The proposal to include what they referred to as *Childhood* Minutes, dramatic historical reconstructions and biographical testimonies, represented a departure from convention. While these *Childhood* Minutes originated early in the series' development, their realization was a point of contestation throughout the production process. The producers agreed that a historical perspective was critical to *Childhood*. Indeed, much of the motivation and material for the original treatments came from historians responsible for reconsidering scholarship about the treatment and conceptions of children and childhood life through different historical periods.[26] Phillipe Ariés's seminal work on childhood's past, *Centuries of Childhood* (1962), invigorated the discipline of childhood and family history, resulting in scholarship rethinking conceptions of childhood.[27] The series made use of this material in its development, including historians Ray Hiner and Robert Wozniak (a specialist in the history of the psychological study of childhood life) as principal advisors. Haines-Stiles explained:

In our approach to the series we always said that the historical perspective was useful because it looked back in our own culture, as opposed to the anthropological record which looks, by definition, at the others. By looking at Western European culture out of which the shaping aspects of American society at least came, we thought we could say if there are changes within our own society that are radical and profound, then that accentuates the idea that childhood is indeed a construct. It's a supplementary force. On the other hand I think that the Linda Pollock sort of points show that because we are one species and because in terms of evolution it's hard to see fifty thousand years worth of evolution having changed us that much, except in culture as opposed to biology, that there may indeed be habits of mind which should transcend culture. How some things will change and some things won't change. That's a quick overview of the history of childhood. (Advisors Meeting, December 13, 1989)

The producers struggled with developing appropriate sequences for articulating this historical material. The debate throughout the development and early production stages considered the contribution of history to the series, the use of both generalizations and historical examples, and how the rendering of these generalizations and examples conformed with this genre of television.

From an academic perspective, history could offer both generalizations about societies through time, and specific anecdotal evidence for supporting those generalizations. Discussion during the history advisors' meeting returned to this dual scholarly role for history, as related by Wozniak:

It's not that you use history obviously to bolster points as much as you do to constrain points. . . . This is obviously a tough line to walk, because as we all know academics love to qualify absolutely every statement they make, and I think that, needless to say, can be taken to a tremendous extreme in this kind of enterprise. By the same token, it seems to me that the historical perspective will give us a chance to, without qualifying, provide a kind of positive qualification, let's put it that way. In other words, instead of saying, "Well, maybe it's this way, maybe it's that way," you can say, "It was this way and it was this way in another location and another period and time, and now, in general, it's this way." And in a sense you can convey the sense of qualifying generalizations without having to sound like you're always backing off from every point you make. I think that's really crucial. (Advisors Meeting, February 19, 1990)

Anthropologist Mel Konner drew parallels between the use of historical data and the use of anthropological data and pushed the group to reach a consensus on the consequences of a broad historical narrative of change in childhood life over time. The result was some agreement about the impact of modernization on childhood life (i.e., the decline of childhood mortality and mortality generally, increase in growth rate and body size, earlier onset of puberty, decline in birth rate). With this consensus reached, they spent much of these two days of meetings discussing specific historical periods and anecdotes, continually returning to the problem of how "history" could contribute to this form of television.

The producers felt history should offer specific stories that would enable them to dramatize the texture of life from other times and illustrate abstract points they intended to make. Producer Gene Marner voiced this view, but was opposed by Konner, who wanted to separate the telling of stories from the laying out of general principles:

> GENE MARNER: It seems to me that what Ray [Hiner] said earlier about the strength of what they have to offer us being in the fact that they tell stories is really the point. I mean, we do have to tell stories, and each of our programs is a story, and that's what they can do for us. We have to tell the story. I think if we get trapped in trying to lay out data with general principles, it means we won't be telling the story.
>
> MEL KONNER: I think you're underestimating the viewer. Why can't you just tell the stories and let the viewer decide . . .
>
> MARNER: We can present the possibilities for generalizing, but I think really what we have to do is choose very carefully and wisely the stories that are going to lay out the complexity of . . . I mean the general principles, we don't want to fire them at the people, I think they want them to somehow be in our minds, and always we will then be advocates for a point of view. (Advisors Meeting, February 20, 1990)

Historian John Demos, brought in as a consultant for one day of the meeting, supported Marner's views after Hiner, Wozniak, and he resisted the kind of generalizing that Konner and Haines-Stiles had encouraged: "I do think the issue of stories is key, and it seems to me the stories ought to have a lot to do with making good films, and I think the issue is which stories are the most helpful. I mean you've got stories from anthropology, stories from present-day life in this country in here, and some stories from history. Maybe there could be more. So the issue is really struggling with where specific ones might fit" (Advisors Meeting, February 20, 1990).

Haines-Stiles, dissatisfied with both the historians' ability to make and hold to generalizations about childhood life in the past and their inability to contribute useful illustrative stories to the series, expected history to do more than "constrain points" and provide a "positive qualification":

> There's two things that come out of this that I think is actually where we want to be at this point. One is that I think that some of the stories that have merged their way sideways into the episodes are just not good enough stories. Cotton Mather is a good enough story. It really is juicy. It has a connection which leads us to the contemporary world. It does something that a building block for a television show really should do. Some of the other things that are sort of wimp-

ing around, and we'll rely on you guys, through the course of the rest of the day, to sort of say, "Well, gee, there's this circumstance that I know of that's really interesting." But what I was afraid yesterday is that there's not enough passionate saying, "That's a dumb story, that's really boring. This is a much more illuminating story. Even if it's somewhat contradictory." What I was coming to yesterday was a lot of the on-the-one-hand, on-the-other-hand, so that you end up not being able to make TV sequences. And you can't really make interesting history, either, out of it. You end up putting so many caveats on screen you have no stories to tell. (Advisors Meeting, February 20, 1990)

Haines-Stiles voiced his frustration about integrating historical material into the series and the advisors' inability to offer them the kind of powerful anecdotes they needed to "bring to life" childhood experience in other times and places and provide "a coherent and dramatic visual presentation out of the partial sources that are there." The limitations of what history could offer stayed with the project as it moved further into production.

From the treatments onward, the producers proposed three different formats for illustrating historical material in the series: dramatic reconstructions with actors on sets reading and interpreting the narratives of specific, well-known historical figures; on-camera testimonials delivered by living celebrities, illustrating aspects of childhood life; and texts read by a narrator, accompanied by either artwork or still photographs. A particular scene under consideration, a "*Childhood* Minute," might shift between the strategies, hoping to provide

> an economical way of giving a twist to a different place, without going into a full-scale historical re-creation. To us, the *Childhood* Minutes are pretty much verbatim autobiographical or diary material, or it could be something as mundane as a verbatim clip out of the U.S. government's Bureau of Child Health Manual, the Infant Care Manual. It is something which is verbatim from the past brought to life by some kind of visual, ranging from stills to an actor in costume reading on camera. So that those are things we're also looking out for. (Advisors Meeting, February 20, 1990)

These sequences would allow the producers to include material that is more personal, literary, and easily accessible to their audience than the scientific sequences, to dramatize expository and abstract concepts, and to provide a useful change of pace.[28] Throughout the early stages of production and script writing, the production staff and advisors contemplated and researched various texts and personalities as candidates for *Childhood* Minutes, and proposed placements for these scenes. Early scripts proposed (among others) Dick Gregory's description of being ridiculed in school, Charlie Chaplin's telling of entertaining his schoolmates, excerpts from Cotton Mather's diary narrating the loss of several of his children, and a Sumerian father's words of encouragement to his son attending school. Advisor and writer Jonathan Cott criticized the "Euro-centric" nature of these choices, and, partly in response, the producers considered *Childhood* Minutes from non-Western sources: South African writer Mark Mathabane, Japanese writer Junichiro Tanizaki, and Japanese filmmaker Akira Kurosawa.

The producers simultaneously debated strategies for rendering these *Childhood* Minutes. These ranged from the most simple and inexpensive (either a narrator or celebrity reading text over still images) to more involved approaches (an actor playing a famous person from the past, performing in direct address to camera) to the most elaborate (full-scale dramatic re-creations). Although planned to take up merely four minutes of screen time per program, these historical sequences generated much commentary and disagreement. For example, the British co-executive producer, Peter Montagnon, expressed skepticism about the dramatized episodes:

> In a way, that was where I thought the original proposal was very weak, that the dramatized episodes bore little relation to the very tough material, intellectually tough material that surrounded them. They were of a different cut, as were the *Childhood* Minutes. And I think there again, it's getting better, because I think we are saying more toughly, "What's it really doing and what's it, is this really the right one?" That sort of reassessment, I think, is actually going on really very well. (Interview with Peter Montagnon, August 1, 1990)[29]

Although staff spent a lot of time researching and planning these *Childhood* Minutes, they had a difficult time integrating them into the programs. Both the demonstration tape and the final series included a prototype sequence with Dr. Benjamin Spock remembering his mother's influential advice, a sequence filmed with Dr. Spock in a neutral studio setting, cut with archival images. Later, Haines-Stiles directed the shooting of two *Childhood* Minutes in dramatic re-creation, with actors playing the colonial New England Minister Cotton Mather and British author Elizabeth Jocelin. After extensive preparation, these two scenes were shot in one day with fully dressed sets and costumed actors, and with a crew working in a mode similar to a dramatic production—expenditures of time and labor out of scale with the other documentary material.

These turned out to be the only scripted dramatic scenes they would shoot, though, and did not survive the editing stage. Too great a departure from the documentary scenes, the producers felt that they were not executed properly. Later, Erna Akuginow directed several sequences shot in Colonial Williamsburg, an elaborate theme park and authentically reconstructed colonial town in Virginia. They employed an unusual hybrid of documentary and dramatic methods, with a relatively large crew and the cooperation of the Williamsburg staff. The officials at Williamsburg stipulated certain criteria of historical accuracy and the use of their staff "actors" demonstrating activities

Figure 4.2 Geoff Haines-Stiles working with an actor and cinematographer Dyanna Taylor during the shooting of the Cotton Mather *Childhood* Minute sequence, a dramatic historical re-creation which was not used in the series. (Photograph © Kate Kunz.)

as they ordinarily do for the public, thereby limiting the pool of possibilities to what was already in place. Although Akuginow had control over placement and action, she was guided by the Williamsburg staff, who had also assisted her in developing the scenes to be filmed. The result was a production style more like controlled documentary, only with the subjects as actors in costume. Akuginow's historical sequences were used in the series, depicting labor apprenticeships in metal and wood shops, children's games (for both Virginia gentry and black slaves), and scenes showing the texture of the lives of children in colonial America.

With the *Childhood* Minutes effectively removed, the series incorporated a more conventional historical mode, using narration over still images (photographs and works of art). Yet even these sequences were greeted by the scientifically oriented advisors with dissension. In the following discussion, Bronfenbrenner, Kagan, Hinde, and Scarr respond to rough cuts of the programs, haggling over a sequence that Gene Marner included in his Program Three/"Love's Labors":

> GENE MARNER: The next thing is this Frederick the Second story, which again was not in the cut you saw, but will be done with artwork. And the point is to,

is so that we can understand that historically the notion that, we shouldn't be so vain as to think that we've just discovered that parents and children have to interact and that people have not known it. And to show that it's something that has been . . .

URIE BRONFENBRENNER: What is the story, I'm sorry?

MARNER: The story is that Frederick wanted to discover, a chronicler from the thirteenth century says that Frederick the Second wanted to discover what language children would speak, and he told the wet nurses not to, to feed them, take care of them, but never to speak. He wanted to discover whether they would speak Hebrew the first language, or Greek, Latin, Arabic, or the language of their parents. But he goes, "But he labored in vain, because all the infants died. For they cannot live without the praise, fondling, playfulness and happy expressions of their nurses." And it seems to me rather striking that in the thirteenth century someone should write what . . .

BRONFENBRENNER: Rene Spitz.

ROBERT HINDE: A, the story isn't true.

MARNER: Of course not.

HINDE: B, it's inconclusive. C, the same point is made much better in the Baka material or anything else. I think this sort of thing is far more remote than the Baka material. And it doesn't add, it takes away from the credibility of the real scenes in the families that we've got.

MARNER: Does it take away? The fact that a thirteenth-century commentator thought that this was an important aspect of child raising? That he had that insight?

HINDE: You don't know anything about it. It just maddens me. I hate it. I just think it isn't real, like the rest of the film is.

MARNER: It's true that it's not a true story. Herodotus wrote the same story about an Egyptian king, so it clearly is not a real story. But I think it shows an attitude toward adults and children.

HINDE: Just because one person thought this in the thirteenth century. I don't think that's such a big deal. You've got the same point which you could easily make in the Baka film or anywhere else, that this is a fundamental issue in mother-child relations.

BRONFENBRENNER: It goes back to the question of what we see the whole series as. My sense is that we are seeing it in terms of, that one of its distinctive features is that while it looks at things cross-culturally, the base is one of attention to careful sources and information and data and so on. That it has a research sort of umbrage about it. It may be that for me there are so many of these historical representations that it raised the question of, "Do we have an agenda and then use anything to beat its drum? Or are we trying to keep the orientation one in which we pay attention to the evidence. (Advisors Meeting, February 3, 1991)

Here, the debate over this historical sequence, eventually incorporated in the program in a form similar to Marner's proposal, provoked a discussion about the formal nature of *Childhood* itself, and about the criteria for acceptability of knowledge and narrative. The use of this literary, "apocryphal" story in the midst of observational documentary scenes seemed perfectly appropriate to the producers and questionable to the social scientist Hinde, who was clearly committed to a different style of presentation. This history of the series' historical sequences illustrates several contentious areas of concern for the producers: the tensions between the uses of historical material as evidence and as story, the force exerted by generic expectations and constraints, and how different agents within the production favor different strategic approaches, depending on their experience as producers and consumers themselves. It also suggests that this genre can only contain this diversity of production styles with a great deal of negotiation and labor.

THE SHAPE OF THE SERIES AS A WHOLE

Semioticians argue that any text can be seen as structured both "syntactically," in relation to a narrative flow across time; and "paradigmatically," as themes that cut across this syntactic flow. This framework illuminates two levels of organization that *Childhood*'s producers constantly balanced and struggled within designing program sequences and structuring the series. On the syntactic level, *Childhood*'s producers organized the series and programs within it as both a sequential whole (with the number of programs changing several times during its life) and as individual units within their proposed lengths (one hour for each program). The producers operated within specific and limiting parameters of time, narrative, and aesthetic convention, and financial constraint that stem from the context of *Childhood* as a high-profile PBS series. They were constantly juggling, substituting, and eventually paring down the overall temporal flow as they moved from scripts to rough cuts to final shows. The paradigmatic level focuses on the thematic dimension of *Childhood*'s content—what ideas, topics, and intellectual positions were to be included, from what points of views, and in what relationships. In constructing programs within this series format, the producers were occupied with the interplay between these two levels of textual organization.

The tensions between narrative and thematic organizational imperatives correlate closely to the broader tensions within the series between dramatic and scientific material, between entertainment and pedagogy. The chronological structure provided a narrative dimension to *Childhood*, intending to involve audience members in the ongoing lives of characters in the families the series follows. The thematic points represent intellectual themes and areas relevant to the scientific and historical study of child development and family life. To balance these organizational logics required the producers to mediate between these sometimes conflicting, sometimes mutually reinforcing imperatives. For its narrative organization, the episodes in the series follow the life span of child development in approximate chronological sequence from birth to adolescence (i.e., Program One/"Great Expectations" covers birth to one year; Program Two/"Louder than Words," one to two-and-a-half years). The influence of the discipline of psychology, the home discipline of several prominent advisors, is evident in this developmentalist structure. The aging of family members, followed over the course of a year of filming, and spaced between episodes, threaded specific characters into the passage of time and supported this developmental scheme. Thematically, each show is organized around an individual developmental issue (Program Two/"Louder than Words" focuses on interaction; Program Five/"Life's Lessons" on formal and informal learning) deemed worthy of lengthy treatment and appropriate for that episode's age segment. The producers designed this paradigmatic level of organization to work in conjunction with the chronological narrative, indicating these themes in episode titles (though sometimes obliquely).

The producers conceded that this dual structure of chronology and theme represented an artificial construction, largely because many issues devoted to a specific age span are relevant at other ages. For instance, *Childhood* presents much of its material on education in Program Five/"Life's Lessons," which roughly covers the age span from five to seven years, but formal learning clearly plays a crucial role for many children at all ages. In addition, scenes depict multiple themes and therefore could be relevant to points made in several programs. This dual structure of chronology and theme, though, offered a viable strategy for organizing the series' complex subject matter.[30] Geoff Haines-Stiles summarized the rationale behind this structure, showing the force of the chronological narrative:

> We thought about different organizing structures for the series, of having like *The Heart of the Dragon*, in fact, I think we talked about that as an example, in which "discipline" or "play" or "sex differences" would be the structuring devices for whole programs. And the more that we talked about it with people like Jerome Kagan and so forth, the more it became clear that it was just getting muddy, because play at two doesn't mean the same thing as play at six doesn't mean the same thing as play at nine, and it was much more the developmental stages that drove the series, than the other way around. So that's how we sort of turned things around and ended up with the developmentally based series that we have. (Interview with Geoff Haines-Stiles, March 2, 1990)

Though developmentally-based, thematic issues still motivated the series structure and focused discussion over specific episodes. The following meeting excerpt indicates the producers' consciousness of both the arbitrary connection of the two organizational schemes and the value of largely keeping to some version of them:

> MEL KONNER: We are creating an artificial connection between a chronological scheme and a thematic scheme. It's okay to do that, to some extent, as long as we know that we're doing it and we don't get seduced into thinking that school really is a big theme for a five- to eight-year-old but not a big theme for a ten-year-old or eleven-year-old. It's the center of their life from five to the end of the series. Likewise peers can be conceived as very important in Program Three as well as Programs Four through Six. Do we want to continue with the thematic orientation of these things and the way they are?
>
> GENE MARNER: You can't talk about everything in every program. You'll see peers, if we shoot kids in a day care center and shoot them in school, you'll see them with peers. In Program Four, you'll see them with peers, you'll see them interacting with peers, but the content of the narration will have a different emphasis.
>
> GEOFF HAINES-STILES: Program Four should be distinguished by the internal changes that are happening. The five to seven shift seems to be a big enough shift, that's worth a program in itself. But the new actors on the kid's stage are the nonfamily adults who represent explicitly what society wants the kids to do. That doesn't have to be in school as teachers, but other adults who are around. But that, I think, are two very juicy things that are right to do here, with the emphasis on the next one being those informal things that happen to kids where the adults are not so important. So we look at the teachers, broadly stated, in this program, and to a lesser extent, although the teachers as coaches or teachers as people who are around the swim teams may well be there in the next, although to a lesser extent than in this program. So I think it's okay. Do you, too, Peter?
>
> PETER MONTAGNON: I think so. I mean, this was the point at which we seem to feel the tug between chronology and theme the most.
>
> HAINES-STILES: Yes, and I think that we switched it around after you left last time to this order. I'd say that the first day of school and the five to seven shift is a great milestone and marker. We were screwing ourselves around by having that left to Program Five and trying to do other things in Program Four. We were jumping ahead indirectly.
>
> KONNER: I think it's fine. I just want to make sure that the age brackets don't become a procrustean bed for the themes. (Advisors Meeting, December 14, 1989)

The producers made presumptions about what design would work well both for viewers who see each show in sequence and for those who see intermittent episodes, leaving them with certain compromises. The consistent viewer, they felt, would appreciate these developmental themes running

[handwritten margin note: NB - different levels of audience participation]

across programs and would follow characters in the families as they age; yet each episode had to stand on its own for the occasional viewer.[31] The narration had to strike a balance, providing sufficient information for first-time viewers while avoiding redundancy for viewers who stay with *Childhood* throughout.

The first and last programs in the series had additional objectives. Program One needed to introduce *Childhood*'s perspective, its principal characters (subjects and hosts), the series' style of exposition and illustration, and the actual range of program elements the viewer would see. The last sequence in Program One introduced the rest of the series, making a transition from its own narrative flow to mention "the milestones that make us all alike, and every one of us unique, as we'll see in future programs." The narrators previewed both themes and narrative moments that would comprise later episodes, and revisited characters this episode introduced, demonstrating the interweaving of topical and chronological structures.

The scope and segmentation of the individual episodes also evolved from early treatments through to the final arrangement for broadcast. As Geoff Haines-Stiles handed me the early *Childhood* treatments, he explained how economic limitations dictated the evolution from ten episodes down to seven:

> There's two different versions of this. They were changed at various times. This is for the ten-part series. We originally started . . . I told David I thought it should be a thirteen-part series. He said he can't afford a thirteen-part series—it had to be a ten-part series. When we had a ten-part series budgeted, it was clear we couldn't afford doing it as a ten-part series. So we went ahead with an eight-part series, and at some point 'NET said, "Well, we can't go ahead with an eight-part series. It will have to be a six-part series." So this is my way—well you keep on hearing me say, "It has to be eight parts; it can't be six parts." It's because I still think it should be a thirteen-part series. (Interview with Geoff Haines-Stiles, March 2, 1990)

Haines-Stiles felt that the series would have greater impact both in broadcast and in its after-broadcast life if it were at least eight programs rather than six, and that the compression of topical coverage necessary to get down to six programs represented a great loss. The producers reduced the ten-program structure by simultaneously expanding the age span covered by each episode and condensing the thematic coverage for the series as a whole. Where ten episodes covered the age span from birth to adolescence in early treatments, six episodes and, later, seven would have to do that work. Though the absence of corporate funding prevented the series from expanding to eight programs, the executive producers were granted approval to move to seven one-hour episodes, splitting the first program into two shows (Programs One and Two).

Narrator (Alex Chadwick): For the first time, a newborn meets the family that will surround her. Michelle Kauffman is welcomed to the community that sustains her family. First care-givers are critically important, but we'll see there are many ways to raise a child. Soon, physical growth brings new perspectives on the world. Mental growth brings first smiles. Then come first steps, and a growing sense of independence.

Narrator/Lynn Neary: We'll see how play and interaction lead to language. We question whether daily care shapes character. We'll see Sue Ellen Oliveira toddle out into an ever wider world.

Chadwick: For Stas Popov, there's a new brother, new hope, new fears, but also new chances for discovery. In every home, and every day, parents teach what's right and wrong.

Neary: In all societies, rituals demonstrate what boys and girls should do. But everywhere, girls and boys begin to differ. Their brains and bodies grow some more, and it's off to school in countries rich and poor, in countries full of tradition and countries bubbling with change.

Chadwick: For Chizuka Nakayama, school is a new arena for achievement. For Benji Gholston, a stage to try on new roles. In northeast Brazil, a place to try to learn. In Israel and everywhere, development gets an assist from siblings. On the streets of Sao Paulo, there's still time for dreams of great achievement. In fights or friendships, we find out who we really are.

Neary: Then come even clearer rites of passage, as girls become young women. Puberty sculpts a new body for Anya Krilov. From adolescent brain and mind comes a new sensitivity, a desire to be different and the same. For Simone Oliveira, there's her first Carnival. For American pre-teens, a first night away from home. In little more than a decade, we change from newborns into young men and women. But childhood is more than just a personal journey. Our children are monuments to our success as humans and as cultures. Living messages to a time we will not see. Childhood is how our future begins.

Figure 4.3 Narration and selected frames from the closing sequence in Program One/"Great Expectations."

This evolution of episodes demonstrates one way the financial constraints on the project had an impact on the text, the practical logic at work in production. The producers had the prerogative to expand the series on their current budget, producing additional programs by cutting back on the expenditures for each episode and for *Childhood* as a whole. This would have either required spending less on overseas filming, using a higher ratio of this material (and therefore being less selective about it), spending less on archival acquisitions, or piling more work on the staff's shoulders. My inference is that the executive producers did not want to dilute "production value" by expanding; they privileged a high level of production value over scope and length. Programming structure represents an area where the constraints of the PBS context were brought to bear on the shape of the series as a whole. Yet this was an area out of the control of *Childhood*'s producers, who would have to exert their influence through WNET executives to obtain what they felt was an optimum program slot. WNET wields substantial power in locating programs where they wish on the national schedule, but these decisions were embroiled in larger scheduling struggles within the system, and WNET could only exert their influence within limits.[32]

MAKING PROGRAMS "WORK": PROGRAM STRUCTURE AND TEMPORAL ECONOMY

Producers' judgments about the overall structure of the series and of the programs within it were guided by their conceptions of the appropriate shape and scope of a program given the parameters of the PBS hour broadcast slot (less than fifty-seven minutes of actual program time), their assumptions about audience attention, and the conventions of making "good television" within this program genre. Gene Marner had criticized the preliminary program treatments structure (see page 103), stressing the importance of "narrative flow" and the marshaling of emotional and dramatic involvement. Although the aesthetic discourse about program structure that I am abstracting here hinges on what seem like obvious terms ("beginning, middle, and end," "overarching themes"), it is instructive to reflect on how producers apply these terms in working through the organization of programs, the temporal and thematic dimension of documentary aesthetics.

Responses to the program treatments often raised the issue of thematic organization, closely tied to temporal structure, urging greater clarity and simplicity: "I think the programs would also benefit from making the episodes somewhat more sharply focused; that is, if the episode themes are more clearly delineated in the beginning and ending of the episode. There is a lot of information in each episode, but the overarching themes and conclusions are not always clear" (memo from Arnie Labaton to David Loxton and

Geoff Haines-Stiles, June 29, 1988). Richard Hutton, too, felt that the message of each episode was unclear: "Finally, and most important, I am concerned about what feels like a lack of a central theme in the shows. Their structure is clear and logical; they are loaded with wonderful bits of information. But when I stop reading, I don't quite know what the take-home message is, what the principle is that is inherent to each episode. It seems crucial to me that one central idea drive each show" (memo from Richard Hutton to David Loxton and Geoff Haines-Stiles, June 20, 1988). Hutton's comment rests on a distinction between the "logical structure" of a program and its "take-home message," which I presume equates the take-home message with a summary and the logical structure with plot.

The challenge facing the producers centered around the complexity of their treatment of the material. They had absorbed a lot of information about an extremely complex subject, initially laid out over fourteen programs, then cut back to eight and later six, and felt compelled to incorporate a great deal of information into each episode. Peter Montagnon spoke about his reactions to the early program outlines:

> But the idea of the points trying to be made, there seem to be actually probably more points in the programs than one could get, in the end, comfortably into a fifty, sixty minute slab of television. [. . .] I was thinking that actually, really, there's an awful lot of information there, and that the main problem is how to make that information into celluloid. By what means and through what examples. And it only comes when one actually takes it program by program. [. . .] I'll tell you what the large question at the back of mind is: is the way forward, given that we want to make a lot of points—let's assume that we try and make all the points that are there and don't argue about how many we can make right now—if we try to make those points, how are they best made? (Advisors Meeting, December 14, 1989)

In a similar vein to Hutton's comments above, Montagnon stressed the necessity of having a coherent structure and continually urged the producer/directors to refine their ideas for programs so that they could fit into a few sentences, or onto a three-by-five index card:

> I'd say that there is a sort of axiom which says that if programs work, even if they're enormously subjective, hardly anybody raises any queries. People largely only raise queries when programs don't work. You could make something which is almost bizarre and get away with it, as long as it's so integral and tight that it works and at the end of it people would barely raise a question: it's a very weird thing. Now I think the problem is that it is very difficult to say at the moment what these programs are about. They are far too long and they are not precise enough. And it should be possible to read the content of the program, actually at this stage, without the commentary upon it, by seeing it. It should also be possi-

ble to write this down on a postcard, what the programs are about. We need postcards, and on these postcards there should be two or three statements about the program, so that there are two or three dominant ideas in each program. And then maybe there is room for a cluster of subordinate ideas. And there should be maybe up to about eight sequences which express these ideas in part or in progressing through. [. . .] And they have to be cut sharper, harder, and more precisely until they actually work and you don't have to spend an awful lot of time explaining what they are about. (Advisors Meeting, February 3, 1991)

Coherence, therefore, is related to clarity and concentration of exposition and some form of narrative and/or aesthetic integrity. Although expository documentary forms have been considered "non-narrative," based on a distinction separating these works from "fictional" or "dramatic" film and television, the above clearly illustrates how practitioners employ theories of narrative in constructing programs, and that the establishment of a coherent organizing principle drives structural considerations in documentary. In the following discussion, the executive producers and producer/directors make explicit these theories of narrative, though employing different terms:

PETER MONTAGNON: You see there is this problem, and two people said it yesterday, the problem that actually although the stuff is mentally stimulating, and covers a lot of ground, a huge amount of ground, and an enormous amount of research has gone into it, it is necessarily disconnected. I mean, there isn't a theme, one can't quite see a theme running through it, a narrative you see. There's a discrete lot of pieces.

PRODUCER/DIRECTOR:[33] If I understand you correctly, there should be a narrative theme that goes from the beginning of each show to the end. We are starting here and at the end of the show we will be there, so there's an emotional arc that you're traversing.

MONTAGNON: Yes, I was wondering now if maybe we had half thought about this.

GENE MARNER: Oh yes, we've had several meetings about that amongst ourselves, and we've talked "from-to"—what's this show, where does it start and where is it going. We've tried to sum it up in maybe a sentence or two. I think one of the things we should try and do today is talk about our "froms-to's" and see what you all think about them. Is this what this program ought to be about?

MONTAGNON: Great. I would find that very helpful. It would give me a lot to think about when I'm back there.

MARNER: It would help us, I think. I mean, I don't want to tell Geoff how to conduct this, but it seems to me that the most useful way of having this meeting today would be to go through the programs one at a time, and not within them in detail, within each program. But just do this: "What is this program about from beginning to end, where does it start and where is it taking us," so that a viewer can feel not that he is just part of a series but has watched an hour television program that had a beginning and end, and perhaps a middle as well. (Advisors Meeting, December 14, 1989)

The producers came up with short tag lines for specific programs (i.e., "From the world of the family to the life of the wide world," for Program Five/"Life's Lessons"), incorporating them as headlines into drafts of the evolving scripts. These summaries represented a thematic flow for a given program, a sequence of connected ideas to be illustrated. The producers debated the appropriateness of these summary descriptions: Did they represent the age-appropriate transformations? Did they depict a logical flow of ideas? Were they trying to include too much material in that episode?[34]

Childhood's producers often spoke about a program's "line," a term related to "storyline," which they also used, but indicating more of a coherent argument, rather than a specific plot, that ideally ran through and supplied a program its structure. Much of the discussion in script meetings and program reviews involved refining the "line" of a specific program. The way Gene Marner expressed it, finding the line was a preliminary step in program construction. They then fleshed out the structure by organizing scenes and sequences around this line, eventually developing into a coherent television program. Montagnon described differences he perceived in the approach of the three producer/directors by referring to how the "lines" of their respective programs might differ, and the tensions involved in shaping a uniform series:

> DORNFELD: How do you see the editing style working out for this?
> PETER MONTAGNON: Well, I think it's important that Geoff sets it; I think it's absolutely right that he should, because he's aiming quite properly for a quite considerable degree of complexity and layering. See, it's got to be there, the complexity and the richness, without confusing people. I think he's got a good grasp on that. I think he's going to be able to do that. And I think that then means that Erna, who is a quite formidable character in her own right and who I increasingly think is making a very big contribution, will I think be able to row along with that. [. . .] Gene's may come out more like classical documentaries, quietistic classical documentaries, and the problem will be whether one can actually shift that around without damaging what is there, in order to make it seem to be very much like the others. So, I would say that maybe Gene's programs are certainly going to have, I'm sure, a very strong line through them, and he's got storytelling skills, and probably best used when he has space to elaborate, let them develop. (Interview with Peter Montagnon, August 1, 1990)

Producers invoked this notion of "the line" in a range of meetings and interactions to describe, criticize, defend, and negotiate the program's evolution. Yet this aesthetic norm brought dramatic and scientific imperatives into potential conflict, since narrative imposes a logic that does not necessarily respect the contingencies of scientific exposition. During these meetings, a producer would often take a discussion through what was essentially a performance of that progression, moving from sequence to sequence and indexing that movement with lexical markers that Marner described as "from-to's." Statements such as, "So far this is very constructive; what are we going to say next?" or "What coherently is the next set of ideas that we're going to tell the viewer?" demonstrate the attention to narrative flow, even with expository material, and propel the process of program evaluation.

An example from a rough cut review meeting illustrates this tension between narrative and exposition. The advisors were quite critical of the version they viewed of Program Three/"Love's Labors," the first of Marner's two programs, which covered attachment, separation, and maturation. The organization of the rough cut took the viewer through a trajectory of developmental topics, a structure that the advisors felt was problematic. Haines-Stiles, Akuginow, and Marner presented an order they felt worked in narrative terms, but the advisors wanted to be sure not to imply any faulty causal relationships through the sequencing of topics. After much debate, Jerome Kagan suggested a restructuring. A few sequences fell out, and others were shortened, in the transition from eighty-minute rough cut to fifty-six minute fine cut. More critically, a clearer line had been drawn through this complex material, conforming the narrative of the program to the more scientifically valid developmental sequence. All the episodes went through this type of editorial evolution through which the producers negotiated the series' dual logics.

Throughout the production, I was struck by the definite sense that producers had about lengths of scenes and sequences they were proposing, shooting, and editing. In discussing scripted material early in the production, they would debate how long a given sequence would likely be, employing a knowledge of the time necessary, working in this particular style, to allow a scene "to play" for it to make sense, to include the salient and necessary narration points, and to avoid audience boredom. Although these projected lengths were certain to change in the editing process, the producers had a confident sense of pacing and duration. The following exchange began as a general consideration of the length of shows and the nature of the material within the shows:

> PETER MONTAGNON: But is it narrative, and if it's narrative, are we willing to accept the penalty that goes with it, that it's going to take more time to cover a point, because once you get into a bit of narration you've got to sort of spell it out?
>
> GENE MARNER: For example, the sequence that I just described. I don't know if anybody else was as taken with it as I was, with that shot of the little girl, but

in order for that to pay off, you need everything that goes around it. So that that material of the family and the making of the sauerkraut, that all has to be somehow used to make other points as well so that the audience can get into that scene and the payoff can be the magical effect on the little girl, or simply the educational effect on the little girl, the developmental effect on the little girl. But so the audience can feel it for its virtually magical quality, it has to develop as a sequence, and not necessarily narrated that much heavily, but, we have to allow that to play and to develop. So we're talking about a two-minute sequence there, and to be efficient we have to make other points. And then those points have to be structured into the script in such a way that the flow justifies making the two different points that are there, at that point. You know what I mean? The integral family in that intimate environment, and then the result for the child. (Advisors Meeting, December 14, 1989)

Marner's comments illustrate both the practical sense of length and the anticipated difficulties of working through a tight economy of program time, considerations that recur throughout the series and affected other program elements. For instance, documentary makers talk about a program having a "tease," a short opening introduction preceding the title sequence, which needs both to set the thematic agenda for that episode and, hopefully, to grab and hold viewers' fickle attentions. The "teases" opening *Childhood*'s episodes last from two and one-half to three minutes, made up mostly of scenes taken from families footage. These sequences simultaneously set the locations, introduce primary characters, and raise thematic questions that will figure largely in that episode. These opening sequences generated substantive discussion, reflecting the feeling that they set the agenda for the programs that followed. For instance, in the meeting where advisors responded to rough cuts, Jerome Kagan suggested that the episode openings were weak and failed to lay out a proper structure for the program that followed. Kagan suggested beginning episodes with several provocative questions, a format the producers adopted in a few programs.

The title sequence, consisting of eight shots, occurs in each program after the opening tease and initial funding credits. It presents a montage of images from different cultural settings showing children of increasing age, overlaid with an animated graphic of silhouetted handprints: a newborn baby in Brazil, a Russian infant crying, a young black American girl, a slightly older Russian boy, a Japanese girl in kindergarten, a Baka boy of about five at play, a young white American boy riding his bicycle, and, finally, a Russian boy opening up a door to a brightly lit room. This last shot is held in a freeze-frame, then the title *Childhood* is superimposed, followed by the episode title. The sequence subtly introduces the viewer to the chronological parameters of the series, and its multicultural subject matter (which I address in the following chapter).

Concluding sequences summarize that episode's material, hoping to reach a resolution and entice viewers into the next episode. In several programs, the closing section actually answers questions introduced during the body of the episode, thereby summarizing the central points in this program.

> NARRATOR (ALEX CHADWICK): So, here's an answer to all our questions about what infant care is best. Bottle or breast, sling, crib or cradleboard, it's responsive interaction that's crucial, not the specific practices.

The summary then briefly leads us to the next program:

> NARRATOR (ALEX CHADWICK): In the beginning, as throughout life, it's humans who make human beings, not simply genes, or history, or advice. As we shall see in future programs, for everyone of us it's the joys and sorrows of human relationships that drive us forward on life's journey. (Narration, Program Two/ "Louder than Words")

This effort toward narrative and temporal coherence supports the broader aesthetic imperative for making television programs that "work," that make, in George Page's words, "compelling television" told "simply and elegantly." In retrospect, Haines-Stiles suggested that these summaries might have been too profound, subtle, and condensed to achieve these parameters.

LANGUAGE AND VISUAL IMAGES

Relationships between words and visual images, most typically between synch-sound observational images and voice-over commentary, occupy a central place in documentary poetics, since it is in the construction of these relationships that significant layers of meaning are encoded. With *Childhood*, these relationships between textual elements become important in three different, though related, areas: (1) the role of narration in the series and the negotiation between illustrative and expository modes of articulation; (2) the use of subtitled synch-sound observational footage and interviews (related to [1]); and (3) the relationship between the series itself and conceptions about how this material could be rendered in written form in the *Childhood* companion book.

Nichols reflects on the conventional function of narration or commentary in documentary exposition, and its relation to what he calls the indexicality of images:

> Here the image's stickiness, its indexicality, provides the evidence, but the commentary guides us toward those aspects of the image that are most important to the argument. At the most general level, this process identifies the documentary text as such: we believe the authenticity of what we see and hear because we are told that what we see is evidence of historical occurrences, not fictional simula-

tions of them. At a more local level, commentary provides a selective anchoring of the image. It selects out some detail and places it within a conceptual frame or explanatory grid. It encourages us to move past questions of construction or fabrication to the brute facticity of the image as historical decal or imprint. (Nichols 1991:154)

For *Childhood*'s producers, narration had to achieve an appropriate level of detail and density: too little labeling and anchoring of detail in scientific explanations would allow them to devolve into the mere novelistic style that Haines-Stiles and the observers wanted to transcend, while too much information would cause the program to become overly didactic, a style that talks down to and thereby repels the audience. Geoff Haines-Stiles, responding to the observers' critique of a shortage of narration in the rough cuts, described this balance well: I think that we do need to make the voice-over terse, but work very hard. I think that the programs are easier for audiences to watch if there are moments in which the pure reality of the family plays itself out. And I know that many people will find segments of the Russian dinner scene charming, cute, entertaining, which will get them into the right frame of mind to notice something later on" (Advisors Meeting, February 3, 1991).

Nevertheless, the tensions remain between the objectives of making programs "easier for the audience to watch" and programs that would have scholarly legitimacy, between illustration and exposition. The following exchange from an advisors' meeting exemplifies these tensions as observer Robert Hinde reacts to a statement that Geoff Haines-Stiles made regarding the amount of commentary in the series.

> ROBERT HINDE: You said one thing that was wrong with the programs was that there was too much talk on them. Are you still committed to the view that the pictures have to speak for themselves, or are you prepared to agree that they need introduction and summary and commentary to say what the point of the scenes is, because that's really vital to my commitment to the series.
>
> GEOFF HAINES-STILES: Okay, then I'll sign you up for the series, because there's no doubt about it that in two different areas we need talk, the right kind of talk. We need signposts that are either on camera or voice-over, that are absolutely explicit, that have an emotional component, have an intellectual component, that guide the audience to what they're seeing, and lets you know what you've seen at the end. I think there are ways of doing it, some places explicitly, some cases allusively, so that you don't feel that you're being preached at, or talked to in the style of didactic teaching films, which this is not intended to be and never was. I said there was too much talk, because in several places, at least in the programs that I sent out to you, I found myself rushing to say things to get them in over the film, and it felt hectoring, it felt rushed, and it's inevitable when you listen to that amount of volume of material that you get overloaded with talk. What I think, I'm doing this again, worked

about portions of the demonstration reel, was that in the Gholstons' throwing-up scene, there was a lot of talk in the beginning, to talk about the deal that had been made, the father had been working, the relatives who were burdening what is in quotes supposed to, in our ideology, be a welcome day [Christmas]. So that when things play themselves out, you, the audience member, knew enough about what was going on that you would understand it for yourself. What I found gratifying about some people's response to that reel was that they found that they were responding in a kind of directed Rorschach way. They were seeing in other people's behavior what they would not have seen if they were doing it themselves. They were seeing things that were seeded by the setup. So I think we clearly need better script and probably less script over Program One-A and One. We need more script and better script over Program Two. And over Erna's program [Five], it's just perfect the way it is. [. . .] So that's answering you two ways. The whole reason why Peter and I from the beginning said that we wanted on-camera observers is that as opposed to *National Geographic* or *Nova* programs, *Horizon* in the UK, we think there's real value in associating opinion, philosophy, syntheses with discrete individual human beings. I think there are a few scenes with the observers where that's working at the moment. [. . .] The answer is, yes, we need more talk and it needs to be better talk.

HINDE: I don't say it has to come from us. I don't care who it comes from. It just needs to be there, that's all.

HAINES-STILES: I agree. I agree. (Advisors Meeting, February 3, 1991)

The functions posited by Haines-Stiles reflect a clear sense of how commentary should operate in the series (as "signposts . . . that guide the audience to what they're seeing"), the tone it should take (not "hectoring" or "didactic"), and what its effect on the audience should be (based in part on responses to the demo tape). Although they reached a resolution in the meetings, some distance remained, in my reading, between Hinde's resistance to observational material ("the view that the pictures have to speak for themselves," "they need introduction and summary and commentary") and Haines-Stiles's desire to let scenes play themselves out after the proper setup. This distance illustrates the differing positions represented by the producers and the advisors.

Narration in Program Six/"Among Equals" exemplifies commentary that seeks to be scientifically sound yet not didactic. Following the opening title sequence, a series of synch sound images show two Japanese boys fishing and two Japanese girls sitting, seeming to watch the boys at play, while the narrators speak:

NARRATOR (LYNN NEARY): In middle childhood, youngsters everywhere venture farther from home. Away from adult eyes, they take more risks. Gender separation increases. More and more, girls and boys prefer to play apart. Both spend much less time with parents. Now, more than fifty percent of waking hours are spent with peers.

NARRATOR (ALEX CHADWICK): Once peers were seen as just playmates. Now research says they are a crucial part of healthy development. (Narration from Program Six/"Among Equals")

In this brief passage, several research studies (on adolescent behavior, gender, and development) have been economically condensed into a simplified but, from the producers' point of view, accurate script, with an abstract relationship to the concurrent images. The images are specific: we see two sets of friends at leisure together in an identifiable location. Earlier narration identified these individuals and their location. Now it "guides us toward those aspects of the image that are most important to the argument," then shifts to a higher level of generality and takes this anchored sequence and "places it within a conceptual frame or explanatory grid" (Nichols 1991:154). Sequences that include similar statements summarizing research studies— "We know now that . . ." and "Cross-cultural observations of play by researchers yield remarkably consistent evidence . . ."—occur throughout *Childhood*, and are characteristic of this genre of educational documentary.

The producers and advisors simultaneously considered the more dramatic and entertaining textual strategy of allowing scenes to play out with extensive subtitled translation. Providing the viewer with a readable transcription of actual speech allows the viewer to experience the program's subjects without the distancing effect of an omniscient narrator. As Haines-Styles explained:

> The footage basically says it with a subtitled translation. I think I'm beginning to state the obvious—the families footage is going to be subtitled, it's not going to be renarrated, so you will hear the intonation of the kids and the parents. And the subtitles will be done like the Baka subtitles, whatever the trick was that they adopted, it knocks the spots off of any other subtitles I've seen on anthropological footage. It just gets to the heart of matters, so that you don't notice that these are guys living in a very alien environment.[35] (Advisors Meeting, December 14, 1989)

The final programs use subtitles with much of the family footage, but in a complex relationship to narration. Where producers wanted the narrators' words to dominate a sequence, they reduced the amount of subtitled speech to avoid conflict with narration. The more observational sequences featuring characters' speech include a greater density of subtitles. In a discussion that took place earlier in the production, Erna Akuginow indicated that the time-consuming and therefore expensive process of subtitling placed limitations on how much material they could handle in this way. In American public television documentary more generally, subtitles are less universally accepted, and many hold the opinion that they turn away viewers.

The relationship between these television programs and the companion book, concurrently written by series observer Mel Konner, raises a third, broader dimension of the word/image relationship and illuminates the pull between evidence and exposition. Several distinctions arose from discussions over the series versus book comparisons. First, there was an intangible sense that certain ideas are more easily articulated in print and others on television despite the intertwining of content designed for the two works:

> GEOFF HAINES-STILES: Interactively, backwards and forwards, as you generate book chapters, we will see those to see how you're weighing ideas that we have, in terms of saying, "Well, this doesn't seem to be as important as this." And based on that we will progressively be doing more and more documentary sequences, some of which will be exactly as you are using them in the book, based on either the original treatments or your own novel research, and some of them will be things that we choose to do because they're good television, that you may choose not to put into the book.
>
> MEL KONNER: Some things might make good book but don't make good film.
>
> (Advisors Meeting, December 14, 1989)

For example, the historical re-creations dropped from the *Childhood* series remained in the *Childhood* book.

Perhaps more illuminating is the amount of verbal density producers feel the written word enables, in comparison to commentary on television. Even with a documentary style that includes a substantial amount of spoken text, the constraints of time are so great that television producers need to work with many fewer words to get across the same intellectual concepts.

> PETER MONTAGNON: Television scripts by themselves are very often quite thin. Not at all like as if you come to it through print. Because there are a surprisingly small number of words in a television program. It's really quite small. So the ability to actually write something with a television script, it's really quite an amazingly small document, which only takes up two or three pages of a journal. There's another thing, that the space for ideas, the exemplification of the ideas, is again very small. So you can with profit put a considerably bigger amount of detail and thought and reiteration into the book, stuff that actually there is just not room for in the program, either in terms of ideas, examples, or words. So the book can with profit, linked to this, can with profit be very much bigger, and include all the stuff we really are not going to have space to put into the program, because in the end a lot of the stuff will have to go out because there won't physically be room. [. . .] But you've probably got far more room for examples in words than we have in our scripts. And we're going to actually feel the lack of that.

KONNER: On the other side you can show something that would take only thirty seconds of beautiful film, but it would take three or four pages to describe it.

MONTAGNON: Yeah, but you are much less strapped for the vital commodity which is either time or word space. We are actually hugely constrained by that in the end. The amount you can actually say in the time.

KONNER: I'm able to deliver a lot more words than you are, but you're able to deliver images that are powerfully explanatory, and bypass a lot of words. I won't repeat the famous cliché, but the problems of exposition . . . [tape ends]. (Advisors Meeting, December 14, 1989)

Konner and Montagnon debated trade-offs between the power of television's imagery and the capacity of written texts to accommodate complexity. The fact that major documentary series are modeled in part after books or lectures adds a level of historical and generic complexity to the comparison. In a sense, the distinction between television programs and books is a distinction between audience segments and viewing practices the authors seek, between television viewing groups and groups who read—potentially different class fragments (though I would venture that many public television viewers are avid readers). Most importantly, this distinction reinforces the constant pulls that *Childhood* feels between education and entertainment (a point I return to in the conclusion), since the producers seek the scholarly legitimacy awarded books along with the breadth of attention entertainment television garners.

NARRATION, AUTHORITY, AND TEXTUAL PRESENCE

Both the producers' and observers' authority can be established through specific textual means, but with different forms of authority for each authorial agent.[36] The tone of narration is often cited as a voice of authority in documentary (i.e., McArthur 1978; Nichols 1991). With *Childhood*, the narrators speak in softer, more inclusive tones than more conventional narration styles, but their script still includes markings of authority, both for the perspective of the series and for the credibility of the observers. The text itself is made authoritative through claims of realism, markers that establish the text's ability to provide a window on the world of the families that make up the primary observational components of the series. (See, for instance, the section of narration in Program One/"Great Expectations" cited earlier in this chapter.) The language the narrators speak seeks to establish the transparency of the text ("we see," "we witness") and the lack of authorial intervention ("our cameras recorded"). This language attempts to draw viewers rhetorically together with the producers and observers "on an expedition of discovery," effacing the work of interpretation and authorial mediation. Au-

authenticity of "being there"

thority is established through what can be described as markings of authenticity, "testifying to the camera, and hence the filmmaker, having 'been there' and thus providing the warrant for our own 'being there,' viewing the historical world through the transparent amber of indexical images" (Nichols 1991:81).

The narrators' voices sound informed and educated, but not pedantic or scholastic. They speak in the first person plural ("We now know that . . . "), bringing producers and viewers into a shared realm of social knowledge. The narrator also gives voice to sentiments, emotions, and cognitive states known and experienced by characters in the production. By wedding together narration and image, the predominant style of the series, the authors reinforce their credibility while guiding the viewer to those expository points that are critical to their argument.

A sequence in Program Two/"Louder Than Words," built from acquired footage of the Baka, a rainforest society in Cameroon, illustrates this relationship between image and commentary. Here, the synch-sound documentary images of routine events in Baka daily life grounds the producers' interpretive framing of the Baka within both an evolutionary argument and a theoretical position about the role of language and environment in development:

NARRATOR (LYNN NEARY): Once, researchers hoped to find a wild child to show human nature unspoiled by culture. Now anthropologists say simpler societies, like the Baka of West Cameroon, show us the environments and way of life all our ancestors might have experienced. Perhaps we all adapted through evolution to such environments. Let's look at how a Baka child spends most of its day. Mother Deni carried Ali, now three, in a sling from birth. In a dense forest with poisonous vines and biting insects, this custom has practical value. But it may also have another effect. Like many simpler societies, the Baka do not talk directly to their infants as much as Americans and Europeans do. But continuous physical intimacy may do more than merely protect and carry. Perhaps the sling attunes the infant to the rhythms of the adult world, and prepares the child to live in close harmony with the forty or so Baka that make up each group.

Kamala, Ali's baby sister, is now eighteen months old. And we can see that this environment encourages independence as well as dependence. Father Likano looks on as Kamala plays at grown-up work. Ali watches as Kamala chops open a gobo nut, a delicacy for the Baka. There's a closeness in Baka relationships, but still many opportunities for a child to take risks and learn to become independent. Eight-year-old brother Yeye learned it's not wise to tease infants wielding machetes. We can see it takes human culture to survive in a rainforest as in a modern city. The Baka and all human societies are children of nurture as well as nature. (Narration, Program Two/"Louder than Words")

The narrators' credibility is reinforced by their identity and tone: Lynn Neary and Alex Chadwick are commentators on National Public Radio's evening news program *All Things Considered*. Many viewers would know their voices, if not their names, and be familiar with the neutral, "objective" public radio style in which they speak.

While the producers' role is textually marked as a distant one, authorial intervention is placed on the shoulders of the observers, who are marked by the text as having opinions and points of view sometimes in conflict with one another, as well as the credibility to convince us to consider their views. Their ability to "show us" elements of the science of child development is critical to the series, but so is their point of view. While the narrators "know," the observers "think." That is, they hold opinions, have perspectives, exhibit biases, all subjectivities that the narrator does not share.

> NARRATOR (LYNN NEARY): Urie Bronfenbrenner, professor of human development at Cornell, grandfather of nine. Bronfenbrenner thinks that the idea of development being either nature or nurture is out of date. He says it's interaction between the developing organism and the total environment that makes human beings human. (Narration, Program One/"Great Expectations")

The mode of direct address the producers employ bolsters the observers' authority. The right to address the camera, as a visual code, is conventionally reserved for individuals with a certain amount of rhetorical power—news anchors and reporters, commercial spokesmen, program hosts—and a degree of ownership over that text. Direct address indicates an authoritative persona, a strong sense of authorship, distinguishing the observers from mere interview subjects who indirectly address an off-camera presence. The producers intentionally gave the observers this persona and authorial role, to gain authenticity for *Childhood* itself. We would need a study of reception to assess whether these strategies for authority are successful. Still, their presence in this genre, and their particular application and reapplication by competent producers, suggests the cultural force of these textual forms.

THE AESTHETICS OF GOOD TELEVISION: ILLUSTRATION, GENERALIZATION, NARRATIVE, AND EXPOSITION

The aesthetic logics considered here address the producers' concern with employing strategies to satisfy the audience and maintain their attention, keeping them watching from one week to the next, and aid them in digesting the core of information the series offers, and conversely avoiding forms that might bore or confuse them, or drive them away. Nichols describes documentary's appeal to audience attention with the concept of epistephilia, explained as "a pleasure in knowing, that marks out a distinctive form of social engagement. The engagement stems from the rhetorical force of an argument about the very world we inhabit. We are moved to confront a topic, issue, situation, or event that bears the mark of the historically real. In igniting our interest, a documentary has a less incendiary effect on our erotic fantasies and sense of sexual identity but a stronger effect on our social imagination and sense of cultural identity" (Nichols 1991:178). Nichols draws a parallel between the pleasures audiences enjoy while viewing fictional, narrative media, and those experienced with nonfiction forms. This "pleasure in knowing" involves a pleasure in knowing about cultural others, and by that engaging our "social imagination and sense of cultural identity," a topic I focus on in the following chapter. Most importantly here, the producers operated with and employed their own sense of how to engage their audience and sought to balance didacticism with televisual inducement in the form of revealing, dramatic, humorous, and humane family sequences and otherwise "cinematic" images. They opposed these pleasurable sequences against more directly lecture-based, scientific material, which the advisors felt were more significant and valid in scholarly terms than the "cinematic" material they labeled as "pretty pictures."

Debates over the "budding babies" sequence, developed to illustrate the physical and cognitive changes children go through in the first few years of growth, reveal this authorial tension. The producers filmed children from different racial and ethnic backgrounds, ranging from birth to three or four years old, either naked or partly clothed against a neutral white studio background. Prompting them to crawl, walk, play with blocks, and engage in other developmentally appropriate activity, they aimed to construct an artistic, illuminating time-lapse montage to demonstrate universal development across cultures and through time. "Budding babies" segments appear in the second and third programs as a sequence of lap dissolves, accompanied by effervescent, humorous music and explanatory narration.

Two of the observers criticized this "budding babies" material, arguing that removing the family setting deemphasized the importance of interaction between the developing child and family members. Both Geoff Haines-Stiles and Gene Marner stridently defended this less scientific material on both pedagogical and rhetorical grounds.

GEOFF HAINES-STILES: I think what we're saying is that in the "budding babies" scene, yes. Are we interested in pretty pictures? Yes. Are we interested in them in such a way that we hope a general viewer will say, "Ah. I see what is distinctive about that, so when I am looking at Vera Kalugin in the middle of a Russian apartment with carpets on the wall and a funny pattern on the bed, I am seeing something which I would not see if it was not juxtaposed with a more abstract approach." I think that that's how those sequences are intended to be used. To the extent to which they're not used that way at the moment, it's our failure as program makers, not our failure as conceptualizers. To the extent to which you are taking that away as the norm, I think that that's a function of us not integrating it properly.

But the intention, the specific intention, was to take the kind of diagrammatic material in Jerry [Kagan]'s Harper and Row films, for example, where he took Piaget tests around the world. We wanted the sort of clarity which comes from a more abstract lablike environment, but not to have that be the overwhelming character of the series.

GENE MARNER: There's a simple point to be made, though, I think, that for an audience, for a television audience, it's a simple shorthand through which people can, just stripped down, so that people are not distracted by the culture, in a way, to show them the incredible rapidity with which children develop the first two years of life. It's really quite astonishing. Every parent knows it, but to see it in this kind of time-lapse way that it moves ahead here is, I think, interesting for the audience. It may not be, of course, we may be wrong. But I don't think we're trying to strip away the idea of interaction. (Advisors Meeting, February 3, 1991)

When, later in the meeting, the producers discussed a second "budding babies" sequence, observers again raised their concern with this material, and asked the producers to defend its use:

JEROME KAGAN: What is the value?

GEOFF HAINES-STILES: The value is seeing the physical transformations that, with proper nourishment and care, as the script says, are almost inevitable in the first year of life. It actually has a sequence in which children are helped to stand by adults, both male and female, politically correct Hispanic and Black and White, and it's a scene which I believe has a filmic essence, and I've already heard the caveats about it.

KAGAN: But just a minute. But Geoffrey, the point is that what can be more banal than that? Everyone knows. It has no purpose. What are you telling them? You're telling them the sky is blue.

HAINES-STILES: I have not heard that response from anybody that has seen the footage . . .

HINDE: I have.

HAINES-STILES: . . . with the proper music and the proper script.

URIE BRONFENBRENNER: All right, then you're telling us there's a substantive point there you're making.

KAGAN: What is the point you're making?

HINDE: That's not what I'm in this film for, I must say.

BRONFENBRENNER: What is it that the script says?

HAINES-STILES: The script is saying, "This is, if you like, the maturational, this is the almost inevitable progression of physical changes which mark the first year."

BRONFENBRENNER: Everybody can remember it, even, let alone know about it secondhand. I think it's a banal statement.

KAGAN: It's totally familiar knowledge.

HAINES-STILES: It may be familiar, but I think it sets an emotional context for a particular program which is useful in program-making terms.

HINDE: Well, we have to bow to your aesthetic judgement. (Advisors Meeting, February 3, 1991)

It is clear in the above passages how both sides of this debate defend their positions by invoking audiences, either real ("I have not heard that response from anybody that has seen the footage"; "I have") or presumed ("Every parent knows it," but it is "interesting for the audience"; "It's totally familiar knowledge"). The estimation of what has "value" for the audience is an equation embedded in authorial assumptions: it depends on where the scene occurs in the flow of the text, what information viewers bring to that sequence, which constellation of viewers is assumed, and a variety of other factors that make these complex processes difficult to predict.

The producers felt that material like the "budding babies" sequence and the family footage—"filmic," "cinematic"—also serves better to prepare the viewer for the expository points they need to absorb. Geoff Haines-Stiles stated that "I think that the programs are easier for audiences to watch if there are moments in which the pure reality of the family plays itself out" (Advisors Meeting, February 3, 1991), a description which parallels Montagnon's metaphor of the Trojan horse in Chapter Three. Montagnon explained the necessity of concealing the academic substance "in an envelope which makes it sufficiently attractive for people just to watch it, otherwise it doesn't work." For *Childhood*, that envelope is constructed primarily from the synch-sound images of the families, accompanied by music and narration, and from sequences like "budding babies" and other stylized elements of the series.

The tension between using the family material as dramatic narrative versus using it as scientific illustration raises the general problem of documentary articulation. *Childhood*'s producers were determined to ground the elements of the series in the relevant research literature, to produce a series that was true to and incorporated contemporary scientific knowledge. At the same time, they intended to produce a series that was enjoyable to watch for a general audience member, and was not didactic or pedantic, issues faced by most documentary producers. One way to articulate this tension concerns the competing drives toward good television and scientific authority, between different logics of inclusion and articulation, one based on projections of audience engagement with dramatic material and the other dictated by standards of scientific exposition. The following discussion began with the producers and advisors considering anthropologist Nancy Scheper-Hughes's controversial descriptions (1989, 1992) of how in impoverished areas in Brazil, with high infant mortality rates, parents intentionally withhold or withdraw love in anticipation of the death of their children.

GEOFF HAINES-STILES: Gene, does that make you feel any different in thinking about the Scheper-Hughes example?

GENE MARNER: No, I think as television it's very dramatic. [Laughter.] No, but I think if we don't generalize too far from it, if we don't say "this is what happens," we don't have to say that, as you just said.

ANN KRUGER (ADVISOR): Well, there are other well-documented cases like this: the Ik. Didn't Colin Turnbull do something on the Ik in which people stopped providing for their children? Certainly not an aberration.

RAY HINER: Maybe if you use it, there would be examples just as you cited, where people are mourning in extreme situations. Maybe that's an appropriate thing to do, to balance that evidence with some reference to people who are maybe not in exactly the same environment, but who are clearly behaving differently when they have high mortality. Maybe that diminishes the good TV, though.

MARNER: No, I don't think it does. But in fact I think we're contrasting it not with people like the !Kung who mourn deeply, but we're contrasting it with ourselves, who don't have this high mortality rate. In general, the PBS audience is an elite audience, and privileged people whose kids probably have pretty high survival rates, and this is going to be, I think, striking, this point. (Advisors Meeting, February 19, 1990)

Clearly they justified certain material on televisual grounds, because of its cinematic, dramatic, or otherwise rhetorical qualities. Other material is justified through a scholarly rationale. PBS documentary poetics provides formal strategies to manage these potentially conflictive goals, to work out approaches that make programs "work" on multiple levels. As Montagnon stated in the epigram beginning this book, "It's easy to think of the right arguments; it's very, very difficult to visualize it and to express it in such a way that it is truly illuminating on the screen" (Advisors Meeting, December 12, 1989). The intent to visualize ideas that are either expository or narrative, or both, is a struggle most documentary filmmakers share and approach through different strategies of production and articulation. The producers constantly search for dramatic material to illustrate intellectual points or to stand on their own. In the end, tensions were played out, more or less successfully, between the "magic" of documentary realism and the edification of expository explanation, between the programs as engaging televisual experience, and the programs as scholarly knowledge, both tendencies mediated by the producers' practical logic and the aesthetic ideologies of program production.

CHAPTER FIVE

Cutting across Cultures

PUBLIC TELEVISION DOCUMENTARY AND REPRESENTATIONS

OF OTHERNESS

PUBLIC TELEVISION is a primary arena in American public culture for the representation of images of cultures outside our nation's borders, or of non-mainstream cultures within them. Even though, as Ginsburg (1988) has argued, a dearth of material on the public airwaves in the United States is produced with the participation of anthropologists, public television presents a steady stream of images representing other peoples from other regions in the world, a multicultural imaginary space. PBS series during this decade—the 1990s—have included *Travels*, based on the journeys of literary figures to less-traveled sites around the globe, *Mini Dragons* (Eaton et al. 1990), short series on Asian economic culture, a cross-cultural examination of expressive movement called *Dancing* (Grauer 1993), a series on Latin and Central America called *The Americas* (Vecchione 1993), and *Millennium* (Grant, Malone, and Meech 1992), a series produced with and about anthropologists that focused on "tribal wisdom in the modern world," as its subtitle indicated. Along with the more than occasional *National Geographic* special on humans, as opposed to the majority focused on animals,[1] the sporadic *Nova* episode in which culture plays a primary role, and additional documentary specials focusing on far-off places and peoples, this represents a significant body of television texts representing cultural others. Indeed, public television's sustained multicultural focus distinguishes this body of texts from those shown on other broadcast networks (which, save for the major evening newscasts and CNN, are surprisingly provincial), and links these representations with other elements of our public culture such as museum exhibits, popular magazines covering travel and social studies, and advertisements for airlines and multinational corporations.

As a fund-raising proposal for *Childhood* reads, the series' producers lodged this "discourse of alterity" at a central place in its thematic concerns: "The CHILDHOOD series takes an inter-disciplinary look across cultures and back through time at the ways in which parents and societies have raised their children" (*Childhood: Series Format, Background Papers: Episodes 1–4*, July 1988, Forward:iii–iv). Much of the productive work of the series—from research and planning, through shooting and postproduction—

concerned the representation of culture and this multicultural articulation: choosing the ethnic, cultural, and national settings *Childhood* would film in and the specific families within these cultures; planning, organizing, logging, and translating the footage; gathering and selecting additional "anthropological" film from archival sources; and designing and implementing structures for editing this material into final programs. This chapter focuses on how *Childhood*'s producers represented "otherness" and "multiplicity" by looking specifically at how the producers went about selecting, steering, and structuring the material they used of the several cultures portrayed in the series. My aim is to explore more generally the formal and intellectual frameworks they employed while negotiating and constructing these images of other cultural sites and practices. I examine how this specific form of PBS documentary articulates cross-cultural comparisons of behavior and attitude, and argue that these representations are part of larger discourses of cultural otherness and difference in American culture.

PUBLIC TELEVISION AS "POPULAR ANTHROPOLOGY"

The various texts and genres in American public culture involved with the representation of cultural others might be considered a form of popular anthropology. These texts articulate either explicit arguments or implicit ideologies about what constitutes the cultures of other places and peoples, what constitutes "mainstream" American culture, and the relationships of difference and similarity between these constructs. As Stuart Hall has argued, cultural identities are produced through these negotiations of sameness and difference: "Identity exists in a hybrid space incorporating both similarity and continuity, on the one hand, and difference and rupture on the other" (Hall 1989:72). Identity is formed at least in part through encounters with difference, and media texts are one primary source of these "encounters," a body of narrative and exposition engaged in making comprehensible unfamiliar behavior in exotic places. The nature and reception of these representations are complex, though, given the intricate ways beliefs about the self are woven into the projection of other cultural worlds. Research and writing on the representation of ethnographic objects in museums (Kirshenblatt-Gimblett 1991), in the texts of *National Geographic* magazine (Lutz and Collins 1993), and the consumption of world cultures through cinema (Shohat and Stam 1994), world music (Feld 1994b), tourist productions (Crick 1989), folk festivals (Bauman et al. 1992), and a myriad of other forms all speak to the fascination Americans have with cultural difference. Americans, perhaps Western culture more generally, seem never to tire of constructing and consuming these sorts of narratives or reports, this "popular anthropology."

Childhood can be located within this terrain of popular anthropology. Mapped along a textual continuum of ethnographic authenticity or responsibility, *Childhood* clearly falls much closer to the pole of the responsible than toward the less scholarly use of cross-cultural material.[2] Although it does not attempt to follow any strict precepts of ethnographic film practice in method or form, the series relies on cross-cultural research and film material to a greater extent than typical educational series broadcast on public television.[3] An anthropological perspective informed and helped to shape *Childhood* from its earliest stages, combining and competing with frameworks from history and, perhaps the most influential, developmental psychology. From the treatments forward, the producers built the series in large part upon the comparison of childhood and family behavior in several cultures and historical periods, and used a large body of observational and archival film of families in these cultures. *Childhood's* Advisory Board included anthropologists Melvin Konner, Richard B. Lee, Jay Ruby, and Thomas Weisner who, with varying degrees of involvement, provided research material and motion picture resources and otherwise consulted with the producers.[4] Konner, one of the key advisors for the series, an on-camera observer, and author of the companion book (Konner 1991), influenced *Childhood's* theoretical perspective and content most fundamentally through his writing and forceful presence at meetings with advisors. In addition to contact with the advisors, the producers utilized a large body of research and film material by other anthropologists and consulted with several anthropologists during production. They drew on classic cross-cultural studies of children from anthropology, such as the Whitings' *Children of Six Cultures* (Whiting and Whiting 1975), portions of the Harvard San project (Lee and DeVore 1976), and Mead and Bateson's work in New Guinea, Bali, and Samoa (Mead 1928 and 1930; Mead and Bateson 1942). Several advisors had conducted their own cross-cultural studies in child development or employed cross-cultural data in their writings (Bronfenbrenner 1979, Hinde 1987; Kagan 1984; Kagan et al. 1979; Konner 1972). The producers also consulted and included recent ethnographic and cross-cultural work, such as research on the resilience of adolescents, conducted in Hawaii (Werner and Smith 1982), Stevenson's comparative studies on Japanese and American schooling (i.e., Stevenson 1986), and Schieffelin and Ochs's work on language acquisition (Schieffelin 1990; Schieffelin and Ochs 1986)

Even so, the producers operated without the daily input of anyone on staff trained in anthropology, and the sociobiological perspective favored by Konner, Hinde, and Kagan strongly influenced their anthropological perspective. The producers continually negotiated their approach to anthropological issues among these experts in other fields. Constrained by practical necessity, and balancing their objectives as television producers, they departed from strictly anthropological frameworks of explanation and theory in their use of cross-cultural material, as I describe later in this chapter. The "discourses of the other" articulated in the series can be seen most prominently in the "families footage," "documentary" scenes shot in other cultures, and commentary from both observers and the series' narrators (off-camera) framing cultural contexts and comparisons. The development of and discussion around each of these textual elements reveals something about both the series' ideology of cultural representation and the logics of production that constrained that representation.

UNITS OF COMPARISON AND COMMONALITY:
FAMILIES FOOTAGE AND DOCUMENTARY SEQUENCES

Childhood's producers structured the comparison of child-rearing practices and children's behavior into the program's basic design and narrative structure, illustrated through scenes of families at home, school, and play in a variety of cultures. They estimated that this "families footage," shot and recorded in what the producers categorize as an observational, cinema vérité style, with the high shooting ratios that typify this sort of material,[5] would comprise slightly more than a third of each program's edited screen time. In the final shows, scenes from the "families footage" increased to even more than this average length per program, comprising close to half the programs' on-air time, in part because some of the historical material fell out of the episodes. Through this families footage, the producers intended to portray and compare a range of social formations, from simple to postindustrial societies in different regions of the world. As a proposal document explained: "We selected these families to reflect a full range of social, economic, political, and religious features. Through them, we will be able to compare and contrast SIMPLE/COMPLEX GROUPS, RURAL/URBAN, SLOW-CHANGING/FAST-CHANGING, SECULAR/RELIGIOUS, CAPITALIST/SOCIALIST ENVIRONMENTS—key factors which are considered significant in the development of the child" (*Childhood: Series Format, Background Papers: Episodes 1–4*, July 1988, Forward:iii–iv).

Early treatments for *Childhood* proposed the selection of families in Brazil, Japan, Zambia, and the rural Midwestern United States.[6] A later treatment was more expansive, while admitting the tentative nature of these preliminary choices, which had both shifted and expanded:

Families:

Throughout the series, we will visit a number of families, carefully selected from the United States, the Soviet Union, Japan, Ireland, India, and East Cameroon. Our families will represent a diverse mix of children of all ages, from birth to puberty, both boys and girls, as well as a wide range of cultures, religions, and family structures. Our families, filmed over an eighteen-month period, will become one narrative backbone of the series, providing dramatic continuity as we follow the development and interaction of individual children and parents and a living example of some of the prominent themes in child development. (*Childhood: Series Format, Background Papers: Episodes 1–4*, July 1988, Forward:i.)

We can read in these proposals the dual objectives the producers had in mind with the family footage: social scientific ("compare and contrast") and narrative ("dramatic continuity"). This proposal went on to describe the potential families. Several were in urban settings and shared the characteristic of a father who worked in an auto factory, others were village-dwelling families in Ireland, India, and a Baka family in Cameroon. An earlier treatment had included a family from the !Kung of Botswana, a traditionally nomadic "hunter-gatherer" society, in place of the Baka group. When the possibility arose of acquiring footage from a body of material filmed with the Baka, they were substituted in place of the !Kung. This material, shot by filmmaker Phil Agland for a series of programs broadcast on Channel Four in England and as a PBS-broadcast *National Geographic* special in the United States, became an important part of *Childhood.*

Peter Montagnon and his company, Antelope Films, spent the fall of 1989 researching potential families for the series, support mechanisms (supplied by a "fixer," a local assistant producer or production manager familiar with the complexities of filming in that country), and permissions for filming in the proposed countries. As plans for production developed, arrangements for filming in India became too bogged down in bureaucratic processes, and Antelope's staff suggested some alternatives:

> Therefore, on speaking to Peter in Moscow, we have come up with a failsafe plan of options other than India. We need an extended family, as all other countries will be nuclear families. The countries that are probably at the forefront of the list are the Philippines and Brazil, with Malaysia as another possibility. Indonesia would be interesting, but very difficult to get into.
>
> [. . .]
>
> The problem with the Philippines and Brazil is getting excellent cameramen and fixers. I will find out from this end who has worked with local crews out there. (Antelope fax from Clare Elliott to Geoff Haines-Stiles, August 21, 1989)

The representational logic they employed called for substitutions between certain national and cultural locations that fit their criteria for inclusion, with these settings cast as thematic resources for the series. The tension between a culturally appropriate setting and one that could facilitate the level of production value that the series required is evident in the planning stages and throughout the experience of working with this family material.[7]

Once the production period started in the late fall of 1989, the producers settled on four countries in which to follow families—Japan, Russia, Brazil, and the United States (in addition to the Baka, Cameroon, footage they acquired). Montagnon made a second round of research trips (termed a "recce" in British production jargon) to Japan, Russia, and Brazil, and, with local assistance, "cast" the actual families *Childhood* would track.[8] Antelope contracted crews in these countries, where they had contacts from previous projects, periodically to film selected families through the long period of the production.

In selecting both foreign and American families, the producers searched for families that were "typical" and "representative," and that had children that covered a broad span of the childhood years. The rationale for choosing "representative" families was to allow the producers to employ a kind of televisual shorthand, highlighting cultural differences between what were essentially national cultures, without having to explain a great deal about cultural or class differences within a country. Peter Montagnon articulated the importance of common features across cultures for family comparisons in a memo sent from Tokyo during this research process:

> Viewer needs to be presented with a comparison structure that makes evident sense within his ordinary terms of reference, and without elaborate explanation. Ideally, structure should be as coherent as possible, i.e., sets of Banks, Schools, Apartment houses, electronic works, Factories.
>
> The units of comparison, i.e., factories, etc., should be as content-rich, as visually interesting, and as multi-layered (in terms of job, skill, and status variations) as possible. (Fax from Peter Montagnon to David Loxton and Geoff Haines-Stiles, September 3, 1989)

The families had to be unambiguously interpretable by the (typical American?) viewer as representatives of the cultures to which they belong, without the "elaborate explanation" Montagnon's letter warned against. As an illustration of this imperative, one family the producers considered filming in Japan included a Japanese mother and an Afro-American father. After some deliberation, the staff concluded that the children's features did not look typically Japanese and their racial and cultural heritage might confuse an audience when the sequence made cultural generalizations. They chose not to use material from that family. This logic of clarity in selection applied locally as well, in the search for the second of two middle-class American families. The staff had already selected the African American family they would film and were searching Westchester County in suburban New York for a representative white middle-class family. The producer in charge suggested they rule out two of the potential families they were considering, indicating, with an explanation directed in part at me, that one candidate was too ethnic, and that another family made too much money. This search for the typical raises the problem of attempting to crystallize heterogeneous national cultures into a small number of families, what a scholarly academic critique would term a form of "essentializing," or simplifying and ignoring difference. The designation of a family as "typical," therefore, is a strategic choice based on a cultural construction of its own in which producers attempt to calculate some form of shared archetype of a cultural or national group and encode this conceptualization in televisual form.

After a research period of several months, the producers settled on families in Brazil, Japan, Russia, and the United States, along with the footage they drew on from the Baka. Since they would not go on location, Haines-Stiles, Akuginow, and Marner drew up "shopping lists" for the families filming, which were sent out to the cinematographers and fixers in these locations.[9] These lists represented the primary form of directorial influence available to the producers during the overseas families filming. The producers revised and added to these lists as they reviewed, with great anticipation, the footage that arrived from the field, and requested stylistic adjustments in shooting.[10] Of course, the producers would exert a great deal of control in shaping this material during the editing stage.

Childhood also incorporated "documentary scenes," sequences representing characters and locations different from the family footage. The producers shot these documentary sequences over a briefer period than the families footage, and consolidated them into the scripts of single programs, rather than across the series. They initially estimated that these sequences would comprise almost as much screen time per episode as the families footage (eighteen minutes out of a fifty-eight minute episode, in contrast to twenty minutes for the families sequences); in the final shows, they averaged less, roughly nine minutes per program. In researching and scripting comparative sequences about topics like education, apprenticeship, and day care practices, the producers weighed possibilities for other parts of the world to travel to and film in to illustrate the conceptual points they intended and include the culture areas they hoped to cover in the series. They filmed sequences in Ghana, Italy, Israel, and Japan (this in addition to families footage shot in Japan), along with additional location scenes in the United States[11]

There were several difficult decisions about what cultures and countries outside of those chosen for the families to include in these documentary sequences. An intense debate concerned whether to film in an Islamic country, an obviously broad culture area not represented in the selection of families. Program Five/"Life's Lessons," which considered a variety of forms of education, provided an opportunity for a scene showing a Quranic school in a Muslim country, depicting a contemporary version of the kind of rote learning characteristic of traditional education. I was given the task of assembling some research material in this area and made contact with a few experts working with Moroccan Quranic education, who confirmed that Akuginow would find the kind of scenes the research suggested and assured us of the feasibility of filming in this setting. The producers had to reach agreement among themselves about the value of investing resources in this location for a sequence.

Both producer/director Gene Marner and historian Ray Hiner, a series advisor, took positions in favor of shooting in Morocco, arguing that a major international series that neglected this pivotal part of the world would be criticized. Peter Montagnon countered that they would have great difficulty including this religious and cultural tradition in the way proposed, given they had limited time in that episode to develop the sequence and location. He felt it would do a greater disservice to describe this culture superficially than to exclude it, arguing that it would be a mistake to portray only this harsh, antiquated aspect of Islamic culture without the balance of more flattering images. Given the lack of agreement on the value of this scene and the potential expense in mounting a production trip to Morocco, the producers ruled Islamic culture out of the series. This decision illustrates how both the economies of production expense and the conventions of documentary television presentation (here, the limitations of screen time) had a strong impact on textual content and cultural representation, whether and how a given culture area would be portrayed in *Childhood*.

THE "VOICE" OF CROSS-CULTURAL COMPARISONS

The issue of "voice" in both written and filmic ethnographies—how authorial point of view is formally encoded in these texts, the relationships between "voice" and authority, and the literal representation of the words of others—is central to how texts represent and convey the beliefs, viewpoints, and practices of the cultures they portray. Shohat and Stam employ a somewhat abstract sense of "voice" in analyzing films, urging us to look at "the interplay of voices, discourses, perspectives, including those operative within the image itself" (Shohat and Stam 1994:214). Their position is something closer to Nichols's in his discussion of "the voice of documentary" as "narrower than style: that which conveys to us a sense of a text's social point of view" (Nichols 1988:50). Shohat and Stam advocate an analytical strategy they term "polycentric multiculturalism," clearly sympathetic with Clifford's description of the production of "voice" in light of the politics of point of view in written ethnography: "Polyvocality was restrained and orchestrated in traditional ethnographies by giving to one voice a pervasive authorial function and to others the role of sources, "informants," to be quoted or paraphrased. Once dialogism and polyphony are recognized as modes of textual production, monophonic authority is questioned, revealed to be characteristic of a science that has claimed to *represent* cultures" (Clifford 1986a:15).

Ethnographic film theorists have long debated the politics of "giving voice" to others, challenged by the models of collaborative and indigenous media productions.[12] In Nichols's phrase, "The Ethnographer's Tale" (Nichols 1994) represents only one possible perspective, and a politically and ethically suspect one at that. While retaining something of the political critique that these broader analyses of voice propose, I want to use the term "voice" in a more linguistic sense here, to focus more literally on whose words both of them structure and are included in the text. The debates in both media studies and anthropology share a belief that the construction and interpretation of "voice" has implications for the articulation of meaning and the attribution of agency (for authors, subjects, and viewers), though given the orchestration of voices in all forms of representation, inclusion does not correlate directly with authorial power.

In *Childhood*, both cross-cultural comparisons and information about other cultural subjects are provided principally by the narrators, and secondarily by the observers (both on and off camera). In addition, the episodes contain some limited interview material with family members, usually parents, describing their attitudes about their children's behavior and personalities, the challenges of parenting, and their wishes for their children, as well as a few interviews with older children. The multiple surrogate authors of the text, not its subjects, deliver most of the content of cultural description. When the subjects' voices are heard, they most typically emerge in observational scenes of "natural" interaction, often interwoven with narration, and rarely in "direct" address. Both technical and conceptual reasons motivated this choice. Technically, the producers were faced with two intrinsic constraints: portraying many subjects too young to speak directly, coherently, and efficiently to an interviewer, and many subjects whose responses would have to be translated into English for American and British audiences. *Childhood* makes use of subtitles to render the speech of non-English-speaking families, but consciously chose to limit the amount of subtitles because of the inconvenience and expense involved in designing them, and the distress they presumably cause viewers.[13] Still, the subjects do speak for themselves to some extent, but are greatly overwhelmed by the "authors'" voices.

Conceptually, I think this can be explained by the producers' ambitious goals for the level and amount of scholarly information the programs should contain. Given the series' broad objectives for presenting scientific and scholarly material, the producers felt constrained in stylistic terms by the practical necessities of the one-hour format, the conventions of presentation, the ambitiousness of the subject matter, and limited expectations about audience understanding (i.e., time constraints, density of message, etc.), and chose to deliver much of the interpretive material through commentary. The following section of narration from Program One/"Great Expectations" illustrates the level of detail and generality contained in the commentary:

> NARRATOR (ALEX CHADWICK): Keno, near Tokyo. Chizuka Nakayama and her class of seven-year-olds begin a new semester. It's the first day after a summer recess that lasted only four weeks. Now the "Happy Wanderers" are brought back into the fold.
>
> Every culture gives things to its members, and asks for things in turn. Japan has made children a priority, but there is a price. This day's events are distinctively Japanese, but all around the room there's evidence of those universal characteristics of first-graders. The worry: "Will I speak up loud enough?" And those missing two front teeth. (Narration, Program One/"Great Expectations")

Interviews with Chizuka and her classmates might have elicited these specific points, but would not have drawn the broader association between the distinctive Japanese nature of these behaviors and their universal dimensions. Other sequences later in the program include phrases such as "birth is biological and universal; the work of nature and evolution" and "human childbirth is shaped by culture, time, and place" (narration, Program One/"Great Expectations"). Given the kind of commentary they were committed to using, the producers were not likely to obtain this level of generality from the families themselves, even if they had hoped to, and certainly not with the rhetorical efficiency they would want. By design, convention, and practical necessity, *Childhood* was bound to be structured around a predominantly monologic narration, a textual mode that, while regarded critically in academic readings of film and video texts, is still a familiar convention in PBS documentary.

JUXTAPOSITIONS ACROSS CULTURES

Childhood's producers and editors structured the footage representing other cultures into two distinguishable types of sequences that I term "extended" and "juxtapositional." By "extended" sequences, I mean edited segments featuring a single culture, following recognizable subjects through a series of events, that combine conventional vérité shooting and editing, and expository narration. Much of the families footage and documentary material employed in the series would fit this category of extended sequences representing other cultural worlds. By the term "juxtapositional," I refer to sequences juxtaposing corresponding practices or events across cultures, constructed by intercutting analogous material from more than one cultural setting. These structures represent two different documentary modalities between which *Childhood* moves. Juxtaposition for cross-cultural comparison occurs throughout the series, where the producers employ sequences made up of

extended vs juxtapositional

(NB - is Childhood doing what Mazzarella argues against - equating social positions across cultures? Is Dornfeld doing this, too?)

brief shots from the several cultures represented to draw out for the audience
both similarities across and differences among cultures. By cutting from one
culture to another, the producers make an explicit associational comparison
in an ethnological mode, as if to say, in Brazil childbirths are like this, while
in the United States, they are like that. Extended and juxtapositional
sequences are not completely discrete categories, however, since extended
sequences themselves are sometimes juxtaposed in longer comparative structures. Still, the distinction allows us to focus on the articulation of cross-
cultural comparisons, accomplished more directly through juxtaposition. In
most cases, these comparisons are framed and reinforced by the narrators'
pointing to both differences and similarities, and by an editing structure that
attempts to match actions across cultures.

The sequence opening Program Two/"Louder than Words" exemplifies
this juxtapositional editing structure. This sequence contains several closely
matching cuts across cultures: from a wide shot of the Kalugin family in
Russia approaching the church where they will baptize baby Vera, to a similarly composed image showing the Oliveira family in Brazil arriving to
christen newborn Simone; from the Baka family anointing baby Kamala
with medicinal paste, to a Brazilian priest christening Simone in her huge
church ceremony; and from the prayers of a New York rabbi conducting a
naming ceremony for Michelle Kauffman, to the Brazilian priest praying for
the christened babies (see Fig. 5.1). The narration through this section steers
attention from the cultural particular to the cross-cultural universal. This
kind of juxtapositional structure, combined with an anchoring, generalizing
narration, is a critical rhetorical device for the series as a whole.

The producers were aware of, and often debated the complexities involved
in making this type of comparison. During a meeting where *Childhood*'s
advisors responded to rough cuts of the episodes, series advisor Robert
Hinde, a scholar of human development who has worked with both cross-
cultural and cross-species comparative research, raised a scientific objection
to the framing of this intercutting for comparisons between cultures: "I think
you want to talk not about cultural differences, but about the variety in the
world, because you can't take a family to specify a cultural difference"
(Robert Hinde, Advisors Meeting, February 3, 1991). Although at the meeting (and I believe in principle) the producers agreed with this assertion, it is
clear that they *did* want the programs to articulate cultural and national differences and make cross-cultural and transnational comparisons, and employ
the families footage to illustrate these differences. For instance, at that same
meeting, Geoff Haines-Stiles described the purpose of the opening sequence
in Program One/"Great Expectations":

That is that rather than having this huffing and puffing introductory material,
which says the Kalugins live here [Russia], the Oliveiras live there [Brazil], so

(NB—Though D. has demonstrated the continuity of producer &
audience categories, he is maintaining the subject as
firmly distinct from both)

and so and so and so, we actually meet each one of our cultures and use them, as we start off with Jerry moments ago, to say, "In the matrix of different cultures around the world that we could have chosen, why did we choose this particular culture or that particular culture." So the combination of scenes that, like the Russian christening and the christening dinner, to me have a cinematic value, where you actually introduce not just the family, but also some aspects of a culture. (Advisors Meeting, February 3, 1991)

The cinematic value Haines-Stiles refers to is just that metonymic extension that Hinde's social scientific caveat warns against. The formal structure the producers often employ to do this—juxtaposition for comparison—is a well-worn but still articulate convention, one found across genres and media. That is to say, that although there is a formulaic quality to these cross-cultural juxtapositions, it seems that the producers proceed with the conviction that viewers respond to these kinds of comparisons, these documentary articulations.

The dissension here can be attributed to differing logics for including material, differing estimations of value, one based on social scientific validity, the other on the effectiveness of documentary conventions and forms. To Hinde, the social scientist (and to the other social scientists present), generalizing from "data," the footage of the family itself, to the culture, a kind of synecdoche, must be avoided or undertaken cautiously. Yet it is just this sort of generalization that the producers counted on in planning, "casting," and editing their families footage. This material is meant to articulate an analogy that the scientist needs to guard against. This type of comparative analogy, what I would call an "ethnological trope," is a foundation on which the producers built the series and a common structure of understanding in popular anthropology. It is arguably a structure essential to how Western cultures construct cross-cultural discourse throughout a variety of representational forms used to depict cultural others.

CONTESTED VIEWS OF REPRESENTING OTHERNESS

Criticisms raised by advisors and WNET staff about the use of both extended and juxtapositional sequences reveal the contested nature of these cultural representations, and a sensitivity about multicultural material in PBS programming. One critique raised during production involved the use of cultural stereotypes, a well-traveled area in literature on the critique of cultural representation. Criticism about the use of stereotypes came up in response to a sequence, included both in the project's demonstration tape and later in Program Five/"Life's Lessons," that cut between contemporary and archival scenes of a Japanese mother dressing up in a traditional kimono for a ritual

Narrator (Alex Chadwick): In Moscow, the old year is ending. New lives are just beginning. Once, such ceremonies were frowned on; now, Sasha Kalugin brings daughter Vera to be baptized.

BRAZIL. Maria Oliveira brings three-month-old Sydney to be christened, and prays for God's blessings on her family.

MANHATTAN. Michelle Kauffman is six weeks old. This naming ceremony is a reform rite, but the spirit is timeless. These ceremonies show adults now expect the child to survive, and carry forward its new name. In times past, they were testaments to the belief in life over death.

continued on next page

Narrator/Lynn Neary: Among the Baka of Cameroon, West Africa, baby Kamala, four weeks old, is anointed with medicinal paste. Caring for the infant comes naturally to our species. But the specifics of care-giving are as varied as the peoples of our planet. But after the ritual words have faded, parents still want to know how to help their children grow.

Chadwick: In the past, it was priests and philosophers who gave advice based on beliefs and guesses about the nature of the newborn. In societies where there was little change or choice, the old ways endured. Now modern parents look to new sources of support and information—medical doctors and scientists.

In this program, we'll explore the characteristics of all infants in their first few months of life. We'll find out if there is a natural way to take care of children, and we'll see how sometimes infants' actions can speak louder than words.

Figure 5.1 Narration and selected frames from the opening sequence in Program Two/"Louder than Words."

before her child's first day of school. In a screening of the demo tape for the project staff, Geoff Haines-Stiles mentioned that somebody at WNET had objected to the stereotypical portrait this sequence articulated. He replied at the screening that "within each culture there's no sense in which we are going only for the clichés." Erna Akuginow added that the ceremonial use of kimonos does not constitute a cliché but represents what the culture really values, basing her credibility on the producers' understanding of the culture. On a separate occasion, she defended the use of these allegedly "stereotypical" cultural images on the grounds of audience comprehension, the importance of avoiding confusion on the viewer's part. Later, in the advisors meeting, Haines-Stiles raised the issue of stereotypy again, in a discussion about a different Japanese family scene:

> . . . the trip of the Nakayama family, Chizuka's family, who we saw going to school. Remember we said they went up-country to meet, that there's a trip in which her parents, who are very savvy, hip graphic designers, and a retired professional woman, go up country to constantly take Chizuka and her twelve-year-old very hip sister back to the traditional environment. That says something about Japan which sounds like a cliché, but I think if you look at the footage and if you've been to Japan you have to say, along with modernity, there is a sense of tradition. (Advisors Meeting, February 3, 1991)

Stereotypy operates as a form of communicative shorthand, allowing the producers to draw comparisons between cultures economically. Several issues were simultaneously at stake here: the line between the typical and the stereotypical, the contestable accuracy of these representations, and the authority to make these sorts of judgments. Haines-Stiles and Akuginow asserted their authority based on their knowledge of Japanese culture and grounding in the research literature, and their conviction both that the producers based these cultural tropes ("Japanese culture as both traditional and modern") in fact and that they were rhetorically convincing.

Two of the series' advisors raised a different and more adamant critique in reaction to a sequence shot in the home of the Gholstons, the African American family *Childhood* features. The sequence in question portrayed the Gholstons' Christmas holiday, a large family celebration in their household.[14] Geoff Haines-Stiles included this sequence in the demo tape and Marner built it into Program Four/"Ties That Bind." It begins with the family preparing for a Christmas meal, with father Felton Gholston doing most of the cooking in preparation for the event, as their many family members arrive. At some point during the hectic evening, Felton promised his two sons (Malcolm and Benji, ages three and five) that he would set up their new train set later that evening, a promise he has to renege on as the evening's events extend way beyond the children's bedtime. When they learn that they will have to wait until the next day, both boys begin to cry uncontrollably, becoming so agitated that they simultaneously begin to throw up, joined by

Avery, their two-year-old sister. The sequence, edited similarly in both the demonstration reel and final program, shows an unusually tense, revealing, family moment, and a difficult situation for a parent to handle, and is a sequence whose significance leaves room for a variety of viewers' interpretations.

Erna Akuginow described to me how advisors Jerome Kagan and Alvin Poussaint, both psychologists (Kagan is white and Poussaint is black), were strongly opposed to the use of this footage, fearing that viewers (both black and white) might read the sequence as an illustration of African American parents mishandling their parental responsibilities. The producers defended the use of this sequence based on how illustrative it was of typical and widely shared parental tensions. They felt the Gholston parents did the best they could given the situation, and that other scenes throughout *Childhood* showed them as responsive, caring, and thoughtful parents, an opinion that Marian Wright Edelman, also African American, supported. Clearly the producers were working with culturally sensitive material and had to weigh viewers potential interpretations of this material carefully, as well as the moral implications of these interpretations. Poussaint eventually agreed to the use of this sequence.

The concern with moral connotations came up at other points in the production. In the following exchange, a few advisors addressed what they saw as the presence of a moral tone in a sequence juxtaposing different cultural practices for carrying infants and the impact these practices have on interaction:

URIE BRONFENBRENNER: That's what disturbed me about that sequence, because even though you don't say it, what happens if you just take this particular feature and show it sequentially . . .

JEROME KAGAN: Sounds like you're moralizing . . .

BRONFENBRENNER: It sounds like you're moralizing . . .

KAGAN: It really does . . .

BRONFENBRENNER: You're saying, "See, these folks do it, possibly these folks find themselves in . . ." Whereas the actual situation is, first of all the reason why this is done elsewhere. The other thing is that there are other kinds of opportunities for the interaction, rather than to convey a message of, "Now we move from primitive to modern."

KAGAN: There is a moral tone in [Programs] One-A and Two,[15] which did bother me and Urie is giving voice to it.

GEOFF HAINES-STILES: Well, to the extent to which that's there, it shouldn't be there, and won't be in there. (Advisors Meeting, February 3, 1991)

It remains an open question whether this comparative material, indeed whether any comparisons across national, cultural, or ethnic boundaries, can be used without an indication of moral value judgment. Anthropologist Lila Abu-Lughod addressed this dilemma when she asked: "Does difference always smuggle in hierarchy?" (1991:146). Clearly the producers wanted to avoid suggesting the superiority of certain cultures (Western, middle-class) and often discussed other cultural practices as critiques of American methods. Yet whether they could put aside their assumptions about the superiority of certain aspects of Euro-American culture (medical practice, family structures, etc.) is a murkier question, one that will depend on and vary with a viewer's readings of the programs. In any case, the text's structure and language seem to encourage these readings.

The producers and advisors expressed a commitment to raising moral questions in the series and articulating a complex moral position: that children's lives have been slighted in the past, that there are better and worse conditions and practices with which to bring up children, that American society and other societies have been guilty of neglect (evident in statistics of infant mortality), and that contemporary societies need to do what they can to improve this situation.

> GENE MARNER: I think, if the question of what kind of society do we want to live in is part of our agenda, then it underlies everything we do, I think.
>
> ERNA AKUGINOW: I don't think that's a question that you or I or Geoff, or even Mel to a certain extent, can answer in terms of the . . .
>
> MARNER: Not answer.
>
> AKUGINOW: Not answer, but even an attempt to . . . that's what we're doing, that's what we're saying to the audience. We're giving you this information now. These are things you need to put together to reach a certain point of understanding to make these kinds of connections. But I don't think that in any way, I mean I certainly don't have . . . nobody's paying me the six million dollars or whatever million dollars to put my viewpoint, Erna Akuginow's viewpoint, and what I think is a socially correct message. That's sort of hubristic of us to assume we can do that.
>
> MARNER: But one of the things that brought me in here was Geoffrey's speaking of the things that he said to me the very first time I met with him, that raising children is so important to the future, and look at the rotten job we're doing.
>
> AKUGINOW: That's right. That was a given.
>
> MARNER: Okay, the given has to be given in the programs. (Advisors Meeting, December 12, 1989)

The producers talked about the need to navigate a careful passage between "describing" and "advising," as Mel Konner put it,[16] between articulating a scientific and informative position and one that implies a stance of advocacy. The decision to include Marian Wright Edelman as an on-camera observer, for instance, brought to the episodes in which she appears a clear voice of advocacy that the British partners (both Peter Montagnon and Gwynn Pritchard from Channel Four) felt was problematic, because of both its American-centered focus and its "preachy" tone (Montagnon characterized one of her scenes as "a sermon delivered to camera"). Other observers spoke from their more "social scientific" frameworks (sociological, ethological, psychological, anthropological), but still moved between descriptive and advocative or advisory modes. The common ground among the staff centered around negotiating a tone for the series that was not overly moralistic, without abandoning something of the producers' and advisors' shared moral position.

POSITING CULTURAL OTHERS OUT OF TIME, AND HISTORICAL ANCESTORS AS CULTURAL OTHERS

Childhood compares both cultures across geographical distance (i.e., Japan and the United States) and cultures across time (i.e., colonial America and contemporary America). Historical comparisons are articulated with some of the same rhetorical structures used by cross-cultural comparison—juxtaposition casting both frameworks of similarity and difference—which attempt to convey changing conceptions and conditions of children's lives. The aforementioned kimono sequence in Program Five/"Life's Lessons," which cuts between black and white archival footage (circa 1950s) of a Japanese mother dressing in a special kimono and contemporary footage of the Nakayama family doing the same, is one of several examples of this editing structure. Instances occur in the series, though, where the producers use material from one cultural setting to make both cross-cultural and historical comparisons simultaneously. When they juxtapose scenes of the Baka, a simple traditional rain-forest society in Cameroon, with contemporary American or Japanese society, the producers both provide an example of a cultural world vastly different from the twentieth-century United States and an illustration of life for predecessors in preagricultural times.

In discussing the theoretical assumptions behind *Childhood's* use of historical material, the producers and academic advisors[17] agreed on the validity of a progressive framework for macrohistory, which posits human evolution developing through a progression of material or subsistence stages, from hunting-gathering through agriculture to industrial forms of society. The producers and advisors concurred in the belief that scenes from cultures like the Baka and the !Kung provide an illustration of an earlier period of human history—the Stone Age hunter-gatherer period—although they acknowledged that this was something of an oversimplification:

GEOFF HAINES-STILES: The Baka, to us, represented not the noble savage, but a hunter-gatherer society where there were no schools, no industrialization. Those kind of grand criteria. We haven't gotten to see the historical periods that are significant for the understanding of how different childhoods have been in the past, categorized by those kinds of differences. Grand changes allow the producer to say that we should situate historical scenes within these periods—that gives us a contrast with how all our societies are operating—except the Baka, who are in some sense out of time, although that's a real oversimplification. (Advisors Meeting, February 20, 1990)

Recent scholarly discussion about hunter-gatherer economies has brought about a rethinking of assumptions about these societies. Some researchers now argue that the previous view of hunter-gatherer societies as essentially frozen in their mode of production, living in the twentieth century in the same fashion they did 10,000 years ago, romanticized these societies and cast them as static and isolated (Myers 1988). These scholars now maintain that hunter-gatherer societies have adopted changing forms of subsistence and economic interaction to accommodate periodic political and economic formations, and had complex relations with agricultural and herding societies. How the current lives of groups like the !Kung and the Baka, to use two examples the series considers, exemplify earlier periods in human civilization is open to a great deal of argument, as is, by implication, the validity of using these societies as examples of an earlier time. Regarding societies like the Baka as living cultural artifacts, illustrating what human life was like at an earlier period in civilization, assumes an evolutionary framework that Fabian (1983) criticized as endemic to anthropological thinking. He argued that assigning a living society to the West's version of the past denies them their existence in the present, and thereby devalues their culture, with potentially destructive political and economic consequences. I would extend this observation beyond academia to the wider discourses of public culture, which share many of these evolutionary assumptions.

The producers were aware of the corrective writing on hunter-gatherer life[18] and raised this perspective during the advisors' meetings:

GEOFF HAINES-STILES: I think in the last program, we are thinking about, not with the Baka, because we don't have the footage, but with the !Kung, of saying that even hunter-gatherers live in history, and that the changes which have characterized the past forty years of !Kung life, in which a fairly humane childhood has been transformed into a much less humane childhood, are happening, and the Baka in fact, have a fairly ongoing relationship with the neighboring villages. They are not quote pure hunter-gatherers. That's true anthropologically. For our purposes, they're closer to the environment of evolutionary adaptiveness than anything else we've got. (Advisors Meeting, February 3, 1991)

Haines-Stiles did not feel uncomfortable with taking a certain amount of social scientific license, arguing the value of scenes or sequences with a different rationale than that of the social sciences, what could be termed a humanistic rationale. He felt that the Baka footage, for instance, evokes a primal human quality in a moving, poetic way and was not primarily concerned with its validity in social scientific terms. Still, the Baka material is used in the series in an evolutionary framework that is both intellectually and politically problematic. In discussing the importance of what the producers refer to as "intimate interactions" in advancing normal child development, a sequence in Program Three/"Love's Labors" moves from documentary footage (in black and white) of Harlow's laboratory experiments on attachment in rhesus monkeys to the Baka family interacting around the campfire, casting the Baka in the evolutionary line from primates to "civilized human society."[19] *Childhood* was guilty of advancing just the kind of evolutionary arguments criticized by Fabian and others.

MEDIATING BETWEEN RELATIVISM AND UNIVERSALISM

In relying on the comparative structure of the cross-cultural trope for representing other cultural practices and comparing them to those of Western cultures, the *Childhood* series articulates a position mediating between what could be characterized as an anthropological cultural relativism and a universalism based both in sociobiological arguments for explaining human behavior and development and in liberal humanist intellectual positions. The following passage of narration, coming late in Program One/"Great Expectations," during a sequence juxtaposing representations of birth positions in a variety of forms and settings, illustrates these broad tensions:

> NARRATOR (ALEX CHADWICK): Birth may be biological, but human childbirth is the product of culture, varying from time to time and place to place. But both Maria [Oliveira from Brazil] and Barbara [Kauffman from New York] are in hospitals, ready for delivery, lying on their backs.
>
> In the past, in many different cultures, other positions were used, and many helpers with nonmedical functions were present. As on the American frontier in the nineteenth century. In Europe, special birthing chairs let a woman bear down strongly. A native American might lean, literally, on her spouse. One African community even decorated its chief's ceremonial chair with many members assisting a squatting mother. A nineteenth-century medical text pictured dozens of similar examples. Contemporary research has verified what ancient Aztecs knew from experience: pushing down with gravity may make active labor one-third shorter, since the size of the pelvic outlet increases.
>
> But there's a trade-off. If there are complications, as in about one-fifth of pregnancies, a doctor can intervene more easily with a woman lying flat on a delivery table. (Narration, Program One/"Great Expectations")

The narration asserts a traditional relativist formulation—"human childbirth is the product of culture, varying . . ."—that different cultural practices can

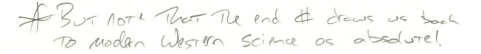
But note that the end # draws us back to modern Western science as absolute!

be understood and justified within, and must be seen as dependent upon their cultural context. This intellectual theme ran through the production process and was woven into the series' expository commentary. Even though, as discussed earlier, the producers and advisors disagreed on the presence of a moral tone in the programs, they expressed and, after some negotiation, seemed to share an overall stance maintaining that the consequences of different cultural practices need to be understood in their cultural and historical context, and that the efficacy of these practices depends on these contextual factors. The sequence of images of childbirth accompanying the narration above takes the viewer through a cross-cultural and historical inventory of childbirth settings and visual representations (illustrations, sculpture), while the narration delivers (American) viewers back to the contemporary world in which they live, returning to Western orthodox medical practices with a conventional childbirth in a New York hospital. That the episode moves next to *Childhood* observer Mel Konner, a trained doctor (and dressed for the part in doctor's garb), scrubbing his hands to prepare for an examination, can be read as an illustration of the limits of these relativist positions.

Indeed, the programs' relativism is most contested when the issues discussed are current and controversial and have more pragmatic and behavioral implications. The producers and advisors used particular caution and concern when portraying aspects of parenting about which potential viewers might be sensitive, since they anticipated that many viewers would expect the series to make recommendations about practices addressed in current parental-advice literature, and might take their statements as expert advice. In designing sequences on the consequences of debates over practices such as breast-feeding versus bottle-feeding, cosleeping, day care, and natural forms of birthing, the producers and advisors agreed that they wanted to articulate the message that there are no absolute precepts, but only different choices, "trade-offs" as the narrator explained when speaking about different birthing positions.[20] They recognized the influence of "objective" factors, such as the health benefits of prenatal care for the newborn or the importance of changes in the medical treatment of childbirth. Yet, the producers were criticized about being less culturally relative in relation to these more current subjects of discussion. For instance, Robert Hinde expressed dissatisfaction with what he perceived as "a terrible American complacency" and lack of "humility" in the series, involving the "denigration of other cultures,"[21] a dissatisfaction echoed by Peter Montagnon on other occasions. We can partially attribute the American-centered approach to the fact that the producers were gearing their work to a predominantly American audience, with the PBS broadcast foremost in their minds. Yet Geoff Haines-Stiles quickly responded to these assertions, saying that the presence of that kind of American-centered tone would have to be eliminated. Surely, part of the authorial process of "pre-figuring the audience" (Smith 1988) discussed earlier involves a presumption about the preconceptions and interests an Ameri-

can audience brings to its viewing experience, and an attempt to frame representations accordingly, particularly on topics of current social concern for
that audience, such as birth practices. Audience members bring to their
viewing of another cultural setting a range of predispositions about that culture. The producers expressed the necessity of being aware of these predispositions and the morally based value judgments that accompany them, and
tried to shape their material accordingly.

The following discussion began in reaction to a sequence that juxtaposed
different methods for carrying and watching over newborns. Cited at length
here, it illustrates the articulation of relativist positions on which the advisors
agree—and hope viewers will infer—and how they debate these positions.

JEROME KAGAN: It seems to me, if I can get my three colleagues to agree, we
ought to say that in these sequences, from Baka to Gholstons, the parents have
to be predictable, they have to present some variety that can be, and they have
to provide a secure attachment. They have to reduce this child's anxieties, so
you can go forward. Then we say, "You see, you can be in the Cameroon, you
can be in Moscow . . . ." That's the underlying . . . You've got to say this.
You can't expect the viewer to infer this. You've got to tell the viewer that,
because it's not in the scene.

ROBERT HINDE: And you can use your split screen stuff in the same place.

URIE BRONFENBRENNER: I would agree strongly, Jerry, if you'd entertain one
addition to that, which you didn't make explicit, that it's got to be back and
forth. It can't be just in one direction.

KAGAN: And reciprocal. Fine.

BRONFENBRENNER: And then by showing reciprocity, in three of four different
modalities, if you will, then we come closer to making the point on the
screen. But I would agree, it's still . . . somebody has to say, "Here's the
golden egg."

KAGAN: And notice that accomplishes what both Robert and Urie were saying.
Then no culture's any better than any other; they provide these resources in
different ways. That's the underlying message your advisors are saying.

[. . .]

HINDE: I think I disagree with my colleagues here, any of you. I think the point
ought to be not that there's something right and something wrong. This is an
instance in which the biological desiderata clash with the cultural desiderata.
What's good for the baby and what's good for the mother clash. What's good
for the mother might be four-hour feedings so that she can do other things,
and get some sleep and all that, and what's good for the baby is something
different. The same issue comes up over day care.

[. . .]

GEOFF HAINES-STILES: Could I ask Robert to follow through on what you just
said, which is more or less the end statement which you said at Cambridge,
which left me, at least, feeling unfulfilled. "There's a conflict between the

biological desiderata and the social desiderata," you actually say more or less that in those words. What comes next, what do you say next?

KAGAN: What are the implications?

HINDE: That this is a balance that's going to be different in different cultures, and that there's no final answer.

KAGAN: Perfect. Amen.

HINDE: You've got to stay unfulfilled, old boy. (Advisors Meeting, February 3, 1991)

The relativist framework is clearly articulated ("no culture's better than any other," "different in different cultures"), but Hinde's biological desiderata offers a different grounding than we would expect from history or anthropology. His comments illustrate the sociobiological epistemology that several of the advisors worked to reinforce and articulate in program form, and which often existed at some tension with culturally oriented forms of explanation.

The discussion continued, defending the importance of articulating a relativist view in sequences on other cultural practices, such as birthing procedures and feeding schedules, and Geoff Haines-Stiles asked the advisors to make explicit what they think an audience member should take away from this sequence:

GEOFF HAINES-STILES: What would you ideally want a mother or a father to take away from what you just said, which is, "it depends."

JEROME KAGAN: That overall—you know, we talk about the greatest good for the greatest number—when we take the average over those first two years, has there been more predictability than nonpredictability, has there been more moments of joy than moments of anxiety. You're looking at the mean; the child is not a fragile piece of porcelain, and so if you've got to schedule-feed because you've got a job, it's okay, if the rest is okay. That's what Urie's saying. And any one of these practices alone is trivial, trivial.

URIE BRONFENBRENNER: And if I were to try to put what I would say, every culture seeks to find a balance here, and it may be, in a culture that is responsive there will be a variety of ways to do that. Other cultures, and this is one way in which American culture has not been too accommodating, it's more difficult to achieve that balance, but the point is, there are a variety of ways of achieving that balance. The principle is: seek that balance, and in particular have social institutions and values that are supportive of seeking that balance. And there we have, I think, a resolution which doesn't emphasize, everybody's got to give something and remain unfulfilled, and life becomes rather decent.

KAGAN: Let me add, and I don't think this is banal, that to the average mother, to tell her, that the message is not in a specific practice will come as a surprise to her. That is an important fact to teach the viewers of this program. (Advisors Meeting, February 3, 1991)

Kagan and Bronfenbrenner articulate conventional relativist viewpoints, mediated and perhaps simplified for an average audience, "an average mother."

Although the producers share these views, they simultaneously feel that much of the appeal of the cross-cultural material to at least a Western audience lies not in its acknowledgment of difference but its expression of an underlying, universally shared similarity. The following exchange, spurred on by Sandra Scarr's concerns that the Baka material would seem too exotic for their audience to identify with, exemplifies the importance of universalism to the producers and the ways in which producers "pre-figure" their audience.

SANDRA SCARR: I've got a question about the Baka material in general.

GEOFF HAINES-STILES: Sorry, what is your question again?

SCARR: My question is whether it's too exotic, that it's too different from the average viewer's knowledge or experience, and will just seem peculiar.

HAINES-STILES: I think that that is not a problem that I'm aware of in somebody responding to the two films that have been made, the three films that have been made by Channel Four, and Gwynn [Pritchard]. Brits are undoubtedly more insular even than Americans. I'm sorry, English people are even more insular than Americans, you can latch on to this and see how people responded in the U.K. But it's my sense that the particular uniqueness of this footage is that it does relate to what Levine would call the environment of evolutionary adaptiveness in a filmic way, and that you can see in enough footage in which there is enough intimate behavior of a similar caliber to that which our cameramen got in Russia or in the U.S., that you can respond to these characters. [. . .] I profoundly believe that, and I would like to just ask maybe Gwynn to just blast that in any way.

GWYNN PRITCHARD: [. . .] I think, and speaking in generalizations in this company is always extremely dangerous, British society is probably less self-consciously racist than North American society. But if that series was going to fall into the trap that you've described, among audiences, that the audience research we did, but anyway the press to the series would have elicited and brought it out pretty obviously and quickly. And indeed, to my knowledge, the universal response in the papers, from the qualities through to the tabloids, was precisely this way, not exactly White Plains but that these are beautiful and charming people, and it was that particular family in the first series, actually concentrated on Ali as a little boy, it was a response actually wonderful. [. . .]

URIE BRONFENBRENNER: It humanized them . . .

ROBERT HINDE: There is a certain sense in which the relation of the Baka to the other families is the same as the relation of your children on an aseptic table is to the other families, they're stripped of all the nonsense of civilization, and here are the same basic processes going on. And you see them more clearly.

(Advisors Meeting, February 3, 1991)

In Hinde's comment the universalisms of biology and humanism come together, as the cultural trappings separating the Baka from Western viewers are "stripped away."[22]

SIMILARITY AND DIFFERENCE: COMPETING FRAMEWORKS FOR TELEVISUAL CROSS-CULTURAL REPRESENTATION

The negotiation between relativist and universalist frameworks does not take place between polar opposites, although these positions are often posed as such. It is more accurate here to think of these intellectual and ideological positions as contending strategies for cultural articulation, based on either social scientific, sociobiological, or humanistic logics that carry with them practical implications for constructing texts. A social scientific logic embodies specific criteria about how to articulate an argument and marshal evidence in its support, undergirded by an antagonism toward discussions of shared human traits across cultures. A biologically based universalist logic proposes specific arguments about the shared dimensions of human development and evolution over time, a baseline for understanding human life. But the tensions between these positions were overridden by a larger overarching tension, between scholarly arguments and strategies for articulation and what I term an ideology of "televisual humanism," a logic and strategy of articulation that shifts authority to the presumed, predicted, and observed response of the audience. This televisual humanism appeals to a sense of equality and empathy by seeing universalism within difference, drawing on both the social scientific and sociobiological positions, but positing these arguments in relation to an ideology of articulation for its particular audience.

With *Childhood*, a project in which the producers worked closely with academic advisors and scholarly material, there were often compromises to be made between these two frameworks of authority and articulation. Geoff Haines-Stiles expressed concern on several occasions about how the consultants would respond to the scientific validity of material, particularly scenes of the families, which he felt worked well as "television." I read his concern over the scientific validity of family scenes, often discussed as the most visually interesting material, as an expression of the conflict over frameworks of authority and a desire to have the series respected both as science and as documentary television.

> GEOFF HAINES-STILES: Do we know that when we focus on a particular family that's having a meal and it's recorded in detail, that that's representative of 60 percent or 80 percent of the population? I think what people who are hard scientists like Jerry Kagan criticize people like Urie Bronfenbrenner for is that

essentially they are novelists in the guise of social scientists. They report interesting findings but they don't have any understanding of whether what they're reporting is based on fact. And the fact that a certain family tends to write a lot, and has a diary, and the family says, "We had a great meal, and we sat around and discussed things, and then went out and had a sleigh ride," that's fine, but is that typical or atypical, and does it matter for us? (Advisors Meeting, December 13, 1989).

The justification for using this "novelistic" material, given its suspect status as science, was often lodged in terms of the audience: holding their interest and providing material they would find appealing, accessible, and with which they could identify.

The producers were more likely than the advisors to win out in conflicts over whether to include scenes that were suspect scientifically, since in the end they were the authors of these texts who had hired the scholars to assist with the series. Nevertheless, the advisors (particularly those who were also observers) had a lot at stake in *Childhood* and exerted the power they had to protect their own notions of authority. For example, the advisors began the meeting in February 1991 (I have cited from it extensively), which was held to discuss their responses to the rough cuts of several episodes, by stating their overall dissatisfaction with the way the programs had come together. They felt, as a group, that the scientific material was being given short shrift, and that there were too many long, uninterpreted sequences of families footage. Haines-Stiles responded during this meeting that much of their dissatisfaction could be attributed to the rough cut stage of the programs, and by the end of the day's meeting the advisors seemed satisfied that the producers would attend to their comments. In my view, what transpired was a negotiation toward a compromise that attempted to balance scientific validity with good television.[23]

Behind these representations of otherness is an attempt to bridge the distancing that Fabian sees as so endemic to anthropological thought. *Childhood*'s producers sincerely hope to convince the viewer of the shared burden of all families, despite the cultural differences, and thereby draw the viewer in to "experience" the worlds of these families, seeking what Abu-Lughod calls "the ethnography of the particular" to balance the distancing discourses of social science (Abu-Lughod 1991). In doing so, though, they risk reproducing what Clifford terms humanist allegories embedded in Western notions and representations of cultural difference.

Cultural and humanist allegories stand behind the controlled fictions of difference and similitude that we call ethnographic accounts. [. . .] Strange behavior is portrayed as meaningful within a common network of symbols—a common ground of understandable activity valid for both observer and observed, and by implication for all human groups. Thus ethnography's narrative of specific differences presupposes, and always refers to, an abstract plane of similarity. (Clifford 1986b:101)

The danger here is that the most appealing form for accounting for the behavior of others (appealing for producers because of its appeal for viewers), particularly in the condensed formats available for television documentarians, involves casting them in a framework of essentialism: "Essentialism posits an ontology to things and, in drawing on observation, proposes transparency between what is seen and the knowable: things are what they can be seen to be. What they are seen to be in ethnography, most frequently, is some version of the family-of-man myth" (Nichols 1981:274).

The communicative form employed by *Childhood*, the aesthetics of public television documentary, pulls us simultaneously in both directions. The expository dimensions of the text move to generalize and distance (the scientific talk of which the advisors wanted more), while the observational tendencies (the "cinematic value" of the families footage) and the more literary or dramatic qualities of the spoken commentary draw the viewer to particularize and participate, "to respond to these characters," as Geoff Haines-Stiles argued. The hybrid text that *Childhood* became contains both of these complexes of meaning, but the primary reference points remain the experience, scientific knowledge, medical practice, and history of American culture.

Reflecting on a cross-culturally comparative sequence in a program made for the British anthropology series *Disappearing World*, David Turton writes:

> It is an excellent thing to demonstrate to the viewer that the subjects of the programme are not *that* different from ourselves, that we share with them a common humanity. . . . But the trouble with this technique of "domestication" is that it locates the focus and chief criterion of humanity in the *viewer*'s cultural experience: *our* behavior legitimates *theirs*. The problem we face in doing anthropology and, therefore, in putting it on television, is how to demonstrate the humanity we share with the people we study without privileging our own, or, as Faris puts it (Faris 1992:174), how to "obliterate otherness while preserving difference." (Turton 1992:291)

In attempting to come to terms with racist discourse, Shohat and Stam suggest that this duality of difference and similarity is part of liberalism more generally, which is both constitutively hierarchical and exclusionary (1994:25),[24] a charge levied at public television more broadly.[25] Their position is reminiscent of Hall's "hybrid space incorporating both similarity and continuity, on the one hand, and difference and rupture on the other" in which identity exists (Hall 1989:72).

We can ask whether these constructions of the other take on Clifford's allegorical function, where "every version of an 'other,' wherever found, is also the construction of a 'self,' and the making of ethnographic texts . . . has always involved a process of "self-fashioning" (Clifford 1986a:23–24). The producers' and advisors' intense and earnest debates about how to represent and compare different worlds of childhood, drawing on knowledge both scholarly and personal, inevitably involve a kind of projection of Western culture onto the world represented. As Annette Hamilton writes, "Imaginary relations at the social, collective level can thus be seen as ourselves looking at ourselves while we think we are seeing others" (Hamilton 1990:17). With documentary media like *Childhood,* the others are undeniably present within the text, but the mediation of their images into a comparative framework reveals concerns about raising children in a changing world, concerns that are both relevant elsewhere and uniquely placed in the twentieth-century United States.

CHAPTER SIX

Public Television Documentary and the Mediation of American Public Culture

THE MULTIPLICITY OF *CHILDHOOD*'S RECEPTION

Geoff Haines-Stiles returned from showing *Childhood*'s demo reel to those gathered at the national PBS meetings in Dallas in June 1990, still a year away from the series' scheduled broadcast date, with the sense that PBS's high-level administrators, the WNET supervisory staff, and the producers all agreed that the series had the potential to reach a level of success comparable to that gained by any of public television's most noteworthy series. Based on the positive reception the working project had received, *Childhood*'s producers believed that PBS would provide ample promotional backing, proper press coverage, and a favorable slot in the prime-time schedule. All of this would result in a high audience rating for a series with the subject matter (family life) and approach (multicultural, scientific) geared to the expanded audience that public television has been desperately seeking.

Their expectations went largely unmet. Although PBS did energetically promote *Childhood*, the system gave priority to another series, *Columbus and the Age of Discovery* (Dor-Ner 1991), scheduled to anticipate 1992s five-hundred-year anniversary celebration of America's discovery. *Columbus* aired during what PBS packaged and presented as its fall Showcase Week, a heavily advertised slate of prime-time programs, and went on to receive higher Nielsen ratings than *Childhood*. PBS scheduled *Childhood* several weeks later, beginning on October 14, and aired the show over seven nearly consecutive Mondays at 8:00 P.M. (Eastern Time), preempted for a special (*Land of the Eagle*; Crawford, Heeley, and Page 1991) between the sixth and seventh weeks. *Childhood* received an average national rating of 2.6, slightly higher than the PBS average prime-time rating of 2.5[1] (Schapiro 1991), but far from the record-breaking ratings garnered by *The Civil War* the previous fall.

The popular press reviews of the series were less glowing than the producers had hoped or expected.[2] *New York Times* writer Carin Rubenstein criticized the series: her review led with the heading, "A Tour of the Wonder Years: It's a Small, Small World," followed by the sarcastic lower-boxed subheadline, "The conclusion of the PBS series 'Childhood'? Kids do the darndest things" (Rubenstein 1991:29). Rubenstein faulted *Childhood* for failing to give useful parental advice (something the producers explicitly wanted to avoid), and glibly compared the observational scenes of family life to home videotapes: "In one program, we see a baby both before and after she learns to speak; another provides a fly-on-the-table view of several families at two consecutive Christmas dinners. It's like viewing your own home videos, only more tedious, because you don't know these people" (Rubenstein 1991:29). She disparaged what she interpreted as self-consciousness on the part of the families filmed and the obvious nature of the observers' on-camera comments. Her review ends with a barbed return to the home-video analogy: "Well-meaning mothers and fathers, trying to do one good thing, may decide to tape 'Childhood.' They could, instead, save the blank tapes and make a few more videos of their own" (Rubenstein 1991:33). The producers, upset with this review, responded with a letter to the editor, printed three weeks later, defending the authenticity of the footage— "Skilled documentary film crews are not Hollywood-style bands but two or three quiet, unobtrusive characters"—and the efforts of the makers of this "ambitious" series (Haines-Stiles, Akuginow, and Marner 1991:4). In personal correspondence, Haines-Stiles criticized Rubenstein's stance as "anti-child, New York trendy" and unrepresentative of the series' intended audience.

New York Times television columnist Walter Goodman's review the following day balanced a few criticisms with several compliments, and gave a more neutral evaluation than Rubenstein had provided.[3] The British magazine New Statesman and Society described the program as "pretty dreary" and criticized its naturalizing treatment of Third World cultures (French 1992), though note that the version of the series broadcast in England differed from the American version (Montagnon cut out eight minutes of material per episode and removed the music track in preparing the British version).

Criticism in other papers varied significantly. Newsweek's reviewer gave Childhood a mixed assessment: "Despite tiresome spurts of simplistic pedagogy, 'Childhood' is often fascinating. . . . Though 'Childhood' imparts no radical news, it has some remarkable and informative segments, particularly those on the acquisition of language—strikingly similar in both hearing and deaf children—and moral development" (Ames 1991).

More-positive reviews ran in other publications, offering discrepant opinions about specific textual features. Rather than "simplistic pedagogy," the critic for USA Today characterized the series as "nifty, delicate, and surprisingly eloquent" (Roush 1991:3) and the writer for the New York Daily News called it "a captivating, illuminating study." The Chicago Tribune's TV critic praised the way "experts . . . pop up at the right moments to explain things" (Kogan 1991:4), and, contrary to Rubenstein's ennui watching these children, the writer for the Montreal Gazette humorously warned that the series "is a real hormone hyper" that would "make viewers want to run upstairs to make babies" (Boone 1991:/F-2). This range of critical opinion for the series' reception, to which I return later in this chapter, raises questions about why the series did not succeed at the level anticipated. Were the typical audience ratings a function of poor promotion and scheduling? Did the public television system and the series producers overestimate the potential interest in this material and approach? Here, the range of reception these reviews represent acts as a check against an analytical reading of these texts.[4]

Despite its disappointing premiere, *Childhood* has had a healthy after-broadcast life. The series has been televised in England, repeated in the United States, and shown in other foreign markets, including Brazil, Australia, and several European countries. Ambrose Video, a major educational distributor, has handled nonbroadcast rights, and the videocassette package circulates in mail-order catalogs for home purchase. In addition, Haines-Stiles oversaw the packaging of the series into *Worlds of Childhood*, consisting of twenty-four shorter modules for classroom use.[5] Educational distribution has been widespread and well received. Still, what emerges from the series' reception (from initial proposal panels to press critics to audience members) is a sense of misunderstanding between the series' producers and their audience, a misunderstanding that Geoff Haines-Stiles reflected on in our correspondence after the series aired.

> Audience expectations are an absolute fact, but they can be managed in two ways—internal to the communication (art and craft of filmmaking) or through setting the scene (publicity, promotion, outreach, etc.) We could have done a better job in both regards. . . . We had too much of a hybrid, too many observers, too many all-be-they accurate and profound thoughts, too many mixed genres. Our audience wasn't ready for us . . . and we weren't ready for our audience—if we mean the mass-sized audience we let ourselves believe we had a shot at achieving. (Letter from Geoff Haines-Stiles to Barry Dornfeld, December 24, 1995).

Though he remains proud of these accomplishments, the disappointment that Haines-Stiles feels in this misunderstanding is evident. Based on the exchange he and I had in response to my analysis of the series, I think we can reframe this misunderstanding by explicating the multiple and disjunctive interpretations of what this series was and could have been, and by extension what American public television documentary and American public culture is, should, and could be.

To do so, I return to some of my observations from previous chapters to contextualize the practical theory and the logic of production practices employed by this group of public television producers and their associates in the making of the *Childhood* series. I then indicate how this kind of analysis of the processes of production can help to illuminate macrostructures of media and society (Corner 1991), a theoretical frame that media scholarship is eager to employ in such analyses. My argument concerns the conceptualization of a shared national public culture in the United States, an entity the public television system has hoped to tap into if not construct. In developing these broader observations, I need to recapitulate the ways this study addresses "how representational strategies are related to the institutional structures in which they emerge" (Morris 1994:4), addressing these relationships in three interrelated areas: the aesthetic, the financial, and the organizational.

AESTHETIC IDEOLOGIES

The narrowest of frames within which I position *Childhood* concerns the aesthetic conventions and generic history of documentary production as they are relevant to this form of public television program. The range of texts and practices considered documentary and the smaller, generally more conventional subset of styles practiced within public television exist as both a pool of aesthetic resources and conventions for documentary/educational program production the producers put into practice, and as a historically legitimated set of expectations and constraints they need to negotiate. My ethnographic analysis of these grounded aesthetics argued that to understand the work of documentary television production that constituted *Childhood*, we need to understand these resources, conventions, expectations, and constraints from the points of view of the agents who put them into practice. Producers' aesthetic ideologies grow out of their experience, and the experience of others prior to them, producing and consuming similar texts, mediated within both the institutional contexts that make up the public television system and the interpersonal contexts within which media production takes place. Their understandings of what constitutes "good television" in this context drove their decisions as they attempted to balance the imperatives of maintaining their viewers' attention while getting across the intellectual material they felt is necessary—all within the formats provided by and allowed for within an increasingly cautious public broadcasting environment.

This aesthetic ideology, rooted in conventions of academic and middle-brow culture, extends as well to the representation of cultural others for American audiences in public television documentary form. Many critics reviewing *Childhood* remarked on the multicultural nature of the series, usually cited as a positive feature, reflecting what are popular pleasures in knowing about cultural others. In constructing portraits of childhood life in other places in the world, in comparing the child-rearing practices of cultures different from our own, and in drawing distinctions between the typical and the stereotypical, *Childhood*'s producers searched out a middle ground between two positions. On the one hand, they occupied what might be termed a position of cultural relativism, the intellectual belief that people in specific cultural worlds and historical periods construct different worldviews of childhood life and engage in a variety of child-rearing practices. On the other hand, they held to a universalism rooted in both a liberal humanistic impulse to see a shared humanity beneath the surface of cultural differences and a scientific belief in the fundamental influence of shared biological characteristics.

The cross-cultural tropes the series relied upon have been a stable motif in public television documentary, just as they have in other forms of public culture, such as television commercials, popular magazines, and museum exhibits. More broadly, they are put to use as one important aesthetic resource in the attempt to negotiate tensions surrounding the series, and public broadcasting more generally, between television programs designed to be educational and television programs aspiring to attract a broader audience. The aesthetics of public television documentary then need to be understood in relation to these two competing models for cultural production: a pedagogical model and a market-driven model. Aesthetic strategies designed to balance the mission of educational programming against pragmatic needs for survival in this historical period need to be seen in relation to the ground of economic and symbolic forces at work in the system, all of which exert their influence on these media representations and practices.

THE ECONOMICS OF PRODUCTION:
"YOU ARE NEVER OUT FROM UNDER THE BUDGET"

Television production is, in most of its forms, extremely capital and labor intensive, requiring specialized equipment, materials, and personnel. *Childhood*'s budget of close to one million dollars per hour of television[7] situates this series within the most expensive levels of production common in public television. Having produced and worked on documentaries completed with budgets one-twentieth of what *Childhood* spent per program, I expected its producers to be relatively unconstrained by financial concerns. They would have a sufficient financial foundation, I reasoned, to proceed without concern for the economic implications of most of their decisions, and could be guided instead by purely thematic or aesthetic imperatives. In fact, this was far from the case. As another public television producer put it to me, these producers too were "never out from under the budget" and always had to weigh the financial implications of their intellectual, aesthetic, and logistical decisions. Indeed, almost every dimension of the series I analyzed in this study can be seen as both enabled and restricted by the available capital resources.

For instance, consider again the development and organization of *Childhood* within the pressures bearing on the PBS system at the time of the series' development (discussed in Chapter Two). *Childhood* originated through negotiations between two well-positioned producers with the institutional resources to obtain the necessary financial support for developing and producing such an ambitious series. Simultaneously, public television's history and present conditions created a situation where the system greatly desired the kind of program *Childhood* represents—a potential "blockbuster" national documentary series with high production values supported by eminent scholars, about a subject with the potential to attract a large, mainstream, and demographically advantageous audience without generating much potential for controversy. One could imagine other trajectories within public television where this kind of expensive programming, devoting extensive resources to a single series, would be undesirable (i.e., a period with severe budget cuts, or a reconfigured mission for public television during which the broadcast of risky alternative programs took precedent over ratings).[8] Still, although the system "wanted the series" and the producers raised much of the money they hoped to, they were not able to raise all the funds they felt they needed, nor as quickly as they hoped. This financial constraint had a profound effect on the evolution of the series, limiting the producers to seven one-hour programs and altering production plans.[9] The production values of the final episodes were given the highest priority, straining personnel resources and production schedules; but the system and the station's investments in *Childhood* obligated and constrained the producers to follow a specific strategy of production.

Budgetary limitations also constrained *Childhood*'s producers in their attempts to transcend the generic limitations of earlier long-form educational series, as I discussed in Chapter Four. Peter Montagnon described some changes in program design to which the producers resorted upon realizing that full funding might not be forthcoming, and the advantages in moving ahead rather than waiting to raise the complete budget they had proposed:

PETER MONTAGNON: So, we decided to go ahead. We then had to revise our plans because there's much less money in the budget, in the overall budget, so the plans to actually, in particular, large dramatized stuff, and overseas shooting, taking crews out, possibly with directors, had to go, because the money was just not there. So I had to reorganize the overall shoot—instead of sending out my ace camera guys I had to go around and try to find the right stringers that could do it.

DORNFELD: I didn't realize that that was partly out of necessity.

MONTAGNON: No. It came really out of the need to cut back, so what we did was, essentially, we cut the number of programs back, we cut the dramatized content back, and we cut the spending on the families back, by not shunting crews around the world, which is a hideously expensive operation. (Interview with Peter Montagnon, August 1, 1990)

The modifications in the plans Montagnon mentions were significant and multilayered. In Chapter Five, I considered how financial considerations influenced the choice of countries in which to film, given that the logistics of production in some countries made them too expensive.[10] Financial constraints also severely limited the methods by which the producers had proposed to treat history in the series, the "dramatized content" Montagnon describes, since they could not afford to stage historical sequences in a style that would provide the desired level of authenticity to work well alongside the documentary material.[11] Fund-raising strategy even impinged on content considerations in the development stages of the project, since potential gains could be made through financial arrangements with television entities in other countries. For instance, a WNET staff fund-raiser suggested to station management and *Childhood*'s executive producers the possibility of arranging a deal with Brazil's TV Globo for contributing to production costs in their country, in return for broadcast rights and the choice of Brazil as a location in which to film selected families.[12]

In the end, the producers had to balance production techniques for planned sequences that were efficacious against those most desirable in program terms, adapting earlier plans to practical constraints. Peter Montagnon saw a benefit from this financial pressure "because it meant that you could examine each one rigorously and say, just consider it, instead of just routinely saying, 'Well, you've got five minutes here, and we'll think about it later on what it's going to be.' One had to say quite rigorously, 'What can we afford to do,' and it's got to really be worth it" (interview with Peter Montagnon, August 1, 1990). These kinds of practical equations confronted the producers in working through many of the aesthetic and topical dimensions of the series: the acquisition of archival footage and stills, the number of days available to shoot the on-camera observer sequences, and the number and type of locations available for documentary scenes. The producers' commitment to the "families footage" represented a significant financial investment on their part, a danger they had been warned of by WNET. Their observational shooting involved extensive travel expenses incurred in finding suitable families and in production logistics, as well as payment to the local camera crews ("stringers") and buying the largest proportion of film stock expended in the series. Logging, synching up, screening, and preparing to incorporate this material in postproduction engaged the labor of assistant editors, translators, and the producer/directors and editors, and required extensive supplies of tape stock and additional equipment. Although the producers had allocated funds for most of these expenses in the production budget, they had not anticipated the complicated procedures that would be necessary to make this material accessible. A point was reached where the project ran out of available funds and time to generate and process more international family footage.

The budget that was available for only certain aspects of the production also constrained the attainable level of craft, an equation mediated by the factor of time. Given the labor expenses involved in production and post-production work, time became a capital resource to be appropriately distributed. An aphorism I heard from freelance crew members on this and other projects, "Speed, quality, or price—pick two" expresses the relationship between time, production value, and expense that is seen as operative in this mode of documentary production, and the tensions, from the freelancers' point of view, arising from producers' expectations. The aphorism indicates that freelancers (1) are only able to deliver a high-quality product quickly if they are given the necessary resources (sufficient time and/or adequate staff and equipment), (2) can find inexpensive solutions to production problems without sacrificing quality if they can take the necessary time to do so (allowing more preparation and shooting time), and, (3) if forced to work quickly with limited resources of staff and equipment, the quality of their work will suffer. In my view, *Childhood*'s producers tried to balance these three kinds of resources, giving the crew members adequate time and sufficient equipment while trying to keep staffing to a workable minimum to economize on expenditures. In the postproduction stages, these relationships intensified as temporal pressures mounted, requiring some modifications and simplifications in the series' content.

POWER, PRESTIGE, AND SOCIAL ORGANIZATION

The hierarchical and processual organization of the production informs the third level of understanding of production frameworks and practices as they are intertwined with aesthetics and economics. Although, as I described in Chapter Three, work on *Childhood* proceeded with a relatively egalitarian structure, a staff hierarchy existed nonetheless, based on an interaction of power and expertise, measured in the resources that individuals brought to the project, their backgrounds and competencies, and their varied levels of commitment and lengths of participation. Compensation in forms of both financial capital (a stepped pay scale) and career capital (the value to be gained from specific credits and experiences garnered from the series) varied as well. I described at length the relationship between producers and advisors, which represents a critical dynamic of power. The fact that the executive producers hired the project's academic advisors, rather than the other way around, influenced the relations of power between these two groups.

The advisors were ultimately at the service of the producers, although their reputations and expertise provided them with a significant amount of symbolic capital and therefore authorial power to exert control over the programs. In a sense they lent their symbolic capital to *Childhood*, which displayed (i.e., through promotional material about the series referring to its impressive advisory panel) and employed (through contributions to the actual programs) that resource, adding to the value of the series. Haines-Stiles and Montagnon, the two executive producers, rested at the top of a pyramid of decision-making, with Akuginow and Marner, the two producer/directors, situated at the next node down. Associate producers, researchers, production assistants, and freelancers were at the lower end. The advisors exerted an authorial force as well. Negotiations of responsibility, strategy, and authority within this social organization influenced the shaping of the texts themselves, and they complicate our understanding of the nature of authorship within this communicative context. The ever-present consideration of the pragmatic, often financial, consequences for this evaluative work evidences a practical logic influencing all evaluative and communicative actions, a point I will return to shortly.

Those working within public broadcasting stand to gain a good deal of status from their labor, but this status comes with a measure of financial penalty. When mapped against other domains of film and television production, work in public television offers lesser financial rewards (lower rates) in return for greater prestige and a kind of moral and intellectual elevation. With *Childhood*, production staff and freelancers were willing to surrender some degree of financial compensation for the privilege of working on the series.[13] At the same time, the production itself could extend its resources in part by utilizing its prestige, at times requesting rate reductions from individuals and production facilities. For staff members, this equation of status versus financial reward was always complicated and calculated in relation to an individual's status with the series and their judgment of how this series might contribute to their individual career trajectories. This status can be seen as related to the building up of a name, a form of personal cultural capital.[14] The staff members either had to be part of a class and occupational fragment that could take advantage of this appropriation of value, or have personal reasons why this perceived disavowal of accumulation is worthwhile. The "profits" gained by those involved with *Childhood* are complex, varied, and speculative: higher audience ratings and funds for PBS and WNET, future projects funded for the producers, opportunities for advancement and for substantive work experience for staff and freelancers, and the potential for a higher-profile publication for me.

The *Childhood* series itself also benefited from its symbolic capital. Staff members used the project's status as a major PBS/WNET series to gain access to people and locations that might have been denied to a smaller, independent documentary or to a commercial production. Early in the production period, a question arose about whether the producers could bring a crew to film in a public junior high school in New Rochelle, New York. The producers had already committed themselves to the choice of the Kirkpatrick family in New Rochelle as one of the two American families they would follow throughout the series and had counted on filming in the classrooms the Kirkpatrick children attended. When arranging for a shoot in Shannon Kirkpatrick's junior high school class, they were told that the school system had a strict policy prohibiting filming in their classrooms, a potential dilemma given that they had already put a fair amount of time and energy into filming this family. Rather than accept this policy as unyielding and risk having to rethink the use of the Kirkpatrick family, the producers mounted a campaign to gain access, faxing letters, a series prospectus, and other information to a school board meeting taking place shortly thereafter. To everyone's surprise, the school system agreed to allow the crew to film, for reasons related to the nature of the series and the status of the project as a production of WNET, and PBS. This kind of cultural power represents a form of "symbolic capital" (Bourdieu 1986:132) that, on occasion, the series expended.

Capital, both financial and social, operates as a locus between the pragmatic dimensions of production practices, the shape of the text itself, and social meaning (interpretation and evaluation). Capital both enables and constrains production, even in a field where profit-making (as conventionally conceived) is not a goal. The importance of these resources to The *Childhood* Project illustrates what Bourdieu has described as the economic logic present even in presumably "disinterested" (economically) cultural fields. With *Childhood*, the stakes for which individuals (at different positions in the project hierarchy) and various institutions (PBS, WNET, Channel Four, The *Childhood* Project, Antelope Films) play will vary as well and analytically merge the nonmaterial with the material. This television text, just as any communicative product or event, is invested with and yields differing values for the various parties involved in its production and broadcast. Such values are intensified with the amount of money and labor invested in a project. The prevailing economic logic, the result of the encounter of a theory of practice with limited resources, constrains practical action and locates the producers and the series within a broader field of cultural production. The success of the series and its value in the careers and histories of the individuals and institutions responsible for it would be measured by a combination of factors including the ratings the series received, its reviews in the popular press, its post-broadcast life in educational and home distribution, and the reactions from relevant scholarly communities.

QUALITY TIME? THE SOCIAL SPACE OF PBS
DOCUMENTARY PRODUCTION

The producers' frameworks for decision making and the strategies and practices they employ are oriented by their positions within the social space of public television production. These positions can be demarcated by various factors: the relevant models for program production the producers value and incorporate, their own previous work and the work they hope to do in the future, their place within the institutional hierarchies and constraints of this territory of cultural production, and their lives within the social spaces they occupy outside their labor. The *Childhood* series itself can also be placed in a social and historical trajectory. We can look at the limitations and constraints imposed on the series by the social field within which it was produced along the dimensions considered in this study—setting, authorship, poetics, and cross-cultural representation—and see choices made by the agents involved in the production from among "the space of possibles" (Bourdieu), defined by the present state of public television programming and the agents' own place within that territory.[15] By looking at the relationships between this cultural production and these broader social forces, we can raise larger questions about the consequences of the series as an example of contemporary public culture in the United States.

The social setting, the conditions structuring public television at the time this program was made, put in place broad parameters within which *Childhood*'s producers worked. PBS's "need" to broaden its audience and strengthen certain demographic segments (including the age bracket of young parents), driven by unstable financial and threatening political circumstances, made a series such as this an attractive opportunity. *Childhood*'s subject matter resonated with the "family values" orientation popular with conservative social movements in the 1990s, and its populist subject matter offered the potential to tap into these underserved audiences. The system's "blockbuster mentality," its strategy for revitalizing its identity, propelled by the success of *The Civil War* series, presented the producers with a model to aspire to and criteria to obtain. The ongoing political attacks on the system—attacks that carry potentially dire financial consequences—limit the kinds of risks that the institutions supporting the series were willing to take and contribute to the definitions of relevant ideas and formats to be presented in televisual form. These tendencies configure with Hoynes's arguments (1994, cited earlier) about public television's increasing market orientation.

The social organization of television production, what we might call the "culture of documentary authorship," influenced the course of production as well. The division of authorial responsibility resulting from a particular hierarchy of personnel was combined with the necessity of creating a series that was coherent and consistent from episode to episode (requiring the sharing of footage and sequences). These procedures led to a production style that discouraged authorial distinctiveness. This authorial ideology was voiced by Geoff Haines-Stiles (see Chapter Three) when he contrasted this PBS series and what he termed "auteur films." Authorship here was seen as collegial and negotiated, among the production staff and between producers and advisors. The orientation of the series toward a broad public audience, including the funding it received, its high visibility as a major PBS series, and its eventual position on the PBS schedule, constrained the producers, who had to work in a style that would accommodate a broad cross section of audience segments and make the material clear for them. At the same time, the series had a more limited set of viewers to appeal to within internal and external institutions of power (public broadcasting organizations, funding agencies, institutions for social policy, and academia). The producers employed a format and style that attempted to balance broad audience engagement with the necessary criteria for what Nichols calls "a discourse of sobriety," that is, documentaries dedicated to disseminating information and knowledge. The construction of these relevant audiences and their interests had a formative impact on the series from its inception through broadcast. Simultaneously, the genre of major documentary series that preceded *Childhood* presented the project with a range of thematic and stylistic strategies from which to choose, and eliminated others. Haines-Stiles and David Loxton designed the series to be comprehensive and global, as previous series from *Civilisation* to *Cosmos* had also been. They felt strongly that *Childhood* had to be rooted in scientific knowledge that was current, even cutting edge. However, the choice of established scholars as advisors and the process of negotiation and compromise around intellectual approaches and issues for inclusion resulted in a construction of the study of childhood that would favor "legitimate" and "accepted" views and avoid more radical perspectives. The genre prescribed proven stylistic strategies—on-camera hosts, observational footage and historical imagery interwoven with omniscient, expository narration, and a high level of production values—and restricted others.[16] The air of conservatism around PBS and WNET further discouraged the producers from innovating within the genre.

On the broadest level, I argue that *Childhood* became the kind of series it did in large part because of its configuration within the present moment of agitation and adjustment in the public television system and within the life history of WNET, one of the highest-profile stations within PBS. *Childhood* was a high-budget multipart series, a form that distinguishes programming on the public television schedule and is undertaken when the system is searching for, or at least reconsidering, its identity in the ecology of broadcast television and grappling for a greater share of certain audiences. The system's support of these national series was described by one writer as "yielding to public television's equivalent of Hollywood's blockbuster mentality" (Schapiro 1991:31), investing significant resources in several large projects and avoiding risky topics. *Childhood*'s existence needs to be seen within this context as part of the public television system's strategy for expanding its audience base. This strategy created three principal imperatives that framed the series in important ways. First, the system wanted to broaden its audience by developing and broadcasting more populist programs, showing material whose subject matter might appeal to a larger demographic proportion of the American viewing audience than the more elitist programs for which the system was famous (or infamous). A series about family life seemed to fit that requirement rather easily. Second, the system looked for programs that would avoid offending conservative political sentiments— programs that were safe. While I do not think that the series intentionally steered away from difficult political topics to avoid offending segments of viewers, the producers did consciously exclude an approach that would dwell on the poor conditions of children's lives internationally and historically. The portrait of the families that evolved did not exclude domestic and social conflict, disease, and poverty but set these negative dimensions as a background to a more positive view of the life of children. In fact, several reviewers remarked upon what came across as the model behavior of most of the families in the series. The producers did their best to avoid a critical and dogmatic tone in the series assessment of the variety of approaches used to bring up children. This second strategy ties in with a third: the desire for a multicultural focus in public television programming. Just as *Childhood* began full-scale production, PBS appointed Jennifer Lawson as its executive vice president of programming and promotion; one approach she stressed in rethinking public television programming was multiculturalism, which she defined as "our commitment to cultural diversity" (cited in Day 1995:303– 4),[17] a statement that is nothing if not multicultural. I hope that this analysis has adequately addressed the construction and evolution of the series' multicultural approach. In large part because of these broader forces, *Childhood*'s orientation became populist, politically neutral, and multicultural. The way the individuals and institutions involved in the series' production constructed and constrained the framing of this material is intertwined with and reveals a great deal about the emergence of contemporary American public culture and the tensions within it: about how public television producers mediate the cultural worlds and bodies of information they represent, how public television conceives of and encodes scholarly and scientific knowledge in television documentary form, and how producers and administrators go about projecting who their audiences will be.

The opposing imperatives of education and commerce, embedded in the structure of public television itself and as an outgrowth of its complex institutional history, pull public television in two directions simultaneously. They are reflected in competing discourses about the purpose of public television, in the texts produced and broadcast, and in the competing authorial stances taken by those who produce them. In the field of television news production, these opposing imperatives take the form of information versus entertainment—that is, the pedagogical function is given less emphasis. Public television, combining an educational mission with a medium consumed in practices of leisure, operates under its own particular and often paradoxical cultural logic, one that attempts to balance education versus entertainment, but education and entertainment seen in specific ways. The structures that facilitate production and distribution of the programs that are broadcast on the PBS system have to mediate this dual logic and inflect the system itself with certain constraints in production.

By stepping back from *Childhood* and considering the series' place, and the place of public television, in the spheres of cultural production in the United States, we are forced to rethink the debates and conflicts over the mission of public broadcasting and its place in our national public culture. At various points in this study, I have characterized the producers' points of view as lodged in tensions between opposing tendencies or imperatives— between education and entertainment, between pedagogical significance and audience engagement, and between social scientific relativism and what I termed "televisual humanism." From the economic perspective considered above, we can argue that these tensions locate this series (and similar material on public television) between highbrow culture on the one hand and something like middlebrow (or middle-to-lowbrow) culture on the other. The crisis in mission and identity burdening the public broadcasting system is reflected in these very tensions, which the system's programming strategies help to perpetuate.

A PBS show such as *Childhood* struggles to traverse the gap between the popular sensibilities historically attributed to and expected from television— characterized by dramatic and narrative satisfaction, character identification, certain kinds of visual and aural aesthetics, the favoring of humor over sobriety, and the demands of "enlightened" educational enrichment—with its scientific authenticity and substantiality, verbal exposition, and extractable intellectual conclusions.[18] Of course, the popular sensibility that public television seeks is not that of the mass audience (which is left to network television), but of the educated, demographically advantaged lay person, the viewer interested in spending some "quality time." But herein lies an unreconcilable tension, since in many class and regional sectors of the United States, the consumption of television is treated primarily as a leisure activity, and intellectual pursuits are resisted as part of this leisure. As Andrew Ross argued (1989), intellectuals and intellectual discourse have historically had a problematic and somewhat marginal place in American popular culture. Pub-

lic television is one primary arena for what Ross described as the recruit-
ment of intellectuals into public culture, where "experts" are given a prominent televisual role. Still, this arena remains constrained in its abilities to
claim more of the social terrain than it already occupies.

If, as Ross argues, "popular culture is the source for most people of the
"common sense" that ideologically absorbs and demystifies the specialist
discourses that saturate these new technologies of knowledge" (Ross
1989:213), then the place of intellectuals within emerging televisual spheres
will be never be one of comfort. Much public television is produced in a
troublesome and unequal collaboration between scholarly experts and the
empowered, educated, but somewhat anti-academic agents who become that
special breed of documentary producers and who hold the ultimate power in
these struggles. Except in rare circumstances, because of their competence in
creating certain forms of televisual discourse and because of their central
place in this escalating field of cultural production, producers control access
to the popular cultural forms that will serve to reproduce this emerging culture. We saw how these tensions continued to bubble up to the surface during the life of the *Childhood* series. On the aesthetic level, the tensions
between information and drama, exposition versus observational sequences,
hard data versus soft illustrations, and sobriety versus engagement resurfaced
repeatedly. Public television in the United States is caught between being a
prominent place for cultural/intellectual improvement and being a technology for the practice of leisure and entertainment. Its very existence is caught
within and perpetuates tensions deeply embedded in the macro-structures
that constitute television's function in American public culture—tensions between discourses of public interest and of corporate-driven entertainment.

This schism, central to American public broadcasting, can be clarified by
comparisons with public broadcasting in other national settings. For reasons
that are both historical and institutionally reproduced, American public television documentary is propelled by an ideology for the encoding of knowledge into televisual form that borrows more from British models of cultural
enlightenment through television than from the orientation of television in
American culture. In fact, several programs that have become mainstays of
public television in the United States, such as the science program *Nova*,
explicitly borrowed from British program ideas. There is some irony here,
though, since the British broadcasting system was explicitly designed to
avoid the commercialism present in American broadcasting. In the United
States, the place of public broadcasting in national cultural life is much more
tendentious and problematic than in other industrialized nations in Europe,
Asia, and North America. In places like Great Britain, Canada, and Australia, vital policy discussion exists over the state funding of television, driven
by the belief that the maintenance of a national cultural identity is at stake.
As Toby Miller described with regard to both Australia and Canada, "there is

little doubt that this desire to form a national identity underlay much of the argument for state subvention of film and television" (Miller 1993:128).

The thrust in these other national settings is to argue for both a moral and a pedagogical function for television, and to bolster this mandate with institutional supports in funding certain forms of programming (educational, public affairs) and restricting others (entertainment-based, imported). The situation is rather the opposite in the United States, where the public broadcasting system has been rhetorically attacked as contrary to our national economic ideology (anti-free market), or as destructive of the kind of value-based moral identity that political conservatives favor. A conflict exists then between the liberal social imperatives behind the founding of the public broadcasting system as part of Lyndon Johnson's Great Society government programs, essentially a social-welfare, anti-market ideology, and the more libertarian, free-market contemporary political/economic climate. Much of the cultural and political conflict can also be traced back to divisions of class and regionalism. Indeed, part of the popular resistance, hostility, criticism, and political contentiousness felt toward public television stems from the perception that it is a system designed by and for cultural elites and political liberals (mostly from the Northeast), a charge that the institutions devoted to the system's vitality simultaneously disavow and embrace.[19]

In fact, the contradictions inherent in the work of public television result from its place in a contested, hybrid field, combining economic and educational motives, similar to other middlebrow institutions recently examined by scholars, such as *National Geographic* magazine (Lutz and Collins 1993) and the Book-of-the-Month Club (Radway 1988b). Unlike forms of cultural production that disavow profit, public television cannot afford to be indifferent to financial concerns and seeks to unite the acquisition of financial and cultural capital. But it does so without the full endorsement and financial support of national cultural or educational policy and is therefore forced to compete through a market-based model of fund-raising, program underwriting, and viewer donations (as Hoynes has argued). The system is hence caught within the contradictory impulses of entertainment and enlightenment, of popular culture and academic culture. Public broadcasting's attempts to find a neutral common ground within this arena, though perhaps a political necessity, contribute to its lack of a clear vision and mission and its marginal success historically.

The irony is that a major PBS series like *Childhood* contains the potential to transcend these limitations and to point the way for a new vision for public media, while it simultaneously reveals the reasons why this transcendence is so rarely reached. Its potential comes from a synergy of real and impressive intelligence and craft with an unusual level of support of financial and cultural resources, committed to producing in a medium that can make important ideas vital and accessible. Yet the pressures on this medium to fulfill several conflicting agendas, to balance the imperatives mentioned above, steer its televisual realization toward positions and articulations that are often politically, intellectually, and aesthetically neutralized, rarely living up to the potential for which those within and without the project would hope. How and in what way these projects will change remains to be seen. Clearly programs like this have a threatened existence in the emerging media landscape as the conditions facing public television endanger its most noteworthy and historically consistent programming fare. Despite their limitations and the work of compromise involved in their production, the loss of PBS series like *Childhood* would be a loss for shared civic culture in the United States.

ELECTRONIC COMMUNITIES, PUBLIC SPHERES, AND NATIONALITIES: RETHINKING MEDIA AS PUBLIC CULTURE

So what can we make of the relative lack of audience attention and mixed press responses for *Childhood*, a series destined and consecrated for success? In its broadest interpretation, the series' lack of national success reflects the problematic place of public television in American public culture. Ultimately, I attribute the mixed reaction the series received to what I perceive as differences between class and regional fragments within American culture, and to related disagreements over what people think public television should be. It would be convenient if we could map the differences between reviews in the *New York Times*, more populist publications like *USA Today* and the *New York Daily News*, and smaller papers like the *Cleveland Plain Dealer* onto social differences between readerships real or perceived. However, frameworks for reception are not usually so easily categorized or linked to demographics or geographies. And though their writing styles classify them as they classify the texts they review, critics are too unpredictable and idiosyncratic to succumb to this simple pigeonholing process. Ultimately most of the critics understood and appreciated the series' intentions, and from this we can conclude that *Childhood* was a typical PBS series. But the differences between critics' assessments of the worth of the series indicate more dissent than agreement over the value of public television documentaries like *Childhood*, and it is this lack of consensus that needs to be explicated. If we extrapolate this diversity of opinion and interest to some body of television viewers, we can see how the issue of consensus dissipates even further.

This line of thinking raises pertinent questions about the constitution of American public culture: Can we locate an abstraction such as "the public sphere" in any empirical basis in the United States? What is the place of public television within such a projection, given the highly commercial and corporate, technologically volatile, and socially fragmented nature of American public cultural life? The issue of nationality and the role that media forms play in the making of national cultures, central to the emerging work in the anthropology of media and other fields,[20] challenges us with regard to the United States. Theories of public culture or the public sphere that look at national media as reflective of some monolithic national identity do not do justice to the conflictive nature of these cultural forces and elide the ways these forces, based in tensions over class and culture, are embedded in the structures and process of cultural production. Unlike the case in many other countries, developed and developing, with state-sponsored television systems, the United States has a unique situation in that the television network the government supports is marginalized in terms of its viewership, representing one choice along the expanding televisual landscape and garnering only a few percentage points of the average national television audience. I would argue that rather than producing a shared national culture (as one might argue the BBC has done with some success), programs like *Childhood* are not only indicative of tensions within American public cultures, but also, crucially, serve to reproduce or even foster them. The various cultural frames that producers, scholars, bureaucrats, critics, and viewers bring to the work of production and reception are reflective of a broader cultural fragmentation than our typical understandings of media acknowledge, and perhaps they serve to produce this very fragmentation rather than construct some shared democratic forum or public sphere.

Commentators either in favor or critical of the public television system tend to share the view of the system as a hybrid and conflictive conglomerate of national policy, borrowing from and loosely based on the British model but with a haphazard history leading to its current state of confusion. It would therefore be problematic to speak of public television as reflective of a dominant national consciousness or political ideology, of a "national imaginary," particularly in light of the vehement and politically and regionally factionalized debates over what public television is and should be, without positing that national imaginary as a multiple and contested one, as some have done (see Ginsburg 1993 and Appadurai 1990). At the same time, the portion of society that both watches and produces the programming, and that supports these institutions, includes a powerful segment of the cultural elite. As *Childhood*'s producers were well aware, this gives public television an important role in the production of the public sphere and in cultural policy. Michael Schudson (1991) has suggested that we need to question the relevance of the very notion of the public sphere. Media critics and advocates cling to the argument that the only path to participatory democracy in the present period of an increasingly technological public culture includes a more progressive and participatory function for electronic communication, holding onto the hopes of what Lewis Friedland termed "the notion of an enlightened public sphere in the realm of broadcasting" (Friedland 1995). While I do not want to seem overly pessimistic, the prospects of television playing such a progressive role seem to me to be fading. Perhaps emerging new technologies can serve to reinvent new possibilities for public discourse and new forms of democracy, though with the increasing concentration and broadening of corporate control over new media technologies and spaces and the ever limiting governmental role for enforcement of public interests, I remain skeptical. What these discourses of public service for electronic communication do illuminate is the extent to which American public broadcasting's place in public culture differs from the experiences of other industrialized nations, and the poverty of our own civic discourse about public media.

Additionally, since television series like *Childhood* circulate outside our national borders, how can we reconcile the potential meanings produced by a diversity of audiences watching these programs, which are often bi- or multinational coproductions anyway? How do works imported from outside national borders contribute to the imagination of a national identity (Anderson 1991)? Anderson's notion of an imagined community is critically relevant here, since the "viewers like you" that the institution of public television is seeking, the audiences it needs to construct, become an imagined community on which it depends. Though this community aspires to some shared national participation, in the end it remains largely a community based in class and cultural exclusions, a community whose hybrid boundaries reflect the culture of production in which it is grounded.

However, to extend this community's influence to the level of the national would misapprehend the increasingly global "mediascapes" (Appadurai) that American media forms are intertwined within, the control of flows of electronic narratives and information. The comparisons to state-dominated mediascapes like those we find in European countries reveal that the media flows in the United States are much more controlled by corporate interests than in other countries.[21] Clearly these differences are eroding, as industrialized countries give over more and more of their broadcast infrastructure to private control and interests (many of them global rather than national, such as Rupert Murdoch's expanding multinational media conglomerate). Corporate and market forces control our dominant national media and leave only a small, marginal space for public interest considerations. This situation has clear historical precedents, since corporate interests have exerted control over broadcasting since the late 1920s, when "they began to sense the immense profitability of advertising-supported broadcasting" (McChesney 1995: 16). Since then, they have dominated policy debates and eclipsed attempts to limit their dominance of the airwaves, constraining public broadcasting in the process. The result, of course, has been a national media ecology dominated by corporate interests—hardly the public sphere that Habermas imagined and which European scholars continue to advocate—or the electronic democracy touted by American pundits. The pressures public broadcasting has always felt are fundamentally determined by its marginal position in our national public culture.[22]

Perhaps a more accurate way to employ the notion of "the public sphere" is not in the sense that Habermas developed the term—as a potential site for the building of a national democracy—or in the way theories of public culture have employed the concept, that is, as the arena through which national identities are imagined and contested. We might better envision public spheres as fragmented and multiple, as extensions of community and class-based discourses (without the geographic orientation we usually refer to when we speak of community). Nancy Fraser has reconstructed the idea of the public sphere with the notion of "subaltern counterpublics" to acknowledge the existence and importance of "parallel discursive arenas where members of subordinated social groups invent and circulate counterdiscourses, which in turn permit them to formulate oppositional interpretations of their identities, interests, and needs" (Fraser 1990:67). This more fragmented and stratified notion of multiple spheres, or mediascapes, allows us to rethink our understandings of media production and consumption as well, to see media texts as emanating from certain cultural, institutional formations (public television producers, independent media makers, conservative religious broadcasters, etc.) and received by multiple communities of audiences involved in forging their diverse identities. Media texts do not *make* these communities or identities (nor do they make national formations) any more than traditional religious rituals make cultures, but both reflect and influence the imaginative and constructive processes by which these identities are formed.

American public culture is a much more contested sphere in terms of class and racial differences than our public debate acknowledges, certainly more than our media texts represent. The way the institutions of public television imagine the communities they reach, or hope to reach, clearly plays a critical role in their members' processes of identity formation. The identities the public sphere's diverse communities are constituted within and serve to re-create are deeply contested ones—contested simultaneously by corporate forces, conservative ideologies, advocates for independent and alternative media practices, and cultural populists on both the left and the right. Seeing media production as this more complex "cultural field" involves an attempt to locate simultaneously and in relation to each other the perspectives, interests, and practices of producers, production staff, PBS administrators, viewers, and the myriad institutions with which they interact, and it allows us to discuss both agency and process in terms of these structural relations. The result, I hope, is an understanding that is more relational, one that positions aesthetic decisions in relation to the social conditions of production, seen in institutional, historical, and financial contexts. In an important sense, this is an argument about agency, an argument to restore the agents of production to a more central place in media theory, a place recently usurped by audiences. However, it is not an argument to restore dominating power to producers or the moments of production, since one of my central points is to see production and reception as completely intertwined, interdependent processes, only separable for transient intellectual or professional purposes.

Analyzing media production through on the ground practices and against the background of institutional settings provides a different kind of qualitative understanding for how media forms make meaning, one that forces us to confront both the symbolic and the material conditions and practices of production. The negotiations producers engage in with administrators, funders, scholars, crew members, subjects, programmers, promoters, critics, and ultimately viewers (though all the previous are important viewers as well) represent acts of mediation that result in media texts. The forms of mediation that result in the production of a television program are socially and historically situated in relation to other public cultural forms. In this sense, television is not just a form of media but a format through which complex acts of cultural mediation take place, and through which a fragmented society produces and reproduces its differences even while it searches for some forms of commonality.

Organizational Chart of the *Childhood* Staff

THIS ORGANIZATIONAL chart roughly maps out the hierarchy of authority and decision-making on The *Childhood* Project staff. Please note that individuals who simultaneously held two separable positions are represented in two places. Freelance production personnel are not listed here but come under the authority of the producer/directors and associate producers. The editors are listed with the program numbers of the episodes they edited; all had assistants who worked under them.

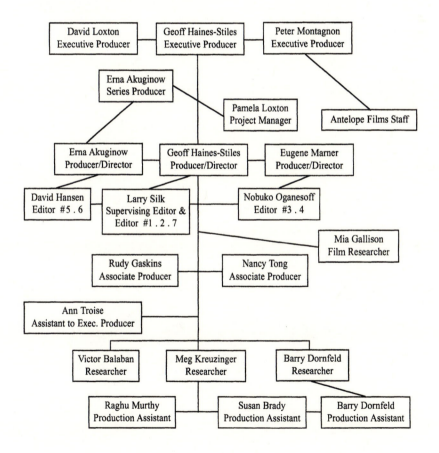

The series credits listed the following:

Executive Producer: Geoff Haines-Stiles (also produced and directed three of the programs)

Producer/Director/Writers: Erna Akuginow (also the Series Producer/Production Manager) and Eugene Marner, both of whom directed two programs

Project Manager: Pamela Loxton

Associate Producers: Rudy Gaskins and Nancy Tong

Assistant to Executive Producer and Art Researcher: Ann Troise

Project Coordinator: Myra Stetser

Researchers: Victor Balaban, Barry Dornfeld, and Meg Kreuzinga

Film/Photo Research: Mia Gallison

Production Assistants: Raghu Murthy, Susan Brady, and Stephanie Howard

Editors: Larry Silk, Nobuko Oganesoff, and David Hanson

Assistant Editor: Jeanne Chien

Associate Editor: Michael Balabuch

Dailies Coordinator: Phoebe Yantsios

Editing Apprentice: Patrick McGuinn

List of Academic Observers and Advisors
(in alphabetical order)

Childhood's Observers (also Advisors)

Urie Bronfenbrenner, Professor of Human Development, Emeritus, Cornell University

Marian Wright Edelman, Director, Children's Defense Fund

Robert Hinde, Professor, Medical Research Council on the Development and Integration of Behavior, Cambridge University, and Master of St. John's College

Jerome Kagan, Professor of Developmental Psychology, Harvard University

Melvin Konner, Professor of Anthropology, Emory University, and an M.D.

Sandra Scarr, Professor and Chair, Psychology Department, University of Virginia

OTHER MEMBERS OF THE ADVISORY PANEL

Elizabeth Bates, Professor of Psychology, University of California/San Diego

Henry Steele Commager, Professor Emeritus, Amherst University

Jonathan Cott, author of *Beyond the Looking Glass* and *Forever Young*

N. Ray Hiner, Professor of History and Education, University of Kansas

Richard B. Lee, Professor of Anthropology, University of Toronto

Lewis Lipsitt, Director, Child Study Center, Brown University

Neil Postman, Professor of Media, New York University, and author of *The Disappearance of Childhood*

Alvin Poussaint, Child Psychiatrist, Judge Baker Guidance Clinic, Boston

Harriet Rosenberg, Professor of History and Sociology, York University

Jay Ruby, Professor of Anthropology, Temple University; Director, Center for Visual Communication

Julius Segal, author and former Director of Public Information, National Institute of Mental Health

Thomas Weisner, Professor of Anthropology and Psychology, UCLA

Robert Wozniak, Professor of Developmental Psychology, Bryn Mawr College

Synopsis of the *Childhood* Series

THE FOLLOWING descriptions are adapted from the Ambrose Video Publishing Catalog, through which *Childhood* is available for home and educational distribution. These descriptions are the promotional announcements for the series; they are excerpted here to provide an outline of program content for the episodes.

PROGRAM ONE: *GREAT EXPECTATIONS*

One of the major themes of the "Childhood" series is introduced and explored—the mutual influence and importance of both "nature and "nurture," the ongoing interaction of time, place, and biology. Highlights of the premiere program include witnessing three births—in Russia, America, and Brazil, to show how different societies approach this universal, yet unique, experience. 57 minutes.

PROGRAM TWO: *LOUDER THAN WORDS*

An infant may not be able to speak, but research clearly shows that the roots of future personality are present from birth. Observer Jerome Kagan shows why shyness and sociability have a distinct biological component. But is biology destiny? We explore how parents' expectations and actions come to shape a child's behavior and character. 57 minutes.

PROGRAM THREE: *LOVE'S LABORS*

An exploration of the fascinating period between six months and three years, when almost every day brings startling evidence of rapid maturation in brain and body—improved coordination, increased mobility, the acquisition of language, and an emerging sense of self. We discover how babies and infants are not powerless but are instead active participants in a world they affect and change almost from birth. 57 minutes.

PROGRAM FOUR: *IN THE LAND OF THE GIANTS*

This program features three- to five-year-olds learning the social and psychological intricacies of family life. Observer Urie Bronfenbrenner characterizes the family as "the most efficient means for making human beings human." As the wider world affects the family, the family in turn teaches children how to view and cope with that wider world as they increasingly interact with it at day care and school. Families use varying models of behavior and codes of discipline to mold their children in their culture's proper social image. 57 minutes.

PROGRAM FIVE: *LIFE'S LESSONS*

Between the ages of five and seven, children enter a new and distinctive stage of development called middle childhood, marked by the phenomenon known as "the 5–7 shift." This change is demonstrated by new abilities and behaviors as children move away from the intimacy of home and family to enter the wider arena of school and work. In sequences showing the first day of school in several countries, this program shows how such universal milestones are recognized by different cultures, and looks at what recent research says makes for effective education. 57 minutes.

PROGRAM SIX: *AMONG EQUALS*

This program explores the importance of peer relationships as a crucial component of development. Peers provide a context for working out moral dilemmas, social relationships, and for developing a strong self-identity. Between middle childhood and adolescence, children often participate in youth groups and team sports—games that sometimes become rehearsals for life. We see how boys of this age usually play with boys, and girls with girls. 57 minutes.

PROGRAM SEVEN: *THE HOUSE OF TOMORROW*

The "Childhood" journey concludes with a look at the many emotional and physical transformations that characterize puberty and adolescence. This program shows how this biological metamorphosis—when boys and girls become men and women—is marked in various cultures. We see that whether adolescence is a time of stress or manageable change critically depends upon how parents and teachers respond to a child's uniqueness throughout the years of childhood. The series concludes by reminding viewers that it matters greatly what we do and say to our children—they are, as Neil Postman once wrote, "living messages to a time we will not see." 57 minutes.

For ordering information contact:

Ambrose Video Publishing, Inc.
1290 Avenue of the Americas, Suite 2245
New York, NY 10104   1-800-526-4663

Chapter One
Studying Public Television as American Public Culture

1. I take up the problems involved in defining and applying this term to American media forms and practices at various points in this study, particularly in Chapter Six.

2. There exists an extensive literature debating the history of public service broadcasting in Great Britain, the role of the BBC in this history, and the place of recently ascending arguments in favor of a greater role of privatization and the market in broadcasting. See Garnham (1990), Scannell (1992), and Ang (1991) for debates about this issue and about the place of public broadcasting in the public sphere and in processes of nationalism. See also Blumler (1991) for a comparative consideration of the changing nature of these forces in the newly emerging televisual landscape.

3. Noteworthy exceptions are Bruce Cumings's _War and Television_ (1992), which examines the WGBH/BBC coproduction _Korea: The Unknown War_ and Dwight Hoover's (1992) study of the PBS series _Middletown_.

4. See Sreberny-Mohammadi (1991) for an interrogation of models of the global and the local in media studies, and for suggestions on how to transcend these problematics.

5. As Jay Ruby writes: "For reasons unclear to me the application of ethnographic methods to the study of mass communication still remains a novel and little used technique. Among some communication scholars it has become chic to talk about and employ some 'qualitative' methods. However, mass communications research is dominated by quantitative methods that are culture blind. Anthropology and communication studies have failed to realize the potential power of ethnography for gaining insight into western culture" (Ruby 1990:35–36). See Spitulnik (1993) for an excellent survey of work that fits within this convergence of anthropology and media studies.

6. See Gross (1981) for an overview of Worth's work.

7. Historically, the field of visual anthropology was slow to take up Worth's summons and has only recently moved beyond a preoccupation with the use of ethnographic film and photography in anthropological teaching to look at the visual dimensions of cultural processes. Ginsburg's "mild polemic" in favor of an anthropology of the media along with her ethnographic writing on the notion and nature of indigenous media exemplifies the turn toward a more politically and culturally rich engagement with the representation of culture beyond the boundaries of ethnographic film proper (Ginsburg 1993, 1994). The ongoing discussions within visual anthropology about ideologies of ethnographic film production (see, for instance, Ruby 1975 and MacDougall 1975, and the essays L. Taylor (1994) collected from the _Visual Anthropology Review_) reflect the roots of this shift and become relevant to my work as a comparative dimension for understanding PBS documentary authorship and practice. Although there is no uniformly agreed upon position among practitioners about

what constitutes a "proper" ethnographic film but rather a critical attack on the notion of ethnographic film itself, there is consensus on the relevant issues: degree of authorial intervention and the place of reflexivity, depth of ethnographic understanding, ethical responsibility about the politics of representation and circulation, questions of subject collaboration, impact of process on product. These issues are pertinent to the work of documentary producers working within public television when one keeps in mind that "ethnographic film" operates largely within an academic context.

8. However, the tendency to ignore the doing of ethnography as a cultural practice itself limits many of these critiques. For instance, Marcus and Cushman explicitly state that they are "concerned with the representation of fieldwork in texts" and that "it is valid to exclude what actually happens in the field from consideration here" (1982:27). By cordoning the ethnographic process out of consideration, they drift toward a framework of literary criticism and rhetorical analysis, neglecting the larger practices of ethnographic production and limiting the possibilities for extending this perspective to other forms of cultural production.

9. Actualities, one of the earliest popular genres of cinema, often took as their topic views of exotic cultures. Before cinema, travelogues and illustrated lectures showed viewers foreign people and places. See Musser (1991) for a discussion of these forms of pre-cinema and early cinema, and Lutz and Collins (1993) for an interesting complementary analysis of *National Geographic* magazine.

10. I am indebted to Toby Miller for this observation.

11. I rely here on Bourdieu's definition of the field of cultural production as "the system of objective relations between these agents or institutions and as the site of the struggles for the monopoly of the power to consecrate, in which the value of works of art and belief in that value are continuously generated," and as "the locus of the accumulated social energy which the agents and institutions help to reproduce through the struggles in which they try to appropriate it and into which they put what they have acquired from it in previous struggles" (Bourdieu 1986:135). Bourdieu's work on cultural production has built on this metaphor of "the field of production." Seeing production as a "cultural field" moves us beyond theoretical limitations present in other approaches to production—from either the ideal-viewer driven perspectives in some film and television theory, the organization-dominated work in the sociology of production or the production-of-culture approach, and from the ideology-driven theories of materialist/critical approaches. By seeing production as a cultural field we attempt to locate simultaneously and in relation to each other the perspectives and interests of producers, production staff, PBS administrators, viewers, and the myriad institutions with which they interact. The field metaphor allows us to discuss both agency and process in terms of structural relations.

12. Turino describes this balance as a methodological dialectic between theory-driven and practice-driven research agendas: "One of the central concerns in the social sciences during the 1980's has been how to come to grips with reporting the dialectic between social determinations—thought of as structures—and the practices of individuals which, at once, constitute the structures and are determined by them. Included here is the dialectic between 'theory' and practice—both internalized versions of the world that influence individual practice, and the theories about the relationship between internalized dispositions and action which are sometimes deduced from observing practices" (Turino 1990:399).

13. I refer here to a broad category that we can term "the anthropology of communication," including visual anthropology and the anthropology of visual communication, aesthetic anthropology, ethnomusicology, folklore, sociolinguistics, performance studies, and the ethnography of communication.

14. Several excellent examples of this work are in the study of musical culture, in which language about music, particularly metaphoric language, is analyzed as a theoretical framework situating musical performance. Feld (1981, 1982), Stone (1981), and Tedlock (1980) all illustrate the intensive study of one culture's ethnotheoretical formulations about music.

15. Agawu has criticized how ethnotheory "reinscribes the dichotomy between 'us' and 'them' in ways that are not politically advantageous to 'them? [. . .] Theirs is ethnotheory (overseen by us, of course); ours is theory" (Agawu 1992:262).

16. Foucault's essay "What is an Author" (1977) exemplifies this theoretical position. He urges us to analyze the "author-function," and "reexamine the empty space left by the author's disappearance" (1977:450).

17. As Janet Wolff argued, "the author, now understood as constituted in language, ideology, and social relations, retains a central relevance . . . in relation to the meaning of the text (the author being the first person to fix meaning, which will of course subsequently be subject to redefinition and fixing by all future readers)" (Wolff 1981:136).

18. This perspective looked at "the processes by which elements of culture are fabricated in those milieus where symbol-system production is most self-consciously the center of activity" (Peterson 1976:10), looking at "culture industries" (Hirsch 1972), "cultural apparatus" (DiMaggio and Hirsch 1976), and "consciousness industries" (Tuchman 1983). Rooted in occupational and industrial sociology applied to the study of "cultural" processes, early writing focused on work practices and strategies within specific domains of production and was concerned with social-structural and organizational issues: how organizations define and condition procedures and routines of work, how these routines provide organizational benefits (efficiency, predictability, training), and what characterizes personnel and roles within organizations. Although this work served as an important corrective to elitist theories of art and culture, from a contemporary perspective it seems to be weakened by a lack of regard for textual meaning and interpretation and by its acceptance "of a narrow, linear, sequential model" for the production process (Tuchman 1983:340).

Silverstone's *Framing Science* (1985), a chronicle of the constraints and negotiations involved in the making of a BBC *Horizon* science documentary, is one of the only full-length accounts of the production of a documentary film. Silverstone was particularly interested in how the translation from a scientific to a televisual discourse dictated a restructuring of intent and objective and was in itself a highly politicized process: "Broadcast television, the culture of the BBC, the genre of the documentary film, the particular history and identity of *Horizon*, the 50-minute slot, the working of ideas into images and of explanations into stories, of competing voices into a single voice, together define an entirely distinct kind of cultural work—obviously sharing much with other kinds of products both on television and more broadly in other media—and equally obviously, constantly changing and adapting to new demands and new opportunities" (Silverstone 1985:167). Silverstone's study of producers' motivations and activities benefits from the ability to observe these processes over time and to reflect on the forces and incidents that shaped the program. As Crane (1992) argues, production of culture theory offers an analytical focus on the (increasing) importance of institutions to a synthetic framework for understanding media culture. Work in this area is strongest when it looks at the production process as an intersection of organizational forces (institutional, occupational, and financial), social and professional practices, conceptual frameworks, and texts, and transcends the limiting theoretical grounding in industrial sociology.

19. As Morley describes in a recent review of audience studies: "In short, the encoding/decoding model was designed to provide a synthesis of insights that had come out of a series of different perspectives—communication theory, semiology, sociology, and psychology—and to provide an overall model of the communication circuit as it operated in its social context" (Morley 1989:18). As Morley acknowledges, Hall's development of the model drew on the work of Frank Parkin.

20. Nicholas Garnham declares that "the bibliography on the producers of culture is notoriously empty" (Garnham 1990:12), noting the swing toward reception studies.

21. Recent writing by Nichols (1991, 1994), Winston (1995), and a collection of essays edited by and Renov (1993) represents a theoretically driven body of scholarship on documentary that is emerging in film studies and cultural studies. Attention has been paid to documentary as a communicative code, how the documentary form constructs and makes use of the symbolic resources available to it, and what the boundaries are between fiction and nonfiction modes, mostly in the form of textual analyses of specific works. They exemplify how close considerations of structural features of documentary reveal the conventionality of the form, its historical development, and the set of textual structures and constraints peculiar to documentary's stance as constructed nonfiction.

22. Some recent work in film studies considers cinematic representations of Third World and minority cultures in a variety of cinematic traditions, addressing issues of nationalism, imperialism, and historical experience (Naficy and Gabriel 1991; Shohat and Stam 1994).

23. One producer I spoke with mentioned his dislike of the book *Photographs of Chachaji* by the Indian-born writer Ved Mehta (1980), about the making of a PBS documentary about Mehta's uncle in a small Indian town. Mehta's account was quite critical of the filmmakers, who are still active in public television. This producer asked me what would prevent me from writing a similarly critical analysis, a charge that was difficult to answer beyond explaining how my social scientific purposes and perspective differed from journalist Mehta's, and assuring my good will. This was the only overt instance where Mehta's book was mentioned, but it is reflective of the kind of skepticism I faced in some of my contacts with producers.

24. During my first conversation with Geoff Haines-Stiles, I was thrown off guard when, after I described my proposed research, my search for a production such as *Childhood*, and status conducting research for my doctorate at the Annenberg School of Communications, he began to laugh. He let me off the hook when he revealed that he had received his master's degree from the Annenberg School years earlier. In responding to my description of my research objectives—some stumbling comments about trying to elucidate the decision-making process in documentary production— Haines-Stiles quipped that the whole process involved capturing the objective truth, a process that left little to investigate. This was the first of many tongue-in-cheek com-

ments of this kind. Clearly, Haines-Stiles understood the origins of the academic perspective of the study and was sympathetic, albeit with some cynicism, toward my objectives.

25. Haines-Stiles had written his master's thesis (Haines-Stiles 1972) at the Annenberg School for Communication on the visual and rhetorical structure of television news.

26. In fact, the impetus for this study developed while I was coproducing an ethnographic documentary film with the administrative sponsorship of a small PBS station, a process that raised complex questions about cultural representation through regional public television. I thought a study of public television documentary would present an opportunity to reflexively examine this kind of documentary production.

27. Ethnomusicologist Thomas Turino writes: "Bourdieu characterizes the elicitation of systems of rules from native informants, and I think in many cases rightly so, as bound to lead to the construction of an artificial account since, if it is not part of the people's normal discourse, the abstracted rule set must be created in doubly atypical verbalizations with an outsider who is often already implicated within relations of asymmetrical power. [. . .] What seems *especially* important in all of this for musical ethnographers is the explicit questioning of the construction of other people's realities in an overly systematized form in our texts: granting privilege to what can be said or shown rather than dealing with the variability and fluidity of actual practices" (Turino 1990:401, 403).

28. Much of my purpose in this research revolves around understanding the nature of agency maintained by those involved with the production of the series. In this attempt, I enter into a problematic of ethnographic writing that has been discussed in recent critiques of ethnography, namely the ambiguous assignment of knowledge and behavior to specific individuals or generic classes of people. In the writing that follows, some attributions are made to specific persons, some to job categories (i.e., "the producer/directors"), and others to the production as a whole ("the production staff" or "The *Childhood* Project"). When I refer to the "producers" I want to indicate a group including the executive producers, the producer/directors, and their staff of associate producers, researchers, and assistants. This term excludes other members of "the production staff," including WNET's administrative personnel, the advisors and on-camera hosts (observers), freelance production crew members, and the editing staff. My intention is to pose different blocks of interest that unite some concerns, behaviors, and knowledge, and need to be seen separately regarding other issues. Appendix A presents an organizational chart of the *Childhood* staff.

Chapter Two
Childhood on the Contested Territory of Public Television in the United States

1. This chapter centers on the circumstances surrounding public broadcasting during The *Childhood* Project's life from the late 1980s into the early 1990s. Since that period, additional battles, debates, and controversies surrounding public broadcasting have surfaced in the press, and a concerted attack on public television programming by conservative politicians and commentators has taken place. The attacks these critics make, that public television has liberal political and socially elitist biases and that it supports and broadcasts programs that go against traditional family values, are

not new assaults. But they are issued with greater vigor given recent shifts in American politics toward the conservative right and the push for restraints on federal expenditures. The movements to defund and privatize the public broadcasting system are part of broad-based conservative attacks on what are thought of as liberal agendas for government programs. These specific pressures were not as vehement at the time *Childhood* was produced, and hence are not addressed in this chapter. But I will return to these attacks later when considering the place of public television in American public culture.

2. As an article in *Newsweek* reported: "Fourteen million Americans, more than the entire population of the Confederacy, gave themselves over to 'The Civil War' last week—a modest television audience by network standards, but a blockbuster for an 11-hour documentary on PBS. For the five nights it was shown, it averaged a rating of just below 9 (and an audience share of 13 to 14 percent) compared with a typical public television rating of between 2 and 5" (Adler 1990:58–59).

3. Producers now talk about designing programs in the style of *The Civil War*, referring to the use of still photographs and static images, accompanied by readings from diaries and letters, over a bed of music. In addition, PBS first experimented in scheduling *The Civil War* with a strategy they refer to as "stacking," that is, programming two episodes per night over the course of a week, rather than spreading episodes over successive weeks.

4. See, for instance, articles by Rowland (1986) and Rowland and Tracey (1990) for fuller discussion of these systemic forces.

5. Hoynes (1994) discusses the multiple views of public television's mission.

6. Such histories are, arguably, closer to the "liberal view" and represented by the works of writers such as Witherspoon and Kovitz (1986 and 1987) and the reporting in *Current*, public broadcasting's monthly trade newspaper, which published this history.

7. Those who advocate an autonomous, nontaxpayer source of federal support often call for either the setting aside of funds from an auction of unused and highly sought-after commercial common carrier broadcasting frequencies or a usage fee levied on present license holders. See Somerset-Ward 1993:31–32.

8. Powell and Friedkin go so far as to argue that this congressional funding process has actually been counterproductive to the goal of insulating public television from political and fiscal vulnerability: "In a curious and unanticipated manner, we believe that the advanced funding mechanism has exacerbated public television's budget problems. For the past years the federal government has been operating under continuing resolutions rather than actual budgets. This means that no budget figures are actually fixed. They can be changed every time Congress extends the continuing funding resolution. Under such a process, the fact that PTV funds are set in advance only means that there is more opportunity to change them" (Powell and Friedkin 1983:417).

9. This overt political pressure periodically erupts into public awareness during moments of political stress, and at these times critics of the system invoke specific programs as examples of how the system has erred. Recently, conservative critics attacked a BBC series, Armisted Maupin's *Tales of the City*, broadcast on PBS in 1994, referring to its portrayal of gay lifestyles and the inclusion of some frontal nudity. Despite his defense of how sensitively the system handled the program, new

PBS president Ervin Duggan will likely look hard at similar programs in the future. Historically, the most systematic attack on public broadcasting came from President Nixon, who was particularly suspicious of public television. David Stone's (1985) study of PBS during the Nixon years details the president's war with public broadcasting.

10. A feature article in the *New York Times*—"Public TV Takes Its Nose Out of the Air" (Schapiro 1991)—describes how PBS turned to a strategy of multiculturalism in designing some recent programs as a step toward establishing a new identity. The system's claims to be multicultural, however, have been attacked by producers of color, who decry the system's predominantly white administrative power structure (Haddock and Mullins Lee 1993).

11. Kinsley writes:

Chevron already had a traveling exhibit and various brochures and ads touting the notion of "creativity," and it proposed that Moyers do a show on the subject.

"In one of those flashes of inspiration sometimes identified as creativity but often, in my business, no more than a desperate act of grantsmanship," Moyers wrote with admirable frankness in *Smithsonian*, "I fired back a letter asking: 'Why not a series?'" (Kinsley 1983:13)

12. For instance, Peter Davis, the executive producer of the series *Middletown*, broadcast on public television in 1982, yielded to pressure from the Xerox Corporation to withdraw the program *Seventeen* from the series (see Hoover 1992; McLagan, n.d.). Other examples include *Tongues Untied* (Riggs 1989), a program about African American gay identity that several stations refused to broadcast, and *Stop the Church* (Hilferty 1991), a documentary about a protest by the AIDS activist organization ACT-UP, which the executive producer of the series *P.O.V. (Point of View)* withdrew from its scheduled broadcast.

13. The Annenberg/CPB Project was designed to develop and fund series suitable for both classroom use and for national broadcast, goals that were often incompatible. It now stresses educational distribution over broadcast.

14. Several internal memoranda projected figures for the series' revenue-generating potential from ancillary distribution based on the performance of series such as *The Ascent of Man*, *Cosmos*, *America*, and *The Brain*.

15. From letters written in early 1987, it became clear that the full amount initially committed by PBS through the Program Development Fund would not be forthcoming and would be cut back to $100,000. In a letter that reveals the interdependent relationship between the producers of a major series and the PBS system, David Loxton put a significant amount of pressure on the director of this fund to come up with the full amount:

If P.D.F. holds to $100,000, that means we would have only $250,000 in hand. But the budget simply cannot be slashed another $50,000 if we are to do the job properly, let alone at all. The start of pre-production would be delayed while we search for the remaining money, thus damaging CHILDHOOD in several alarming ways:

• By delaying pre-production, we would be unable to assure completion of the series for the 1989/90 season.

• The delay would represent a severe setback in our negotiations with foreign co-producers, who require a demonstration of forward motion and substantial commitment by the public television system if this project is to be taken seriously by them.

• We could possibly jeopardize the availability of some of our key creative personnel. Geoff Haines-Stiles is an independent producer and has cleared his time based on an understanding of a specific schedule.

Therefore, we implore you to provide the full $150,000 set aside by P.D.F. The system wants the series. Please, let's not destroy the gathering momentum. If for any reason PBS cannot provide the full amount, can P.D.F. and CPB together cover the additional shortfall of $50,000?

Clearly, we are either at an exciting juncture or a crucial point of jeopardy for CHILDHOOD. PBS has been an enthusiastic backer from the beginning. We need your fullest support now more than ever. (Letter from David Loxton to Suzanne Weill, January 13, 1987)

16. This rough time line is based, in part, on a series of "Updates" written for The *Childhood* Project by researcher and writer Harriet Reisen, a source for internal circulation that might not be strictly accurate.

17. The Challenge Fund was put in place by the CPB to fund extended format series like *Childhood*. "The intent of the plan is to make sure that each spring and fall the Public Broadcasting Service season contains a major blockbuster such as 'The Brain' or 'Vietnam: A Television History'" (Anon., *Variety* 1986:34).

18. WNET's difficulties have not diminished in the time since *Childhood*. There have been further layoffs and loss of production opportunities (see Carter 1994, 1995).

19. During The *Childhood* Project's development period, Geoff Haines-Stiles was still located in Los Angeles, working on other projects, some through PBS affiliate KCET, and Loxton was at WNET. Both devoted time to research and write for *Childhood*, with Haines-Stiles supervising most of the research and the contact with scholars, and Loxton the fund-raising, planning, and negotiations with WNET. Haines-Stiles moved to the East Coast late in 1988, and in September 1989 David Loxton died of cancer. With the scheduled start of production near, Haines-Stiles and the WNET staff decided to continue as close to schedule as possible. However, there would have to be substantial restructuring, as I describe below.

20. I must confess, though, that the actual interactions between *Childhood's* producers and upper-level staff members at WNET were mostly outside of the limits of my research access. Except for a few large meetings I was able to attend, and some interoffice memos I found in the files, I only learned of the frequency and content of exchanges between WNET and *Childhood* secondhand.

21. For instance, *Childhood's* upper-level staff hired independent production and postproduction personnel rather than station staff (although a number of these people had connections through WNET projects), contracted almost all of its services from outside the station, and administered its own day-to-day financial affairs. Haines-Stiles maintained an independent relationship with the series' funders, the relevant PBS programming departments, and the British coproduction partners. *Childhood* also was responsible to Channel Four in England, which had put up $750,000 for the series and had a voice in certain decisions. Gwynn Pritchard, the supervising editor at

Channel Four, made at least two trips to New York to consult with the producers and offer his opinions. He spoke at some length in the meeting, reviewing the rough cuts of programs and urging the producers to avoid an overly American-centered focus in the series.

22. In Europe, coproduction partnerships have been even more typical, and are increasingly relied upon.

23. The possibility of coproduction became a hot issue in the 1980s: "Although Peter McGhee, programming manager for national productions at WGBH-TV Boston, says co-production is not a new alternative for his station, he—and representatives of all the major PBS producing stations—agreed it's an essential one. Their comments bore out that view: 'For some series it can't be done without.' 'Virtually every project of any scale requires an international partnership in order to proceed.' 'We're very interested in them, because in this time of dwindling resources it makes sense to get many pools of money together.' 'The number of co-productions has increased exponentially'" ("Co-productions . . . ," 1986:68).

24. It was actually the series *Civilisation* that Peter Montagnon was largely responsible for, not *Ascent of Man.*

25. A letter from Arnold Labaton, senior vice-president and director of WNET's Production Center, announced to CPB and PBS that production on the series was to commence even though it had not achieved full funding, with WNET guaranteeing the remainder of the funds until corporate money was raised: "While we still have a significant shortfall in the revenue needed to make us whole on this project, we have committed to its production and expect to have it ready for broadcast in the Fall of 1991" (Letter from Arnie Labaton to Jennifer Lawson, head of the CPB Television Program Fund, and Barry Chase, vice president of PBS programming, July 18, 1989).

26. The likelihood of broadcast to audiences in these additional countries (in which the producers had searched for potential coproduction partners) forced the producers to consider how these audiences might regard the cultures represented in the series. Chapter Five considers some effects on the design of the series stemming from the anticipation of foreign audiences.

27. The series included *Paul Jacobs and the Nuclear Gang* (Landau and Willis 1989), winner of an Emmy; *Pesticides and the Pill* (Richter, 1981), winner of a DuPont Columbia Award, and *The Times of Harvey Milk* (Epstein and Schmeichen 1983), winner of an Academy Award.

28. DORNFELD: So, how did you decide to split up the responsibilities?

PETER MONTAGNON: Well, I think Geoff thought rightly or wrongly that I had quite a lot of experience or was better at location filming, in terms of trying to get cine-vérité material, of the people, which is possibly true. Actually, most of that really comes from organizing the thing in such a way that you can actually do it, and of course we couldn't really do that. The most key thing is actually the cameraman. But I certainly know quite a lot about it, spent a long time doing it. And I also know quite a bit about filming abroad, and what the snags are and the rest of it, so we thought this would be quite a good idea if I took on the families. Which is coherent in the sense that you could deal with that separately, and it wasn't going to pose any logistical problems that you could see right from the start. And then the material would come back to New York, come back into a common pool for the editors, a common lab and all of those things like that. (Interview with Peter Montagnon, August 1, 1990)

29. Documents indicate that the resumés of the candidates that the executive producers chose for producer-director positions were shown to WNET executives; other staff members were chosen without oversight.

30. I was not privy to much of the discussion about these choices, but clearly the decisions about who would appear on camera in the series were related to both the expertise of the advisors and to their potential performance capabilities as on-camera personalities. Both the role of the "observers" and the nature of filming the "observers" filming are taken up in later chapters.

31. Eric Michaels's model of "teleported texts" (Michaels 1991), discussed in Chapter One, endeavors to accomplish a similar goal, transcending the processual linear production-consumption model of television texts, designed to situate the text in relation to the various contexts of interpretation and circulation through which it passes.

Chapter Three
Negotiating Documentary Production

1. Not surprisingly, these assumptions are based on a combination of research (audience ratings statistics that have become increasingly important in programming decisions and the administration of PBS stations) and folklore (information derived from experience and word of mouth).

2. During one discussion, Channel Four's representative, Gwynn Pritchard, maintained that sequences about infant mortality, problems of teenage pregnancy, and the lack of prenatal care presented by on-camera observer Marian Wright Edelman, head of the Children's Defense Fund (a national organization located in Washington, D.C., advocating and lobbying for children's rights), seemed like "sermons" to an exclusively American audience. Pritchard and British co-executive producer Peter Montagnon felt that focusing on problems most pressing in the United States would both narrow the impact of those scenes for audiences outside of the United States and date the series' material. These scenes also were thought to communicate in a more didactic style than the rest of the series' expert commentary, which employs a more distant, scholarly voice, not surprising given Edelman's occupational identity. These sequences with Edelman remained in the series.

3. The response to the aforementioned recent report on the state of public television sponsored by the Twentieth Century Fund (Somerset-Ward 1993) reflected this tension. Some of the report's readers questioned the report's assertions about the diverse nature of the PBS audience (i.e., Lapham 1993). In my view, the statistics used to refute charges of elitism (Somerset-Ward 1993:126), an argument based on the broad demographic spread of viewers who tuned in at least once a month, hide the fact that this spread is not reflective of more frequent prime-time viewers, who are more concentrated in the higher income brackets. Hoynes's research (1994), including interviews with staff at WGBH, illustrates the concern about lack of audience diversity shared by public television professionals.

4. Geoff Haines-Stiles did, however, disagree with Montagnon's statement when he read my manuscript, a point he made in correspondence after reading it.

5. Montagnon's assumptions are echoed in André Singer's (1992) reflections on the success of the anthropology series *Disappearing World*, produced by England's Granada Television. Singer calls for accepting the limitations of pedagogy available in a format that is designed for entertainment.

6. This concern resonates with the issue of PBS ratings raised earlier in Chapter Two. Although the series was not required to bring in the sort of audience ratings that network television would, and would be measured in other terms (reviews, influence, ancillary sales), the increased awareness of program ratings within the system and the high expectations for the series were not easily dismissed. Geoff Haines-Stiles agreed that these pressures and expectations influenced the production. He wrote in retrospect that "we should have cut our coat to fit our cloth, taken steps to understand our audience more, built a more attractive Trojan horse to appeal to the audiences we found, and been more realistic in our expectations" (letter from Haines-Stiles to Barry Dornfeld, December 24, 1995). Of course, the desire for ratings was intertwined with the desire to make "good television" within the parameters of public television, a term the producers used to characterize an approach to documentary that was both scholarly sound and aesthetically inventive and dynamic.

7. This connection between producer and viewer is indexed in the way the authors addressed their presumed audience within the text, setting up a structure of identification shared between author and viewer, a rhetorical strategy to which I return in Chapter Four. It was interesting to see how members of the production staff differentiated themselves through a conception of their relation to the audience. The editors felt that their role was more that of a proxy for the audience, keeping the producers, who from the editors' point of view were slightly out of touch with their viewership, on track. The fact that editors came from a somewhat different class position—less advanced education, union membership, freelance occupation, affiliation with independent film culture (as opposed to network television)—might have something to do with this distancing. Still, the gap between producers and freelance staff does not approach that between production staff and on-camera subjects, American or other.

8. Research on expressive culture in ethnomusicology, folklore, and communication has looked at this metalanguage as an avenue into understanding native models of aesthetic experience. As Feld argues, "The linguistic dimension of musical discourse concerns the relationship of musical terms, their semantics, and the theoretical postulates of the musical system, to which they refer. Systematic links between one semantic field and another make it possible to approach musical theory as metaphorical thought coded in a metalanguage" (Feld 1981:23). While this approach runs the danger of being excessively cognitive, we can search for the application of these conceptual terms in production practice.

9. The analogy of musical sampling, the work of the contemporary pop music composer, is instructive in considering the nature of producing this material: "The increasing use of sampling devices and preprogrammed synthesizers means that as producers musicians are, in fact consumers, working with commercial sounds that have been made for them" (Frith 1988a:120). The documentary producer operates at least some of the time as a sampler or bricoleur, assembling, arranging, and reframing material from a variety of sources, all with regard to the aesthetic economy of their use.

10. I admit to being surprised at the sophisticated sense of television form displayed by a few of the observers as they suggested changes to the rough cuts. I expected the observers to make exclusively "academic" (dry, literal, expository) rec-

ommendations, but they did make suggestions that were driven as much by a sense of the televisual as of the scholarly.

11. It is worth noting that Gene Marner, who has shot a lot of his own material in the past, chose to take on the shooting for several of the production days he also directed. He explained that even though he respected and trusted the freelance cinematographers the series employed, he preferred, when possible, to have control over this element of authorship.

12. Hollywood editor Ralph Rosenblum's popular and entertaining book about editing feature films, *When the Shooting Stops* (Rosenblum and Karen 1979), is full of these sorts of narratives. See also Vaughan (1983).

13. Although it is difficult to be precise about what Montagnon means by "controlled setups," it is clear that he contrasts them with an observational, vérité style of shooting that made up much of the material for the series. Controlled setups would include observers speaking to the camera, an interview with a family member, or the illustration of an experiment for the camera.

14. The phrase "It is not your father's PBS" is a humorous reference to a television commercial, popular at the time of the production, that had the refrain "This is not your father's Oldsmobile."

15. Tulloch takes this idea further, drawing connections between the producers' professional and everyday lives and raising the issue of "media power" or agency more directly:

"There are also similarities between textual practice and ordinary day-to-day activity. Both are grounded in conventional routines and practical consciousness, the products of which escape the intentional input of its creators. [. . .] "Authors," then, are both social observers and audiences. [. . .] The point is, of course, that we are, all of us (TV dramatists, media academics, adult members of the television audience) necessarily engaged in *both* the pleasure of knowledgeable observers (questioning, monitoring, watching, bringing to light) *and* the pleasures of knowledgeable actors (evading, fleeing from and fooling this power). We need to be aware of both pleasures in *all* the institutional and agentive situations to which we customarily relate. (Tulloch 1990:17–18; emphasis in original)

16. For example, when PBS broadcast *The Civil War* series (Burns 1990) in the fall of 1990, there was a great deal of conversation about that program in the *Childhood* office. They felt that *Childhood*'s success would be compared to the reputation of *The Civil War*, so the staff was interested in the program from a professional perspective.

17. I thank Faye Ginsburg for her comments about this contrast, based on her research with British producers of ethnographic film for television (Ginsburg 1988).

Chapter Four
Public Television Documentary Parties

1. This latter perspective, common in film studies, bases analysis more on a literary or rhetorical model. As described by Bordwell, these two paradigms share a general purpose: "A poetics—derived from *poeisis*, or 'active making'—puts at the

center of its concerns the problem of how art works are constructed to have certain effects and uses. The artist's craft, including both abstract principles and particular practices, takes on major importance" (Bordwell 1988:51).

2. Neale adapts the Russian formalist idea of a dominant aesthetic device on which basis "particular genres can be characterized, not as the only genres in which given elements, devices and features occur, but as the ones in which they are dominant, in which they play an overall, organizing role" (Neale 1990:65–66). Although there remains the problem of ascertaining which formal features are dominant in a work, and from whose point of view, particularly in a hybrid text like *Childhood*, this approach provides an appropriately flexible and broad beginning for a definition of genre.

3. For instance, Turow, writing about the behavior of mass media industries, points to the tensions between innovation and risk in media practices and the tendency toward conservatism. He characterizes producers' work as "a kind of balancing act between the need by creators to search for novelty and their need to limit that search in the interests of predictability and efficiency" (Turow 1984:151). Turow's model is concerned with the potential costs that innovation poses for a firm's profitability. This concern is less critical for public television, where "profit" is redefined and decisions are driven by a fusion of symbolic capital and financial capital. Still, the model applies and emphasizes the issue of agency within institutions.

Neale offers an extension of the industrial model, more applicable when the genre under consideration diverges from the formulaic structures and categories of film and television: "It may at first sight seem as though repetition and sameness are the primary hallmarks of genre: as though, therefore, genres are above all inherently static. But as Hans Robert Jauss and Ralph Cohen (and I myself) have argued, genres are, nevertheless, best understood as *processes*. These processes may, for sure, be dominated by repetition, but they are also marked fundamentally by difference, variation and change" (Neale 1990:56).

4. Urban and Sherzer describe how "the genre concept places more emphasis on the meaning or function of the discourse as the basis for differentiating ways of speaking, as in the contrast between myth and folktale or story and song" (Urban and Sherzer 1988:286). They emphasize the genre/style distinction in language performance, but this issue is less problematic in film studies, where genres are more conventionally defined by practitioners, and style is seen as a more limited category.

5. Altman writes:

Before semiotics came along, generic titles and definitions were largely borrowed from the industry itself.

Genres were always—and continue to be—treated as if they spring full-blown from the head of Zeus. It is thus not surprising that even the most advanced of current genre theories, those that see generic texts as negotiating a relationship between a specific production system and a given audience, still hold to a notion of genre that is fundamentally ahistorical in nature. (Altman 1986:28)

6. As Fiske has argued, research on genre needs to explore the importance of genre in the processes of production: "Understanding works of art generically, however, locates their value in what they have in common, for their shared conventions form links not only with other texts in the genre, but also between text and audiences,

text and producers, and producers and audiences. Generic conventions are so important in television because they are a prime way of both understanding and constructing this triangular relationship between producer, text, and audience" (Fiske 1987: 110).

7. It would certainly be valuable to know whether this genre exists in the same sense in the expectations of those who consume it, but this insight could only result from reception research with public television audiences, work that remains to be done.

8. That these tensions have always been present in public television programming is reflected in histories of the medium, such as Day (1995) and Engelman (1996).

9. As Neale states, "Genres are inherently temporal: hence their inherent mutability on the one hand, and their inherent historicity on the other" (Neale 1990:56)

10. Comments cited from the Corporation for Public Broadcasting Advisory Panel Meeting, F.Y. 1989, in a letter from program officer Lynae Berge to Geoff Haines-Stiles, August 16, 1990.

11. My initial research proposal anticipated finding this "folk historical" awareness, which Geoff Haines-Stiles confirmed in his reading.

12. One useful point of comparison was between the series itself and *Childhood in America*, the follow-up program planned and produced by The *Childhood* Project that departed in intent and structure from the series. *Childhood in America*, an issues-oriented public affairs program, incorporated a panel discussion with an investigative "magazine" format. It focused on current problems confronting childhood life in the United States, issues that the series intentionally avoided addressing in detail. Geoff Haines-Stiles distinguished *Childhood in America* from the rest of the series by comparing the former to *Sixty Minutes*, an investigative television journalism network format that the producers wanted to avoid for the *Childhood* series itself. A primary distinction concerned the "observers" on-camera technique the series implements, compared to expert interview and panel discussion formats typical of other related nonfiction genres.

13. Following this exchange, the producers agreed that nonconventional points of view could be summarized or paraphrased by the narrators or observers, though the particular positions suggested above were not included in the series. Conventions of the genre itself seem to guard against nonmainstream views. The controversy surrounding the PBS/BBC series *The Africans* (Mazrui 1986) corroborates this suggestion, since that series did employ a subjective style of commentary to voice nonconventional political views and was criticized by some for doing so.

14. The preceding citations are taken from my field notes.

15. Although its present usage dilutes the original intent of the term, cinema vérité has come to indicate an observational style of camera and sound recording that favors long takes, mobile, hand-held camera work, and a minimal use of artificial lighting; it eschews voice-over, narration, and formal interviews in constructing programs. The terms "vérité" or "direct cinema" are also used to refer to this style. See Winston (1988) for a clear, though critical, discussion of these terms.

16. In commercial cinema and advertising, the techniques commonly discussed as markers of high production value include extensive dolly or moving camera shots, stylized lighting setups and composition, and well-dressed period sets. These criteria shift somewhat for modes of documentary, though they include polished camera

movements and careful composition. Cinema vérité documentaries, by contrast, eschew these same levels of production value in an attempt to look more authentic and realistic.

17. "And so the independents have struggled on with grants from the NEH, the NEA, and various arts councils, knowing that when their films were completed they stood a fair chance of being screened on public television if they were of any quality. Unfortunately, the returns for such local screenings are at best minimal, ranging from $200 to $1000 per broadcast hour, which is unlikely to make the independent jump for joy—especially in view of the millions spent on 'Cosmos,' 'Heritage,' and 'The Brain'" (Rosenthal 1988:350).

18. Even though the end product is a television broadcast, the result of shooting on film is a different texture for image and sound that practitioners argue either surpasses the quality obtained from working with videotape as the originating format, or provides an aesthetic texture more appropriate to the documentary form.

19. The producers were concerned that they not use too much archival film footage and, in the case of the Baka material, not use much of the footage that was included in the National Geographic program that PBS broadcast, for these same reasons.

20. The unorthodox approach of combining modes taken up in the series called for a mix of production strategies appropriate for specific sequences: cinema vérité or observational style filmmaking requires a very different directorial approach and production organization than that needed for the filming of dramatic re-creations or for the filming of observer stand-up scenes. I will consider shooting strategies later in this chapter.

21. Series such as *Eyes on the Prize* (Houpton 1986), about the American civil rights movement, and *Making Sense of the Sixties* (Green and Hoffman 1991) are exceptions to this generalization. They employed a mixture of interviews and omniscient narration to propel the exposition. *The Civil War* series was something of a middle ground, since it was characterized by a regular on-camera presence whose persona fell somewhere between that of host, narrator, and expert interview subject and who was complemented by others on camera.

This format was defended by Ward Chamberlain, the president of WETA, Washington D.C.'s PBS station: "As public-television viewers know, the most successful method of covering an immense subject has been to use a single host/narrator/editor, such as Kenneth Clark in 'Civilisation,' Jacob Bronowski in 'The Ascent of Man,' and Abba Eban in 'Civilization and the Jews.' It is inherent in such a cinematic form that one person's distinctive style comes to the fore" (Chamberlain 1986).

22. Much of the discussion of the choice of the observers for *Childhood* occurred before I began this research. However, I did observe a few exchanges concerning their selection, and gained some insight from file documents.

23. Chisolm described a modified teleprompter device he constructed that reflected an image of the producer on a one-way mirror in front of the lens, designed to comfort the observer being filmed. Another observer, Urie Bronfenbrenner, was concerned enough about his performance to enlist a videographer to tape practice performances and to help him polish his on-camera technique. The producers also expended extra energy and attention working with the observers on the set, and on occasion simplified their shooting plans, limiting the use of extended camera moves and gath-

ering appropriate props for the observer to work with. The quality of the performances was not problematic enough to consider entirely abandoning the use of the hosts. In postproduction, the editors were able to cut between sections from repeated takes of observer scenes to accommodate and conceal performance errors, cutting away to associated scenes and using voice-over sections to work with these performances.

24. WNET producer Richard Hutton expressed doubt about the likelihood of *Childhood* succeeding in recording these moments: "If there was one thing I learned while I was filming babies for 'Development' in THE MIND, it was that you cannot overestimate the number of babies you will need to film a desired behavior. In any case, the two variables for filming children are: numbers of children and time. With fewer babies available, the structure you propose will, in my opinion, require an enormous number of filming days, with cameramen constantly at the ready in all family locations—*An American Family* filmed six times over. Otherwise, you're not going to get the behaviors you want (memo from Richard Hutton to David Loxton and Geoff Haines-Stiles, June 20, 1988). *Childhood*'s producers felt that they succeeded in obtaining the specific kind of observational footage they needed through the strategies they put in place, though they did devote significant resources to the family filming.

25. Cited from memo of George Page to David Loxton and Geoff Haines-Stiles, June 23, 1988. A third WNET respondent to the treatments doubted the likelihood that producers would gather "appropriate" and "engaging" footage and, like Page and Hutton, questioned the dramatic value of these sequences, suggesting they would take on a repetitive quality. "My most serious concern deals with the structure of the programs as they are presented in the proposal. Because each of the programs seems so dependent on footage of the subject families, I am worried that the programs will all begin to look alike from week to week. This structure also makes every episode dependent on having the good fortune to have filmed family material which is not only appropriate but engaging—a heavy weight to carry. I would try to leave open opportunities for producers to deal with the subject areas somewhat more flexibly and not have every episode so dependent on so many family stories" (memo from Arnie Labaton to David Loxton and Geoff Haines-Stiles, June 29, 1988).

26. When Haines-Stiles introduced WNET's George Page at the History Advisors Meeting, Haines-Stiles stated that "it was actually the history of childhood that we sold him on" (History Advisors Meeting, February 20, 1990).

27. See the work of Linda Pollock, which critically reexamined art-historical evidence that Ariès used (Pollock 1983, 1987), and *Childhood* advisor Ray Hiner's compilation of research on the world history of childhood (Hawes and Hiner 1991).

28. During the history advisors' meeting, the staff discussed the possibility of devoting a single program to the history of childhood rather than spreading historical material throughout the episodes, but they did not pursue this option.

29. WNET's Richard Hutton, producer of the series *The Mind*, had earlier been skeptical of these sequences in his reading of *Childhood's* treatments. "The childhood minutes and dramatic recreations feel haphazardly laid in. Both are extremely dangerous forms; if you are going to use them, you should use them sparingly and only when absolutely necessary" (memo from Richard Hutton to David Loxton and Geoff Haines-Stiles, June 20, 1988).

30. Documentaries often rely on chronological structures for their organization. This raises the broader issue of narrative organization that I return to throughout this chapter. As Nichols describes: "A tendency in recent writing on documentary is to stress its link to narrative. Documentaries are fictions with plots, characters, situations, and events like any other. They offer introductory lacks, challenges, or dilemmas; they build heightened tensions and dramatically rising conflicts, and they terminate with resolution and closure" (Nichols 1991:107). Nichols seeks to distinguish documentary from narrative modes by examining the kind of "fiction" that documentary represents.

31. This last requirement meant that each program had to include at least a cursory introduction to *Childhood's* major characters (family members and advisors), cultures, and locations as they were introduced. For instance, when the Baka make their first appearance in Program Six, the narrator provides information that viewers who had seen previous programs would know: "NARRATOR (LYNN NEARY): The rainforests of the Cameroon. . . The Baka are hunter-gatherers. The Baka live in small villages in igloo-shaped huts" (narration, Program Six/"Among Equals").

32. The proposed programming schedule for the series had an important impact on decisions about the number of programs and their structure, since placement on the national PBS schedule is a commodity intensely contested for by affiliates. At one point in the postproduction stage, the producers mentioned the possibility of having programs air on consecutive nights, a technique called "stacking" that PBS had first employed for *The Civil War* and had used subsequently to profile certain programs. Later, the decision was made to run *Childhood* one night a week. During the fall when *Childhood* aired, PBS broadcast the series *Columbus and the Age of Discovery* in this consecutive-night format. I can only speculate on whether PBS chose to feature *Columbus* in place of *Childhood*, or if reasons argued for *Childhood's* once-a-week schedule.

33. I cite here but avoid identifying a producer/director who was asked to resign early in *Childhood* 's life. I avoid identification because of some apprehension s/he expressed about participating in my research project.

34. Early in the production process, the producers developed a list of short outlines in paragraph form to describe the flow of ideas within each of what would be six programs and to organize the scene sequences within that program. Program One was described in the following six sentences: "Program One takes us from the newborn to a milestone that occurs at about three months: the first 'social smile.' We compare the diverse customs and rites that surround birth and the immense variety of childrearing practices. We examine new scientific evidence that children are born with distinct personalities and temperaments. But is biology destiny? How do parents' expectations and actions come to shape a child's behavior and character. And how is 'childhood' itself defined in the varied countries we will visit" (Program Update: Outlines). These summaries condense complex questions in brief lexical form. As I became familiar with the working scripts, I learned that there was a metonymic relationship between these descriptions and the evolving programs. Each sentence, phrase, or theme was linked to a sequence of scenes under some form of consideration (i.e., "the immense variety of child-rearing practices" indicated a sequence of visual art objects depicting different methods of childbirth over time and across cultures). By debating the summaries for a given show, the producer/directors were simultaneously debating

where a complex of sequences should occur in relation to one another. In discussing the overall shape of each episode, they would often return to these narrative summaries, changing them as programs developed.

35. I was unsure of what Geoff Haines-Stiles meant when he praised the subtitles in the Baka films. In the *National Geographic* program, the subtitles provided an unobtrusive summary translation of speech, but this did not strike me as an unusual accomplishment. He responded that, in his view, Channel Four's version of the program was informal, colloquial, and wonderful.

36. Foucault points to the way a text bears signs of authorship: "However, it would be false to consider the function of the author as a pure and simple reconstruction after the fact of a text given as passive material, since a text always bears a number of signs that refer to the author. Well known to grammarians, these textual signs are personal pronouns, adverbs of time and place, and the conjugation of verbs. But it is important to note that these elements have a different bearing on texts with an author and those without one" (Foucault 1977:4).

Chapter Five
Cutting across Cultures

1. Though National Geographic recently ended its ongoing contract with public television and now produces material for network television.

2. The less scholarly end of the continuum would range to include works of cultural exploitation, such as the infamous film *Mondo Cane* (Jacopetti and Prosperi 1963). See Staples 1995 for a review of the fascinating film genre that she calls "Mondo Cinema."

3. Three major anthropology series have been broadcast on public television in the United States: *Odyssey* (Ambrosino 1980), *Faces of Culture* (Abrams 1983), and *Millennium* (Grant, Malone, and Meech 1992). Ginsburg (1988) reviews some of the early efforts to develop anthropological material for television, comparing American, British, and Japanese programs.

4. That some of these consultations were strained reveals something of a conflict in stance between the producers and a more rigorous anthropological perspective. For instance, Jay Ruby, a visual anthropologist, criticized the proposal to use the body of footage shot with the Baka people in Cameroon, since he regarded it as methodologically suspect. The producers disagreed with this assessment, though, and relied on this Baka material throughout the series. Also, a meeting of anthropologists on the Board of Advisors scheduled for the spring of 1991 was canceled and never rescheduled.

5. In film and video production, "shooting ratio" refers to the rough proportion of the total length of original material filmed to the final length of time used in the edited show. A one-hour show made from twenty hours of original footage has a twenty-to-one shooting ratio.

6. *Childhood: A Proposal for an Eight-Part Television Series, Part II* (1986).

7. By the beginning of September 1989, the producers had committed to filming in Brazil in place of India. A later fax from Antelope's production manager outlines the logistical arguments in favor of Brazil, in addition to its suitable family and class structure:

The reasoning behind Brazil is as follows:

1. Extremely good locations are available for both car and electronic factories. The electronic factories in particular are highly recommended as there are a lot of large families who work in them and live in the nearby shanty towns (favelas). This is Peter's first choice.

2. We have found a very efficient production company called Neon Studio, who are able to give us extremely good deals. Having filmed many times over a period of years in these electronics factories and established good relations with them, they will be able to offer us a good negotiated discount.

They have supplied us with extensive lists of suitable factories to film in, good 16mm cameramen and crews, plus all other necessary requirements that we need to adhere to. (Antelope fax from Fiona Freed to David Loxton and Geoff Haines-Stiles, September 2, 1989)

8. The two American families, located in the suburbs of New York City, were scouted by the New York production staff.

9. For instance, Erna Akuginow's list of scenes that she hoped to obtain for her programs included the following: "Would like to ask all expectant mothers whether they care if it's a boy or girl? How many children would they like? Are they nervous about delivery? What is their fondest wish for child? What is their greatest fear/concern for child? [. . .] Once the infant is moved out of delivery and into nursery, we want the camera to widen out so we can see the infant in relationship to its environment—the quality and quantity of the human interactions, the physical environment—stimulating, sterile, or overloading. . . . We then need to widen our scope to other babies in the nursery—are there safe generalizations about ethnic type (the docile Oriental baby) or culture-bound practices (swaddling). Need to see ample evidence of these cultural variants in nursery context" (memo from Erna Akuginow to Peter Montagnon, December 1989).

10. These adjustments ranged from critical decisions, such as replacing the original cinematographer in Japan with a resident American cameraman who works regularly on films for public television, to logistical considerations, such as requesting that the Russian sound person identify the sound reels more clearly.

11. For instance, Jonathan Cott, a series advisor, suggested that the producers film a traditional "drumming school" in Ghana, West Africa, to use in a sequence on apprenticeship and education for Erna Akuginow's shows (Program Five/"Life's Lessons" and Program Six/"Among Equals"). The producers were interested in the subject and asked me to do some further research after I mentioned having some familiarity with Ghanaian music. I contacted the American ethnomusicologist, David Locke (a former teacher of mine), who directed the project to Abubukari Luna, a Dagomba master drummer in Tamale, a city in northern Ghana, whose teaching program producer/director Gene Marner and associate producer Rudy Gaskins eventually filmed. Marner undertook directing this shoot, even though these scenes would be used in Akuginow's programs, because of the efficiency of adding this location to his upcoming production trip to Israel and Italy, and because of his familiarity with filming in this region. He and Gaskins traveled to Ghana to film Luna's apprenticeship program and the additional sequences that Akuginow added on to this location shoot (one showing children's games and a second apprenticeship of weavers in Kumasi).

Akuginow incorporated these scenes into the scripts she was refining for those episodes and later worked the footage into the edited shows.

12. See, for instance, discussions by Asch et al. (1991), Ginsburg (1994), and Ruby (1991).

13. See MacDougall (1995) for a discussion of the authorial implications of employing subtitles in ethnographic documentary.

14. This event was one of the first sequences shot with the Gholstons and turned out to be among the most memorable and frequently discussed, though it was a sequence that the producers debated shooting. They had experienced some trouble arranging for the cameraperson they wanted to shoot this event, given the short notice they had to make arrangements. There was some tension about whether to go through with the shooting or to postpone it for the following year.

15. Programs One-A and Two became Programs Two and Three in the reorganization of episodes.

16. At the Advisors Meeting, December 12, 1989.

17. In the specific meeting I refer to, three historians and anthropologist/observer/advisor Mel Konner were present.

18. Perhaps because of Myers's (1988) article, which I brought to the project's attention. See also Wilmsen (1989) and Gordon (1992) for an expanded discussion of the mythology propagated by research on the "hunter-gatherer" societies of the Kalahari in southern Africa.

19. See Haraway 1989 for a discussion of the social politics of research on primate behavior.

20. Robert Hinde at the Advisors Meeting, February 3, 1991, said: "The other thing, the business about 'there's no right way,'" which goes right through all the programs, again comes up over the birth business, about the natural birth, the quicker birth in squatting, and yet the greater difficulty for doctors over complications, and that's such a good point to make, right at the beginning of the series."

21. Hinde's comments were made at the Advisors Meeting, February 3, 1991, in reference to how a section of narration characterized Russian culture.

22. It is important to avoid casting the producers and advisors as either unsophisticated, insensitive to, or unaware of the complex issues surrounding cross-cultural representation and the criticisms lodged against these representations. For example, the producers adamantly opposed the use of the word "primitive" by one of *Childhood's* advisors, and raised this issue during the Advisors Meeting of February 3, 1991:

> URIE BRONFENBRENNER: I worry particularly about the use of words such as primitive, certain things are primitive. I think it's much more exciting if we were to speak about this as, 'This is a species that is unique in its capacity to create the environments that in turn shape it.' And that this has been a long history of cultural change, and from that perspective, the Baka indicate not a perspective in terms of primitive to here, but rather how culture has evolved, not necessarily for the better, and it's a very exciting story.
>
> GEOFF HAINES-STILES: It's not a story of primitive man versus nonprimitive man. I do not believe that in either Gene's program or in my program we ever

use the word primitive about the Baka; if we do, it's by accident. I certainly don't think that's the way we intend to use it. (Advisors Meeting, February 3, 1991)

23. This is a well-worn debate within ethnographic filmmaking, where some have argued about the anthropological value of observational filmmaking against an ortho-doxy biased toward intellectual and objectivist models of how to employ the images in relation to spoken commentary.

24. Shohat and Stam write: "Racism thus juggles two complementary procedures: *the denial of difference* and *the denial of sameness*. While obfuscating differences in historical experience, it denies the sameness of human aspiration" (1994:24).

25. See, for instance, the attack by Mullins and Lee (1992) on the monocultural makeup of production organizations getting funded to produce multicultural program-ming.

Chapter Six
Public Television Documentary and the Mediation of American Public Culture

1. Each ratings point represents 921,000 households, meaning that *Childhood* aver-aged close to two and a half million viewers each night of its broadcast. *Columbus* was reported to have a rating of 4.6.

2. Although I did not do any substantive research on the program's reception, I did collect reviews of the series and tracked its publicity campaign. Geoff Haines-Stiles sent me a packet of reviews, press material, and excerpts from viewers' telephone responses to the series.

3. Goodman's review, however, takes issue with the ethics motivating an intense and troubling cross-cultural moment: "Next week's hour begins with a vivid scene that raises questions about the people behind the cameras. A young New Guinea woman is seen enduring labor pains and giving birth without any assistance. Did the rules of anthropology prevent the production team from trying to help out? Then she covers the baby, which the narrator says she did not want, with leaves and goes away. After a while she comes back and begins to mother it. How long would the producers have left the baby under the leaves?" (Goodman 1991:C18). In fact, the attribution of blame to "the producers" is misplaced if it means to refer to *Childhood*'s producers, since this sequence was acquired from the German ethnographic filmmaker, Eibl Eiblesfeldt. This scene was also the focus of a more generally critical review in the British magazine *New Statesman and Society* (French 1992), published the following March after Channel Four aired the program in England. The British reviewer ex-pressed a good deal more dismay at the use of that sequence, criticizing the ethics of filmmakers who would stand back and observe that act without intervening (this is a more complicated issue than the reviewer describes) and at the authorial implications of using material that attempts to efface the presence of the camera crew and fails to explain the relationship between author and subject: "This is perhaps a matter of nuance, but shooting and then broadcasting the New Guinea footage was shamefully degrading. One might have thought it a matter at least of professional, if not moral, integrity to make clear the status of what we were seeing. I would not imagine that a

woman who planned to reject her baby would be eager to be observed, so, at the very least, the filmmakers should clearly have explained the form of consent the woman had provided for them" (French 1992:8).

4. These reviews constrain our analytical readings in more specific ways as well. Certain features that I raise issues about or regard as problematic were rather seen as successful aspects of the series, or else ignored by reviewers. For instance, the complex issue of stereotypy discussed in Chapter Five in regard to the portrayal of a traditional basis for Japanese family practices was cited as a positive sequence articulating cultural differences in the *Montreal Gazette* review (Boone 1991).

5. Distributed by GPN and the PBS Adult Learning Service.

6. This rough figure includes overhead costs to WNET, the sponsoring station, as well. Actual production costs totaled around $600,000 per episode, a level of expenditure in line with other PBS documentary programs.

7. A PBS producer with whom I spoke while searching for this research site said this, summing up our conversation about the financial pressures on public television documentary production.

8. Schapiro's assessment of PBS's difficulties questioned this blockbuster mentality as a production and programming strategy: "'PBS should provide an alternative to commercial TV,' says Dai-Sil Kim Gibson, an independent producer on the PBS Programming Policy Committee, a panel appointed to advise [PBS program director] Ms. Lawson's office. 'That means a greater willingness to take risks, even though this may be in conflict with the need to increase the audience'" (Schapiro 1991:31).

9. For example, the producers attempted to save money by keeping personnel costs down to a workable minimum. In fact, as I discussed in Chapter Two, when one of the three producer/directors was let go early in the production stage, Geoff Haines-Stiles chose to take on the two programs under that person's charge in addition to his own responsibilities as executive producer. Although his decision was not entirely financial (Haines-Stiles mentioned the difficulty of finding producer/directors appropriate to the project), the financial advantages of saving a relatively high salary expense were significant. Haines-Stiles agreed in retrospect that this decision increased his production responsibilities and cut into the time he had had available for fundraising, administration, and promotion, and therefore had a detrimental effect on the series as a whole.

10. As I discussed in Chapter Five, the producers' capacity to incorporate material from prominent world culture areas was constrained by the budget. Their decision to cancel a possible sequence on Islamic education in Morocco was largely an economic one, since it would have required an expenditure of tens of thousands of dollars.

11. As mentioned earlier (Chapter Four), the producers incorporated history into the series in two more cost-effective forms, in sequences designed as narration over still photographic and artwork, and in material shot in Colonial Williamsburg. Narration and still sequences require little raw film stock and can be efficiently designed and executed, saving production resources. Williamsburg, a historical theme park in Virginia, provided preformulated sets and actors, allowing the producers to shoot in something more of a documentary fashion with little preproduction time devoted to locating talent, costumes, and "sets" compared to more typical "dramatic" filmmaking practices.

12. "Might one of the four families be Brazilian and could we ask Globo to pay

for all production costs in their country. [. . .] If you think this is worth discussing (strikes me that it is), I would like to send them a copy of the CHILDHOOD proposal with an indication of possible Brazilian content" (Memo from Hugh Price to David Loxton, Arnie Labaton, and Marian Swaybill, November 18, 1986).

13. The relationship between the staff and freelancers illustrates a different version of the trade-off between financial and symbolic capital than between producers and advisors. Freelance crew members (cinematographers, sound recordists, assistant camera operators) receive greater financial compensation, based on a daily rate, for a brief association with the project, than do staff members, who benefit from their long-term relationship. The series' postproduction staff falls somewhere in between these positions, since they are more like long-term freelancers, paid less per day than crew members but over a longer period of time. Staff members articulated how they willingly traded off the higher financial rewards they might gain from comparable commercial work for various forms of symbolic capital they could accrue, either in the form of career advancement after their association with *Childhood* or a more abstract personal sense of fulfillment from being associated with a substantive, well-intentioned, ambitious educational series.

14. This form of personal capital is similar to what Bourdieu describes for workers in the arts: "For the author, the critic, the art dealer, the publisher or the theatre manager, the only legitimate accumulation consists in making a name for oneself, a known recognized name, a capital of consecration implying a power to consecrate objects (with a trademark or a signature) or persons (through publication, exhibition, etc.) and therefore to give value, and to appropriate the profits from this operation" (Bourdieu 1986:132).

15. Bourdieu describes these equations as "defined in relation to the *space of possibles*:" "The literary or artistic field is a *field of forces*, but it is also a *field of struggles* tending to transform or conserve this field of forces. The network of objective relations between positions subtends and orients the strategies which the occupants of the different positions implement in their struggles to defend or improve their positions (i.e. their position-takings), strategies which depend for their force and form on the position each agent occupies in the power relations" (Bourdieu 1983: 312–313: emphasis in original).

16. For instance, reflexive revelations about the role of the producers, fairly common in independent works, would not be appropriate in this form of public television documentary (though of course there are some exceptions). See Nichols (1991:69–75).

17. As James Day writes: "In a memorandum to her station constituency, she summed up her seven-point prescription for the newly named National Programming Service. Primary emphasis was to be placed upon 'the creation of a distinctive, culturally diverse variety service demonstrating leadership in children's programming and increasing the visibility of public television's public service and educational role.' The prescription's key word was *multiculturalism*, the fashionable term for the 1990's, which Lawson defined as 'our commitment to *cultural diversity*'—the wish to make certain that all PBS programs 'accurately reflect and serve our society in all its diversity." If the goal had a ring of old coinage—cultural diversity has been a strong element in public television's programming for more than forty years—the emphasis was new: Lawson would have every show proposed for the National Pro-

gram Service vetted for multicultural content" (Day 1995:304–5). The citations from Lawson come from a memorandum entitled *National Program Service 1991 Annual Report*, January 17, 1992.

18. Bourdieu's distinction between popular and bourgeois aesthetic systems (1984) also sets out these tensions, as well as the "middle ground" the producers seek as an attempt to bridge these positions.

19. See James Day's comments on this cultural divide in his reflections on teaching public television to an undergraduate body of working-class students at Brooklyn College (1995:331–332).

20. See, for instance, the special section of essays in *Public Culture*, "Screening Politics in a World of Nations," edited by Abu-Lughod (1993), and Monroe Price's recent book, *Television, the Public Sphere, and National Identity* (1995).

21. See Avery 1993 for a series of essays comparing institutions of public service broadcasting across national boundaries.

22. McChesney points out that "the major function of nonprofit broadcasting in the Untied States from 1920 to 1960 was, in fact, to pioneer new sections of the electromagnetic spectrum when the commercial interests did not yet find them profitable," referring to AM broadcasting in the 1920s and to FM radio and UHF television in the 1940s and 1950s. "In each case, once it became clear that money could be made, the educators were displaced and the communications companies seized the reins. This may also be the fate of the Internet, which was pioneered as a government-subsidized public service by the nonprofit sector until capital moved in" (McChesney 1995:17).

References

Abu-Lughod, Lila
1991 "Writing against Culture." In *Recapturing Anthropology: Working in the Present*, ed. Richard G. Fox, pp. 137–162. Santa Fe, N.M.: School of American Research Press.
1993 "Editorial Comment: On Screening Politics in a World of Nations." *Public Culture* 5(3):465–468.
Adler, Jerry, et al.
1990 "Revisiting the Civil War." *Newsweek*, October 8, pp. 58–64.
Agawu, Kofi
1992 "Representing African Music." *Critical Inquiry* 18:245–266.
Altman, Rick
1986 "A Semantic/Syntactic Approach to Film Genre." In *Film Genre Reader*, ed. Barry Keith Grant, pp. 26–40. Austin: University of Texas Press.
Ames, Katrina
1991 "It's a Small World, after All." *Newsweek*, October 14, p. 65.
Anderson, Benedict
1991(1983) *Imagined Communities: Reflections on the Origin and Spread of Nationalism*. London: Verso.
Ang, Ien
1991 *Desperately Seeking the Audience*. London: Routledge.
Anonymous
1986 "Hey, Big Spender! C.P.B. Pledges Help on $24-Mil Fund." *Variety*, May 21, p. 34.
Appadurai, Arjun
1990 "Disjuncture and Difference in the Global Cultural Economy." *Public Culture* 2(2):1–24.
1991 "Global Ethnoscapes: Notes and Queries for a Transnational Anthropology." In *Recapturing Anthropology: Working in the Present*, ed. Richard G. Fox, pp. 191–210. Santa Fe, N.M.: School of American Research Press.
Appadurai, Arjun, and Carol A. Breckenridge
1988 "Why Public Culture?" *Public Culture* 1(1):5–9.
Ariés, Phillipe
1962 *Centuries of Childhood*. New York: Vintage.
Arlen, Michael
1969 *Living Room War*. New York: Viking.
Asch, Timothy, with J. I. Cardoza, H. Cabellero, and J. Bortoli
1991 "The Story We Now Want to Hear Is Not Ours to Tell." *Visual Anthropology Review* 7(2):102–106.
Aufderheide, Pat
1984 "TV Worth Paying For?" *The Progressive*, May, 1984, pp. 33–36.
1991 "Public Television and the Public Sphere." *Critical Studies in Mass Communication* 8 (June):168–183.

Avery, Robert, ed.

1993 *Public Service Broadcasting in a Multichannel Environment: The History and Survival of an Ideal.* White Plains, N.Y.: Longman.

Barnouw, Erik

1978 *The Sponsor: Notes on a Modern Potentate.* New York: Oxford University Press.

Barthes, Roland

1972 "The Great Family of Man." In *Mythologies*, pp. 100–102. New York: Hill and Wang.

Bauman, Richard, and Charles Briggs

1990 "Poetics and Performance as Critical Perspectives on Language and Social Life." *Annual Review of Anthropology* 19:59–88.

Bauman, Richard, et al.

1992 *Reflections on the Folklife Festival: An Ethnography of Participant Observation.* Bloomington: Indiana University Press.

Becker, Howard

1982 *Art Worlds.* Berkeley: University of California Press.

Bird, S. Elizabeth

1992 "Travels in Nowhere Land: Ethnography and the "Impossible" Audience." *Critical Studies in Mass Communication* 9:250–260.

Bluem, William

1965 *Documentary in American Television.* New York: Hastings House.

Blumler, Jay G.

1991 "The New Television Marketplace: Imperatives, Implications, Issues." In *Mass Media and Society*, ed. James Curran and Michael Gurevitch, pp. 194–216. London: Edward Arnold.

Bolton, Roger

1992 "Disturbing Wishes." *Sight and Sound*, February 1992, p. 29.

Boone, Mike

1991 "Documentary on Kids Will Steal Hearts and Hype Hormones." *Montreal Gazette*, October 13, p. F-2.

Bordwell, David

1988 *Ozu and the Poetics of Cinema.* Princeton, N.J.: Princeton University Press.

Bordwell, David, Janet Staiger, and Kristin Thompson

1985 *The Classical Hollywood Cinema: Film Style & Mode of Production to 1960.* New York: Columbia University Press.

Bosk, Charles L.

1979 *Forgive and Remember: Managing Medical Failure.* Chicago: University of Chicago Press.

Bourdieu, Pierre

1983 "The Field of Cultural Production, Or: the Economic World Reversed." *Poetics* 12:311–356.

1984 *Distinction: A Social Critique of the Judgement of Taste.* Trans. Richard Nice. Cambridge, Mass.: Harvard University Press.

1986 "The Production of Belief: Contribution to an Economy of Symbolic Goods." In *Media, Culture, and Society: A Critical Reader*, ed. Richard Collins et al., pp. 131–163. Beverly Hills, Calif.: Sage Publications.

Brenner, Daniel

1990 "Era of Reconstruction: Life Exists for Public TV after The Civil War.'" *Current*, December 17, p. 31.

Bronfenbrenner, Urie

1970 *Two Worlds of Childhood: U.S. and U.S.S.R.* New York: Russell Sage Foundation.

1979 *The Ecology of Human Development: Experiments by Nature and Design.* Cambridge, Mass.: Harvard University Press.

Bronowski, Jacob

1973 *The Ascent of Man.* Boston: Little, Brown.

Bunce, Alan

1990 "PBS: the Best and Room to Grow." *Christian Science Monitor*, August 29, p. 13.

Carnegie Commission

1967 *Public Television: A Program for Action.* New York: Harper and Row.

1979 *A Public Trust: The Landmark Report of the Carnegie Commission on the Future of Public Broadcasting.* New York: Bantam Books.

Carter, Bill

1994 "For 13, Change Brings a Chill." *New York Times*, October 18, p. C15.

1995 "WNET Braces for Cuts or Worse." *New York Times*, January 25, p. C13.

Caughie, John

1986 "Popular Culture: Notes and Revisions." In *High Theory/Low Culture*, ed. Colin MacCabe, pp. 156–171. New York: St. Martin's Press.

Chamberlain, Ward

1986 "Public Funding for 'The Africans.'" *Washington Post*, October 21, p. A17.

Clifford, James

1986a "Introduction: Partial Truths." In *Writing Culture: The Poetics and Politics of Ethnography*, ed. James Clifford and George Marcus, pp. 1–26. Berkeley: University of California Press.

1986b "On Ethnographic Allegory." In *Writing Culture: The Poetics and Politics of Ethnography*, ed. James Clifford and George Marcus, pp. 98–121. Berkeley: University of California Press.

Clifford, James, and George Marcus, eds.

1986 *Writing Culture: The Poetics and Politics of Ethnography.* Berkeley: University of California Press.

Colford, Steven

1990 "PBS Hawks Itself on Network TV." *Advertising Age*, September 24, p. 18.

"Co-productions Now Dominate Public Television"

1986 *Broadcasting*, September 22, p. 68.

Corner, John

1991 "Meaning, Genre and Context: The Problematics of Public Knowledge in the New Audience Studies." In *Mass Media and Society*, ed. James Curran and Michael Gurevitch, pp. 267–284. London: Routledge.

Corry, John

1987 "Why It's Time for Public Television to Go Private." *New York Times*, November 1, p. 35.

Crane, Diana
1992 *The Production of Culture: Media and the Urban Arts.* Newberry Park, Calif.: Sage Publications.

Crick, Malcolm
1989 "Representations of International Tourism in the Social Sciences: Sun, Sex, Sights, Savings, and Servility." *Annual Review of Anthropology* 18:307–344.

Cumings, Bruce
1992 *War and Television.* London: Verso.

Day, James
1995 *The Vanishing Vision: The Inside Story of Public Television.* Berkeley: University of California Press.

Demos, John Putnam
1986 *Past, Present, and Personal: The Family and the Life Course in American History.* New York: Oxford University Press.

DiMaggio, Paul, and Paul M. Hirsch
1976 "Production Organizations in the Arts." In *The Production of Culture*, ed. Richard A. Peterson, pp. 73–91. Beverly Hills, Calif.: Sage Publications.

Edelman, Marian Wright
1987 *Families in Peril: An Agenda for Social Change.* Cambridge, Mass.: Harvard University Press.

Engelman, Ralph
1996 *Public Radio and Television in America: A Political History.* Thousand Oaks, Calif.: Sage Publications.

Fabian, Johannes
1983 *Time and the Other: How Anthropology Makes Its Object.* New York: Columbia University Press.
1990 "Presence and Representation: The Other and Anthropological Writing." *Critical Inquiry* 16 (Summer):753–772.

Faris, James C.
1992 "Anthropological Transparency: Film, Representation, and Politics." In *Film as Ethnography*, ed. Peter Crawford and David Turton, pp. 171–182. Manchester, U.K.: Manchester University Press.

Feld, Steven
1981 " Flow Like a Waterfall: The Metaphors of Kaluli Musical Theory." *Yearbook for Traditional Music* 13:22–47.
1982 *Sound and Sentiment: Birds, Weeping, Poetics, and Song in Kaluli Expression.* Philadelphia: University of Pennsylvania Press.
1994a "Communication, Music and Speech about Music." In *Music Grooves*, by Charles Keil and Steven Feld, pp. 77–96. Chicago: University of Chicago Press.
1994b "From Schizophonia to Schismogenesis." In *Music Grooves*, by Charles Keil and Steven Feld, pp. 257–289. Chicago: University of Chicago Press.

Ferguson, Andrew
1990 "Not with My Money." *The Washingtonian*, July, pp. 61–67.

Fiske, John
1987 *Television Culture.* London: Methuen.

Foucault, Michel
1977 "What Is an Author?" In *Language, Counter-memory, Practice: Selected Es-*

says and Interviews by Michel Foucault, ed. Donald Bouchard, pp. 446–464. Ithaca, N.Y.: Cornell University Press.

Fraser, Nancy
1990 "Rethinking the Public Sphere: A Contribution to the Critique of Actually Existing Democracy." *Social Text* 25/26:56–80.

French, Sean
1992 "Diary." *New Statesman and Society*, March 13, p. 8.

Friedland, Lewis
1995 "Public Television and the Crisis of Democracy: A Review Essay." *Communication Review* 1(1):11–128.

Frith, Simon
1988a "Video Pop." In *Facing the Music*, ed. Simon Frith, pp. 88–131. New York: Pantheon Press.
1988b "The Pleasures of the Hearth—the Making of BBC Light Entertainment." In *Music for Pleasure*, by Simon Frith, pp. 24–45. New York: Routledge.

Garnham, Nicholas
1990 *Capitalism and Communication*. London: Sage Publications.
1993 "The Mass Media, Cultural Identity, and the Public Sphere." *Public Culture* 5(2):251–267.

Ginsburg, Faye
1988 "Ethnographies on the Airwaves: The Presentation of Anthropology on American, British and Japanese Television." In *Cinematographic Theory and New Dimensions in Ethnographic Film*, ed. Paul Hockings and Yasuhiro Omori, Osaka: Senri Ethnological Studies 24.
1994 "Culture/Media." *Anthropology Today* 10(2):5–15.
1993 "Aboriginal Media and the Australian Imaginary." *Public Culture* 5:557–578.

Goodman, Walter
1991 "Many Faces and Crises of Childhood." *New York Times*, October 14, p. C18.

Gordon, Robert
1992 *The Bushman Myth*. Boulder, Colo.: Westview Press.

Gross, Larry
1974 "Modes of Communication and the Acquisition of Symbolic Competence." In *Media and Symbols: The Forms of Expression, Communication, and Education*, ed. David Olson, pp. 56–80. Chicago: University of Chicago Press.
1981 "Introduction: Sol Worth and the Study of Visual Communication." In Sol Worth, *Studying Visual Communication*, ed. Larry Gross, pp. 1–35. Philadelphia: University of Pennsylvania Press

Grossberg, Lawrence
1987 "The In-difference of Television." *Screen* 28(2):28–45.

Habermas, Jürgen
1989 *The Structural Transformation of the Public Sphere: An Inquiry into a Category of Bourgeois Society*. Cambridge, Mass.: MIT Press.

Haddock, Mable, and Chiquita Mullins Lee
1993 "Whose Multiculturalism? PBS, the Public, and Privilege." *Afterimage*, Summer, pp. 17–19.

Haines-Stiles, Geoffrey
1972 "A 'Construct' Analysis of Television Newscasts: A Method and Its Applications." M.A. thesis in Communications, University of Pennsylvania, Philadelphia.

Haines-Stiles, Geoffrey, Erna Akuginow, and Eugene Marner
1991 "Letter to the Editor." *New York Times*, November 10, p. 4.

Hall, Stuart
1980 "Encoding and Decoding." In *Culture, Media, Language*, ed. Stuart Hall et al., pp. 128–138. London: Hutchinson.
1989 "Cultural Identity and Cinematic Representation." *Framework* 36:68–81.

Hamilton, Annette
1990 "Fear and Desire: Aborigines, Asians, and the National Imaginary." *Australian Cultural History* 9:14–35.

Hammond, Charles Montgomery
1981 *The Image Decade: Television Documentary, 1965–75.* New York: Hastings House.

Hawes, Joseph M., and N. Ray Hiner, eds.
1991 *Children in Historical and Comparative Perspective: An International Handbook and Research Guide.* New York: Greenwood Press.

Hinde, Robert A.
1982 *Ethology: Its Nature and Relations with Other Sciences.* New York: Oxford University Press.
1987 *Individuals, Relationships, and Culture: Links between Ethology and the Social Sciences.* Cambridge, U.K.: Cambridge University Press.

Hirsch, Paul M.
1972 "Processing Fads and Fashions: An Organization-set Analysis of Cultural Industry Systems." *American Journal of Sociology* 77 (4):639–659.

Hoachlander, Marjorie E.
1977 *"The Ascent of Man": A Multiple of Uses?* Vol. 1: Summary, vol. 2: Research Report. Washington, D.C.: Corporation for Public Broadcasting.

Hoover, Dwight
1992 *Middletown: The Making of a Documentary Film Series.* Philadelphia: Harwood Academic Publishers.

Hoynes, William
1994 *Public Television for Sale: Media, the Market, and the Public Sphere.* Boulder, Colo.: Westview Press.

Irvine, Reed
1986 "Give Up on Public Broadcasting." *Wall Street Journal*, March 28, p. 22.

Jensen, Joli
1984 "An Interpretive Approach to Culture Production." In *Interpreting Television: Current Research Perspectives*, ed. Willard D. Rowland, Jr., and Bruce Watkins, pp. 98–118. Beverly Hills, Calif.: Sage Publications.

Kagan, Jerome
1984 *The Nature of the Child.* New York: Basic Books.

Kagan, Jerome, et al.
1979 "A Cross-cultural Study of Cognitive Development." *Monographs of the Society for Research in Child Development* 44(5). Chicago: University of Chicago Press.

Karp, Ivan, and Steven D. Lavine, eds.
1991 *Exhibiting Cultures: The Poetics and Politics of Museum Display.* Washington, D.C.: Smithsonian Institution Press.

Kingsbury, Henry
1988 *Music, Talent and Performance: A Conservatory Cultural System.* Philadelphia: Temple University Press.

Kinsley, Michael
1983 "None Dare Call It Commercial." *Harper's*, March, p. 9, 12–13.

Kirshenblatt-Gimblett, Barbara
1991 "Objects of Ethnography." In *Exhibiting Cultures: The Poetics and Politics of Museum Display*, ed. Ivan Karp and Steven D. Lavine, pp. 386–443. Washington, D.C.: Smithsonian Institution Press.

Kogan, Rick
1991 "The 2nd Chance: 'Childhood' Probes the Influences That Mix to Make Us What We Are." *Chicago Tribune*, October 14, sec. 5, p. 4.

Konner, Melvin
1972 "Aspects of the Developmental Ethology of a Foraging People." In *Ethological Studies of Child Behavior*, ed. N. Blurton Jones, pp. 285–304. Cambridge, U.K.: Cambridge University Press.
1982 *The Tangled Wing: Biological Constraints on the Human Spirit.* New York: Holt, Rhinehart and Winston.
1990 *Why the Reckless Survive, and Other Secrets of Human Nature.* New York: Viking.
1991 *Childhood.* Boston: Little, Brown.

Lapham, Lewis
1993 "Adieu, Big Bird: on the Terminal Irrelevance of Public Television." *Harper's*, December, pp. 35–39.

Lashley, Marilyn
1992 *Public Television: Panacea, Pork Barrel, or Public Trust.* New York: Greenwood Press.

Lee, Richard B., and Irven DeVore
1976 *Kalahari Hunter-Gatherers: Studies of the !Kung San and Their Neighbors.* Cambridge, Mass.: Harvard University Press.

Leerhsen, Charles
1990 "Avoiding Gridlock at Gettysburg." *Newsweek*, October 8, pp. 62–63.

Le Guin, Ursula
1971 *The Lathe of Heaven.* New York: Scribner.

Lewyn, Mark
1990 "Is PBS Really Worth It?" *Newsweek*, December 24, p. 10.

Liebes, Tamar, and Elihu Katz
1990. *The Export of Meaning.* New York: Oxford University Press.

Lidz, Charles
1977 "Rethinking Rapport: Problems of Reciprocal Obligations in Participant Observation Research." Paper presented at the Eastern Sociological Association meeting, New York, March.

Lutz, Catherine, and Jane Collins
1993 *Reading National Geographic.* Chicago: University of Chicago Press.

MacDougall, David

　　1975 "Beyond Observational Cinema." In *Principles of Visual Anthropology*, ed. Paul Hockings, pp. 109–124. The Hague: Mouton.

　　1995 "Subtitling Ethnographic Films: Archetypes into Individualities." *Visual Anthropology* 11(1):83–91.

Marcus, George, and Dick Cushman

　　1982 "Ethnographies as Texts." *Annual Review of Anthropology* 11:25–69.

Marcus, George, and Michael M. J. Fischer

　　1986 *Anthropology as Cultural Critique: An Experimental Moment in the Human Sciences.* Chicago: University of Chicago Press.

McArthur, Colin

　　1978 *Television and History.* London: British Film Institute.

McChesney, Robert W.

　　1995 "America, I Do Mind Dying." *Current*, August 14, pp. 16–19.

McLagan, Meg

　　N.d. "Mediating Muncie: Middletown, *Seventeen*, and the Politics of Representation." Unpublished Manuscript.

Mead, Margaret

　　1928 *Coming of Age in Samoa.* New York: Blue Ribbon Books.

　　1930 *Growing Up in New Guinea.* New York: Blue Ribbon Books.

Mead, Margaret, and Gregory Bateson

　　1942 *Balinese Character: A Photographic Analysis.* New York: New York Academy of Sciences.

Mehta, Ved

　　1980 *The Photographs of Chachaji: The Making of a Documentary Film.* New York: Oxford University Press.

Michaels, Eric

　　1991 "A Model of Teleported Texts (with Reference to Aboriginal Television)." *Visual Anthropology* 4:301–323.

　　1994 *Bad Aboriginal Art: Tradition, Media and Technological Horizons.* Minneapolis: University of Minnesota Press.

Miller, Toby

　　1993 *The Well-Tempered Self: Citizenship, Culture, and the Postmodern Subject.* Baltimore: Johns Hopkins University Press.

Moffat, Michael

　　1992 "Ethnographic Writing about American Culture." *Annual Review of Anthropology* 21:205–229.

Morley, David

　　1981 " 'The Nationwide Audience'—a Critical Postscript." *Screen Education* 39(Summer):3–14.

　　1983 "Cultural Transformations: The Politics of Resistance." In *Language, Image, Media*, ed. Howard Davis and Paul Watson, pp. 104–117. New York: St. Martin's Press.

　　1989 "Changing Paradigms in Audience Studies." In *Remote Control: Television, Audiences, and Cultural Power*, ed. Ellen Seiter et al., pp. 16–43. London: Routledge.

1991 "Where the Global Meets the Local: Notes from the Sitting Room." *Screen* 32(1):1–15.

Morris, Rosalind C.
1994 *New Worlds from Fragments: Film, Ethnography, and the Representation of Northwest Coast Cultures*. Boulder, Colo.: Westview Press.

Murdock, Graham
1989 "Critical Inquiry and Audience Activity." In *Rethinking Communication*, vol. 2, ed. Brenda Dervin et al., pp. 226–249. Beverly Hills, Calif.: Sage Publications.

Musser, Charles
1991 *The Emergence of Cinema: The American Screen to 1907*. New York: Charles Scribner's Sons.

Myers, Fred
1988 "Critical Trends in the Study of Hunter-Gatherers." *Annual Review of Anthropology* 17:261–282.

Nader, Laura
1974 "Up the Anthropologist: Perspectives Gained from Studying Up." In *Reinventing Anthropology*, ed. Dell Hymes, pp. 284–311. New York: Random House.

Naficy, Hamid, and Teshome H. Gabriel
1991 "Introduction: Consuming the Other." *Quarterly Review of Film and Video* 13(1–3):i-iii.

Neale, Steve
1990 "Questions of Genre." *Screen* 31(1):45–66.

Nichols, Bill
1981 *Ideology and the Image*. Bloomington: Indiana University Press.
1988 "The Voice of Documentary." In *New Challenges for Documentary*, ed. Alan Rosenthal, pp. 48–63. Berkeley: University of California Press.
1991 *Representing Reality: Issues and Concepts in Documentary*. Bloomington: Indiana University Press.
1994 *Blurred Boundaries: Questions of Meaning in Contemporary Culture*. Bloomington: Indiana University Press.

Ortner, Sherry
1984 "Theory in Anthropology since the Sixties." *Comparative Studies in Society and History* 26 (1):126–166.

Peterson, Richard A.
1976 "The Production of Culture: A Prolegomenon." In *The Production of Culture*, ed. Richard A. Peterson, pp. 7–22. Beverly Hills, Calif.: Sage Publications.

Pollock, Linda
1983 *Forgotten Children: Parent-Child Relations from 1500 to 1900*. New York: Cambridge University Press.
1987 *A Lasting Relationship: Parents and Children over Three Centuries*. Hanover, N.H.: University Press of New England.

Powell, Walter W., and Rebecca Friedkin
1983 "Political and Organizational Influences in Public Television Programming." *Mass Communication Review Yearbook* 4:413–438.
1986 "Politics and Programs: Organizational Factors in Public Television Decision

Making." In *Nonprofit Enterprise in the Arts*, ed. Paul DiMaggio, pp. 235–269. New York: Oxford University Press.

Price, Monroe E.
1995 *Television, the Public Sphere, and National Identity*. New York: Oxford University Press.

Public Broadcasting Report
1991 "APTS Annual Meeting Teleconference." *Public Broadcasting Report* 13 (14):4–5.

Radway, Janice
1988a "Reception Study: Ethnography and the Problems of Dispersed Audiences and Nomadic Subjects." *Cultural Studies* 2(3):359–376.
1988b "The Book-of-the-Month Club and the General Reader: On the Uses of 'Serious' Fiction." *Critical Inquiry* 14:516–538.
1989 "Ethnography among Elites: Comparing Discourses of Power." *Journal of Communication Inquiry* 13(2):3–11.

Renov, Michael
1993 *Theorizing Documentary*. New York: Routledge.

Rosenblum, Ralph, and Robert Karen
1979 *When the Shooting Stops . . . the Cutting Begins*. New York: Penguin Books.

Rosenthal, Alan, ed.
1988 *New Challenges for Documentary*. Berkeley: University of California Press.

Ross, Andrew
1989 *No Respect: Intellectuals and Popular Culture*. New York: Routledge.

Roush, Matt
1991 "On PBS, *Childhood* around the Global Village." *USA Today*, October 14, sec. D, p. 3.

Rowland, Willard D., Jr.
1986 Continuing Crisis in Public Broadcasting: A History of Disenfranchisement. *Journal of Broadcasting and Electronic Media* 30(3):251–274.

Rowland, Willard D., Jr., and Michael Tracey
1990 "Worldwide Challenges to Public Service Broadcasting." *Journal of Communication* 40(2):8–27.

Rubenstein, Carin
1991 "A Tour of the Wonder Years: It's a Small, Small World." *New York Times*, October 13, sec. F, pp. 29, 33.

Ruby, Jay
1975 "Is an Ethnographic Film a Filmic Ethnography?" *Studies in Visual Communication* 2(2):104–111.
1990 "The Belly of the Beast." *Continuum* 3(2):32–52.
1991 "Speaking For, Speaking About, Speaking With, or Speaking Alongside—an Anthropological and Documentary Dilemma." *Visual Anthropology Review* 7(2): 50–67.

Said, Edward
1979 *Orientalism*. New York: Random House.

Scannell, Paddy
1992 "Public Service Broadcasting and Modern Public Life." In *Culture and*

Power: A Media, Culture and Society Reader, ed. Paddy Scannell, Philip Schlesinger, and Colin Sparks, pp. 317–138. Beverley Hills, Calif.: Sage Publications.

Scarr, Sandra
1984 *Mother Care, Other Care*. New York: Basic Books.

Scarr, Sandra, Robert Weinberg, and Ann Levine
1986 *Understanding Development*. San Diego: Harcourt, Brace, Jovanovich.

Schapiro, Mark
1991 "Public TV Takes Its Nose Out of the Air." *New York Times*, November 3, pp. 31–32.

Scheper-Hughes, Nancy
1989 "The Human Strategy: Death without Weeping." *Natural History*, October, pp. 8–16.
1992 *Death without Weeping: The Violence of Everyday Life in Brazil*. Berkeley: University of California Press.

Schieffelin, Bambi B.,
1990 *The Give and Take of Everyday Life: Language Socialization of Kaluli Children*. New York: Cambridge University Press.

Schieffelin, Bambi B., and Elinor Ochs, eds.
1986 *Language Socialization across Cultures*. Cambridge, U.K.: Cambridge University Press.

Schudson, Michael
1991 "The Sociology of News Production Revisited." In *Mass Media and Society*, ed. James Curran and Michael Gurevitch, pp. 141–159. London: Edward Arnold.

Seiter, Ellen, et al.
1989 "Introduction." In *Remote Control: Television, Audiences, and Cultural Power*, ed. Ellen Seiter et al., pp. 1–15. London: Routledge.

Shattuck, Roger
1980 *The Forbidden Experiment: The Story of the Wild Boy of Aveyron*. New York: Farrar, Straus, Giroux.

Shohat, Ella, and Robert Stam
1994 *Unthinking Eurocentrism: Multiculturalism and the Media*. New York: Routledge.

Shorenstein, Stuart Alan, and Lorna Veraldi
1989 "Does Public Television Have a Future?" In *American Media: The Wilson Quarterly Reader*, ed. Philip S. Cook, Douglas Gomery, and Lawrence W. Lichty, pp. 229–241. Washington, D.C.: Wilson Center Press.

Silverstone, Roger
1985 *Framing Science: The Making of a BBC Documentary*. London: British Film Institute.

Singer, André
1992 "Anthropology in Broadcasting." In *Film as Ethnography*, ed. Peter Crawford and David Turton, pp. 264–273. Manchester, U.K.: Manchester University Press.

Smith, Barbara Herrnstein
1988 *Contingencies of Value*. Cambridge, Mass.: Harvard University Press.

Somerset-Ward, Richard

1993 *Quality Time: The Report of the Twentieth Century Task Force on the Future of Public Television.* New York: Twentieth Century Fund Press.

Spitulnik, Debra

1993 "Anthropology and Mass Media." *Annual Review of Anthropology* 22:293–315.

Sreberny-Mohammadi, Annabelle

1991 "The Global and the Local in International Communications." In *Mass Media and Society*, ed. James Curran and Michael Gurevitch, pp. 118–138. London: Edward Arnold.

Staples, Amy

1995 "An Interview with Dr. Mondo." *American Anthropologist* 97(1):110–125.

Stevenson, Harold, Hiroshi Azuma, and Kenji Hakuta, eds.

1986 *Child Development and Education in Japan.* New York: W. H. Freeman.

Stone, David

1985 *Nixon and the Politics of Public Television.* New York: Garland.

Stone, Ruth

1981 "Toward a Kapelle Conceptualization of Music Performance." *Journal of American Folklore* 94(372):188–206.

Taylor, Clark

1987 "KCET to Launch Series on Childhood." *Los Angeles Times*, September 1, sec. 4, p. 9.

Taylor, Lucien, ed.

1994 *Visualizing Theory: Selected Essays from Visual Anthropology Review, 1990–1994.* New York: Routledge.

Tedlock, Barbara

1980 "Songs of the Zuni Kachina Society: Composition, Rehearsal, and Performance." In *Southwestern Indian Ritual Drama*, ed. Charlotte J. Frisbie, pp. 7–35. Albuquerque: University of New Mexico Press.

Tedlock, Dennis

1983 "The Analogical Tradition and the Emergence of a Dialogical Anthropology." In *The Spoken Word and the Work of Interpretation*, pp. 321–338. Philadelphia: University of Pennsylvania Press.

Todorov, Tzvetan

1981 *Introduction to Poetics.* Brighton, U.K.: The Harvester Press.

Tuchman, Gaye

1979 *Making News.* New York: Free Press.

1983 "Consciousness Industries and the Production of Culture." *Journal of Communication* 33(3):330–341.

Tulloch, John

1990 *Television Drama: Agency, Audience and Myth.* London: Routledge.

Turino, Thomas

1990 "Structure, Context and Strategy in Musical Ethnography." *Ethnomusicology* 34(3):399–413.

Turow, Joseph

1984 *Media Industries: The Production of News and Entertainment.* Philadelphia: Annenberg/Longman Books.

1985 "Cultural Argumentation through the Mass Media: A Framework of Organizational Research." *Communication* 8:139–164.

Turton, David
1992 "Anthropology on Television: What Next?" In *Film as Ethnography*, ed. Peter Crawford and David Turton, pp. 283–299. Manchester, U.K.: Manchester University Press.

Urban, Greg, and Joel Sherzer
1988 "The Linguistic Anthropology of Native South America." *Annual Review of Anthropology*, pp. 283–307.

Vaughan, Dai
1983 *Portrait of an Invisible Man: The Working Life of Stewart McAllister, Film Editor*. London: BFI.

Werner, Emmy, and R. S. Smith
1982 *Vulnerable but Invincible*. New York: McGraw-Hill.

Whiting, Beatrice B., and John W. M. Whiting
1975 *Children of Six Cultures: A Psycho-cultural Analysis*. Cambridge, Mass.: Harvard University Press.

Wilmsen, Edward
1989 *Land Filled with Flies: A Political Economy of the Kalahari*. Chicago: University of Chicago Press.

Winston, Brian
1988 "Documentary, I Think We Are in Trouble." In *New Challenges for Documentary*, ed. Alan Rosenthal, pp. 21–33. Berkeley: University of California Press.
1995 *Claiming the Real: The Documentary Film Revisited*. London: British Film Institute.

Witherspoon, John, and Roselle Kovitz
1986 *A Tribal Memory of Public Broadcasting: Missions, Mandates, Assumptions, Structure*. Prepared for the Corporation for Public Broadcasting.
1987 *The History of Public Broadcasting*. Washington, D.C.: Current.

Wolff, Janet
1981 *The Social Production of Art*. London: Macmillan.

Worth, Sol
1980 "Margaret Mead and the Shift from Visual Anthropology to The Anthropology of Visual Communication." *Studies in Visual Communication* 6:15–22.
1981 *Studying Visual Communication*, ed. Larry Gross. Philadelphia: University of Pennsylvania Press.

Worth, Sol, and John Adair
1972 *Through Navajo Eyes: An Exploration in Film and Anthropology*. Bloomington: Indiana University Press.

Filmography

Abrams, Ira
  1983 *Faces of Culture*. Alexandria, Va.: PBS Adult Learning Satellite Service.
Adato, Perry Miller
  1989 *Art of the Western World*. New York: WNET.
Ambrosino, Michael
  1980 *Odyssey*. Boston: WGBH.
Barzyk, Fred, and David Loxton
  1980 *The Lathe of Heaven*. WNET.
Bronowski, Jacob, and Adrian Malone
  1973 *The Ascent of Man*. BBC-TV and Time-Life Films.
Burns, Ken
  1990 *The Civil War*.
Clark, Kenneth, and Michael Gill
  1969 *Civilisation*. London: BBC.
Cooke, Alistair, and Michael Gill
  1972 *America, A Personal History of the United States*. BBC-TV and Time-Life
  Films.
Crawford, Peter, David Heeley, and George Page
  1991 *Land of the Eagle*. New York. WNET and BBC-TV.
Dor-Ner, Zvi
  1991 *Columbus and the Age of Discovery*. Boston: WGBH.
Eaton, Leo et al.
  1990 *Mini Dragons I*. MPTV and Film Australia.
Epstein, Robert and Richard Schmeichen
  1983 *The Times of Harvey Milk*. Pacific Arts Corporation.
Eyre, Ronald and Peter Montagnon
  1978 *The Long Search*. BBC-TV and Time Life Films.
Ferris, Timothy, and Geoffrey Haines-Stiles
  1985 *The Creation of the Universe*. Alexandria, Va.: PBC Video.
Grant, Michael, Adrian Malone, and Richard Meech
  1992 *Millennium: Tribal Wisdom in the Modern World*. Los Angeles: KCET and
  BBC-TV.
Green, Ricki, and David Hoffman
  1991 *Making Sense of the Sixties*. Alexandria, Va.: WETA.
Grauer, Rhoda
  1993. *Dancing*. WNET with R. M. Arts and BBC-TV.
Grubin, David, and Bill Moyers
  1982 *Creativity with Bill Moyers*. New York: WNET.
Hampton, Henry
  1986 *Eyes on the Prize*. Boston: WGBH.

Hilferty, Robert
   1990 *Stop the Church*. New York: PDR Productions.
Hutton, Richard
   1988 *The Mind*. New York: WNET.
Jacopetti, Gualtiero, and Franco Prosperi
   1963 *Mondo Cane*. London: Times Film Corporation.
Labaton, Arnold, and Mark Siegel
   1984 *Heritage: Civilization and the Jews*. New York: WNET.
Landau, Saul, and Jack Willis
   1979 *Paul Jacobs and the Nuclear Gang*. New York: Center for Documentary Media.
Mazrui, Ali
   1986 *The Africans*. Washington, D.C.: WETA.
Montagnon, Peter
   1983 *Heart of the Dragon*. London: Channel 4.
Richter, Robert
   1981 *Pesticides and Pills, for Export Only*. New York: WNET.
Riggs, Marlon
   1989 *Tongues Untied*. Los Angeles: KCET.
Sagan, Carl
   1980 *Cosmos*. Los Angeles: KCET.
Sameth, Jack
   1984 *The Brain*. New York: WNET.
Vecchione, Judith
   1993 *Americas*. Boston: WGBH, and UK: Central Television Enterprises for Channel 4.

Index

Abu-Lughod, Lila, 155–56, 165, n220
aesthetic criteria, convention, or ideology, 44, 58, 68, 100, 102, 104, 126–35, 139, 171–72, 187
Africans, The, 76, n210
Agawu, Kofi, n199
agency, 10, 13, 15–17, 28, 29, 32, 69, 148, 187–88
Agland, Phil, 144
Altman, Rick, 91, n209
Ambrose Video, 52, 170, 195
Anderson, Benedict, 32, 61, 186
Annenberg School for Communication, 20, 52, n200–201
Ang, Ien, 13, 61
Antelope Films, 46, 54–55, 59, 83, 144–45, 177
anthropology of media, 8, 18, 185
anthropology in *Childhood,* 7, 56–57, 68, 97, 112, 142
Appadurai, Arjun, 9, 11–13, 18–19, 185–86
Ariés, Phillipe, 110, n212
Arlen, Michael, vi, 5
Ascent of Man, The, 42–44, 49, 93–95, 97, 104, n211
audience (viewers), 18, 29–33, 36, 38, 40–43, 46–47, 60–62, 119–20, 129–30, 132, 135, 154, 155, 163–65, 168, 170, 186–87
—American: 5, 7, 41, 63–65, 145, 148, 160–61, 171
—British: 7, 63–64, 163
—for *Childhood*: 62–67, 76, 80–82, 98, 105–6, 110, 122, 127, 138–39, 145, 160–61, 163–65, 168–70, 176, 179–81, 184–85
—demographics: 29, 33, 41, 62, 87, 173, 178, 180–81
—studies of: 13–16, 26, 29, 69, 81, 87, 188
Aufderheide, Pat, 39

Baka family, 31, 116, 127, 131, 144–46, 150, 157–59, 161, 163, 164
Bateson, Gregory, 142
Bauman, Richard, 89, 141
Becker, Howard, 67, 73

Bordwell, David, 17, n208–9
Bosk, Charles, 25–26
Bourdieu, Pierre, 12, 24, 32, 60, 62, 86, 177–78, n198, n219–20
Brain, The, 43, 45, 95, 102, 106, 109, n211
Brazil, Brazilian family, 4, 49, 55, 62, 68, 108, 127, 139, 143–46, 150, 159, 170, 174
Brenner, Daniel, 36, 41
Briggs, Charles, 89
British Broadcasting Corporation (BBC), 38–39, 42–44, 49–51, 88, 95, 100, 104, 182, 185
Bronowski, Jacob, 42, 44, 95–96, 104–7, n211
"budding babies" sequence, 136–38
Burns, Ken, 36, 40

cable television, 35, 39–42, 90
Cameroon, Cameroonian family, 4, 134, 143–45, 157, 161
Caughie, John, 15
Chamberlain, Ward, n211
Channel Four, 45–46, 49–51, 54, 59, 144, 156, 163, n214
Chicago Tribune review, 169
childbirth practices, 12, 57, 83, 108, 149–50, 159–62, n216
Childhood
—book: 48, 51, 85, 132–33, 142
—funding: 35, 44–52, 63, 95, 98, 120, 173, 179
—Minutes (historical sequences): 101–4, 110, 113–15
—reviews: 168–70
—staff: 69–81
Childhood in America, n210
cinema vérité, 44, 54, 83, 94, 98, 100, 102, 109, 143, 149, n210
cinematographers (camera operators), 55, 71, 78–79, 100, 107, 146, 173
Civilisation, 42–44, 54, 76, 93, 95, 97, 102, 104, 179, n211
Civil War, The, 30, 36–37, 40, 42, 168, 178, n202, n208, n211, n213
Clark, Kenneth, 42, 54, 95, 104–7, n211

Cleveland Plain Dealer, 184
Clifford, James, 147–48, 165–67
Collins, Jane, 32, 141, 183, n198
Colonial Williamsburg, 114–15, n218
Columbus and the Age of Discovery, 168
communities
—of consumption: 14, 61
—electronic: 18, 184
—imagined: 32, 186
—of viewers: 61, 187
Corporation for Public Broadcasting (CPB), 26, 33, 35–36, 38–39, 43, 45–46, 49, 63
Cosmos, 30, 43–45, 76, 94–95, 97, 101, 104–6, 179, n211
cross-cultural comparison, 10, 31, 47, 116, 131, 141–43, 147–51, 154, 157, 160–67, 172, 178
cultural difference, 5, 7, 10, 31–32, 140–41, 145–46, 150, 156–57, 163–66, 172, n217
cultural stereotypes, 151–54, n218
Cushman, Dick, n198

Dancing (television series), 140
Day, James, 180, n219–20
documentary
—poetics: 92
—theory and research: 9, 12, 14–19, 29, 84, 90, 92, 124, 135–36, 171
—economics of documentary production: 172–75, n218

editors, 54, 68, 77, 79–81, 149, 174
Eiblesfeldt, Eibl, n217
ethnographic film, 22, 68, 85, 142, 147–48, n217
ethnography, 9, 11–12, 19–21, 23–25, 27, 87, 141–42, 147, 165–67, 171
—of audiences: 16, 26
—of communication (speaking): 8, 89–91
—ethnography, popular: 9–10
—of media: 5, 7, 10–13, 24–28
—and stance and role: 22–27
ethno-theory, 12, 30, 97
evaluation, by producers, 14, 16, 29, 60, 67–69, 81, 86,
evolutionism, 158–59
exposition, expository modes, 18, 29–33, 64, 82, 89, 94–98, 104–10, 113, 120, 124, 128–29, 132–35, 138–41, 149, 160, 166, 179, 181
Eyes on the Prize, 42, 76

Fabian, Johannes, 9, 158–59, 165
family footage, 68, 83, 103–4, 108–10, 127, 131, 138, 143–47, 149, 165, 174–75
Feld, Steven, 67, 141, n207
Fischer, Michael, 9, 12
Fiske, John, 90, 92 n209–10
Foucault, Michel, n199, n214
Fraser, Nancy, 5, 187
French, Sean, n217–28
Friedland, Lewis, 185–86
Frith, Simon, 88, n207
fund-raising, 174, n218–19

Gabriel, Teshome, 9–10, n200
Garnham, Nicholas, n200
genre theory, 90–93
Gholston family (U.S.), 4, 109, 130, 154–55, 161, 208
Gibson, Dai-Sil Kim, n218
Ginsburg, Faye, 9, 140, 185, n197, n214, n216
Goodman, Walter, 169, n217
Grossberg, Lawrence, 15

Habermas, Jürgen, 5, 186–87
Hall, Stuart, 16, 90, 141, 166
Hamilton, Annette, 167
Hammond, Charles Montgomery, 93–94
Heart of the Dragon, The (television series), 49, 54, 118
Heritage: Civilization and the Jews, 102, n211
history in *Childhood*, 101–4, 110–17, 132, 174, n218
Hoynes, William, 39, 41, 178, 183, n202, n206
hunter-gatherers, in *Childhood*, 46–47, 144, 157–58, n216
Hutton, Richard, 110, 123, n212

interviews, 148–49
Islamic education, n218

Japan, Japanese families, 4, 49–52, 55, 62, 68, 85, 100, 105, 108, 114, 127, 130, 142, 145–46, 149, 151, 154, 157
Jensen, Joli, 15
Jocelin, Elizabeth, 114
juxtapositions across cultures, 10, 149–51, 155, 157, 159

Kalugin family, 109, 136, 150
Kauffman, 108, 150, 159
Kingsbury, Henry, 23
Kinsley, Michael, n203
Kirkpatrick, 109, 177
!Kung, 47, 139, 144, 157–58

Lawson, Jennifer, 180, n218–20
Lutz, Catherine, 32, 141, 183, n198

Making Sense of the Sixties, 76
Marcus, George, 9, 12, n198
Mather, Cotton, 112–15
McChesney, Robert, 186, n220
Mead, Margaret, 10, 85, 142
Media production, studies of, 5, 7, 10, 13–15, 24–29, 81–82, 87, 91, 187–88
mediascapes, 18, 186–87
Michaels, Eric, 14, 18–19, n206
middlebrow, 181, 183
Millennium, 10, 97, 140, n214
Miller, Toby, 182–83
Mind, The, 43, 45, 96, 102, 109–10, n212
Mini Dragons, 140
Montreal Gazette review, 169
Morley, David, 8, 13, 81, 87, n200
Morris, Rosalind, 171
Moyers, Bill, 41, n203
multiculturalism, 10, 12, 81,127, 140–41, 147, 151, 171, 180, n219–20
Myers, Fred, 158

Naficy, Hamid, 9–10, n200
Nakayama family, 149, 154, 157
narration (commentary), 68, 82, 85, 90, 98, 103–9, 113–15, 119, 120, 126, 128–38, 148–50, 159–60, 179
narrative, 17–19, 30–31, 89, 98, 109, 117–20, 122–28, 135–39, 141, 143–44, 165, 181, 186, n213
National Geographic
—magazine: 32, 141, 183
—television series: 9, 32, 105, 130, 140, 144, n214
National Public Radio, 86, 135
Neale, Steve, 90, 102, n209–210
New Statesman and Society review, 169, n217
Newsweek review, 169
New York Daily News review, 169, 184
New York Times reviews, 168–69, 184

Nichols, Bill, 5–6, 17, 92–94, 128–29, 131, 133–36, 147–48, 166, 179, n213, n219
Nova (television series), 53, 85, 93, 104–6, 130, 140, 182

Ochs, Elinor, 142
Oliveira, 150, 159
on-camera hosts (observers), 22, 55, 57–58, 73–76, 84, 90, 95–96, 101, 103–8, 129–30, 133, 135–37, 157, 169–70, 179
otherness, 140–47, 151, 165–66

Page, George, 45, 102, 110, 128, n212
Pollock, Linda, 111, n212
production, research and theory, 8, 10–19, 24–31, 33, 62, 69–70, 87, 89–93, 122, 171, 178, 181–88
production value, 100–101, 122, 144, 173, 175, 179
public broadcasting, 6, 12, 14, 26, 33–39, 41–42, 52, 61–63, 88, 93, 171–72, 176, 181–83, 186–87
Public Broadcasting Act, 38
Public Broadcasting Service (PBS), 7, 19–20, 32–33, 35–37, 39–44, 47–49, 51–52, 59, 86–88, 92–93, 122, 151, 160, 168, 173, 176–88
public culture, 5, 7, 9–12, 18–19, 33–34, 140–41, 158, 170–72, 178, 180–82, 184–88
public sphere, 5, 13, 33–34, 184–87, n197
public television, 3, 5–7, 9–11, 19, 21, 23, 25–30, 32–45, 47–50, 52–55, 59–61, 66, 71, 87–89, 92–93, 95, 140, 166, 168, 170–73, 176, 178, 180–87
—audience (viewers): 29, 45, 59–66, 87, 139, 168, 178
—documentary: 3, 7, 12, 26, 30, 59, 90–92, 141–49, 166, 170–72, 182, 184
—funding: 6, 26, 35, 38–43, 49, 92, 182–83
—producers: 21, 33, 40–41, 55, 86–87, 170, 172, 178, 180, 187
—programming strategy: 40–43, 160, 178–80
—series: 11, 55, 70, 95–97, 100–101, 104, 117, 140–42, 168, 179, 183–84

Quranic school, 146–47

Radway, Jan, 15, 21, 23, 183
relativism, cultural and social scientific, 11, 33, 159–64, 172, 181

Rosenthal, Alan, n211
Ross, Andrew, 181–82
Rowland, Willard, 38–39
Rubenstein, Carin, 168–69
Ruby, Jay, n197, n216
Russia, Russian families, 4, 49, 55, 57, 68, 81, 85, 100, 108, 127, 129, 136, 145–46, 150–51, 163

Sagan, Carl, 52, 104–7
Schapiro, Mark, 180, n218
Scheper-Hughes, Nancy, 138–39
Schieffelin, Bambi, 142
Schudson, Michael, 185
Seiter, Ellen, 15
Sherzer, Joel, 11, 91, n209
Shohat, Ella, 147, 166, n217
shooting ratio, 143, n214
Shorenstein, Stuart, 36, 40
Silverstone, Roger, n199
Singer, André, 207
Smith, Barbara Herrnstein, 62, 160
social organization of production staff, 175–76, 178–79
social status and prestige, 21, 175–77
Society of the Observers of Man, 73
sociobiology, 57, 142, 159, 162–64,
Spock, Dr. Benjamin, 114
Stam, Robert, 147, 166, n217
Stevenson, Harold, 142

subtitles, 90, 128, 131–32, 140, 148
symbolic capital, 26, 32, 176–77

televisual humanism, 32–33, 164, 181
title sequences, 101, 103, 118, 127–30
Tracey, Michael, 38–39
Tulloch, John, 14, 69, n208
Turino, Thomas, n198, n201
Turow, Joseph, 11, n209
Turton, David, 13, 66, 166
TV Globo, Brazil, 174, n218–19
Twentieth Century Fund Task Force on Public Television, 27, 37, 38, 42, n206

United States, families, 3, 4, 47, 63, 105, 108, 127, 143, 145, 154–55, 157, 177
Urban, Greg, 11, 91, n209
USA Today review, 169, 184

Veraldi, Lorna, 36, 40
visual anthropology, 8, 18, n197–99
voice (point of view), 17, 108, 133, 147–48

Whiting, Beatrice B., and John W. M., 142
Wild Boy of Aveyron, 73
Wild Child, 73
Winston, Brian, n210
Wolff, Janet, 199
Worlds of Childhood, 170
Worth, Sol, 8, 18, n197